Dear Reader:

The book you are about to read is the latest bestseller from the St. Martin's True Crime Library, the imprint *The New York Times* calls "the leader in true crime!" Each month, we offer you a fascinating account of the latest, most sensational crime that has captured the national attention. St. Martin's is the publisher of John Glatt's riveting and horrifying SECRETS IN THE CELLAR, which shines a light on the man who shocked the world when it was revealed that he had kept his daughter locked in his hidden basement for 24 years. In the Edgar-nominated WRITTEN IN BLOOD, Diane Fanning looks at Michael Petersen, a Marine-turned-novelist found guilty of beating his wife to death and pushing her down the stairs of their home—only to reveal another similar death from his past. In the book you now hold, THE MILLIONAIRE'S WIFE, Cathy Scott covers over 20 years of cold-case clues to detail a story of money and murder.

St. Martin's True Crime Library gives you the stories behind the headlines. Our authors take you right to the scene of the crime and into the minds of the most notorious murderers to show you what really makes them tick. St. Martin's True Crime Library paperbacks are better than the most terrifying thriller, because it's all true! The next time you want a crackling good read, make sure it's got the St. Martin's True Crime Library logo on the spine—you'll be up all night!

Charles E. Spicer

Charles E. Spicer,
Executive Editor, St. Martin's True Crime Library

Also by Cathy Scott

The Killing of Tupac Shakur

The Murder of Biggie Smalls

*Murder of a Mafia Daughter: The Life and Tragic
Death of Susan Berman*

Death in the Desert: The Ted Binion Homicide Case

The Rough Guide to True Crime

THE
Millionaire's
WIFE

THE TRUE STORY OF A REAL ESTATE TYCOON,
HIS BEAUTIFUL YOUNG MISTRESS,
AND A MARRIAGE THAT ENDED IN MURDER

CATHY SCOTT

St. Martin's Paperbacks

THE MILLIONAIRE'S WIFE

Copyright © 2012 by Cathy Scott.

All rights reserved.

For information address St. Martin's Press, 175 Fifth Avenue, New York, NY 10010.

ISBN: 978-0-312-59435-0

Printed in the United States of America

St. Martin's Paperbacks edition / April 2012

St. Martin's Paperbacks are published by St. Martin's Press, 175 Fifth Avenue, New York, NY 10010.

10 9 8 7 6 5 4 3 2 1

To the memory of my mother, author Eileen Rose-Busby, who I miss every day and who not only taught me, as a child, the joy of reading and writing, but also the value of researching.

ACKNOWLEDGMENTS

This proved to be an especially challenging book to research and write as I wrestled up decades-old documents and records and sought out sources from New York to Puerto Rico. It could not have been done without the help of many.

Special gratitude goes out to St. Martin's Paperbacks' former editor Allison Strobel, editorial assistant April Osborn, and, particularly, executive editor Charles Spicer for their faith in me. Thanks also to my determined partner-in-crime, literary agent Susan Lee Cohen, for her steadfast support, advice, and friendship.

Big thanks to freelance book editor Deke Castleman for his invaluable input, crime writer E.W. Count for being my backup in New York City, fellow true crime author Kathryn Casey and artist/author Paulette Frankl for their second set of eyes on a draft of the manuscript, and author Sue Russell for her LexisNexis searches.

I thank the Kogan clan for background into their family dynamics and insight into the case, and I give them my condolences for their loss. Thanks as well to Nilda Martinez, whose undying devotion to her brother Manuel and belief in his innocence is commendable, and to Clarissa Barth, who is a true friend to Barbara Kogan. Special thanks to doorman Moses Crespo for physically walking me through the crime scene that unfolded before his eyes so many years ago.

I thank Assistant District Attorney Joel Seidemann for taking the time to talk to me, as well as defense attorneys Barry Levin, Lori Cohen and Jonathan Strauss, and appellate attorney Claudia Trupp.

For her analysis of the case, I thank crime writer and former Deputy District Attorney Robin Sax. Much thanks as well to graduate student Yoav Sivan for his generosity in sharing his research. Also, thanks to journalist Mitch Gelman for his recollections from his early reporting in the case.

A shout-out and thanks, as always, to my core family support: my twin sister Cordelia Mendoza, my big brother J. Michael Scott, and my son Raymond Somers Jr.

Lastly, I thank you, the many readers who have discovered my books. Your kind endorsements and recommendations to other readers are forever appreciated.

CONTENTS

CHAPTER 1

A Cool Manhattan Morning

A light rain fell over Manhattan on a weekday morning like any other. But life can change on a dime, and that's exactly what happened as middle-aged business tycoon George Kogan hurried back to his ultra-chic Upper East Side apartment with a bag of groceries on each arm in anticipation of breakfasting at home with his young lover. The late morning of Tuesday, October 23, 1990, turned out to be anything but a typical day in the city.

On the busy sidewalk, George, who'd recently celebrated his forty-ninth birthday, turned the corner onto East Sixty-ninth Street and headed toward his mid-block building, between Second and Third. As he hurried down the tree-lined street, he didn't notice anything unusual other than the cool morning temperature. He continued walking toward the canopied entrance to the co-op where he'd lived for the last two years with Mary-Louise Hawkins, a twenty-eight-year-old rising star in the public relations world. Across the street, carpenters noisily worked on the new Trump Palace high-rise apartment building. A few blocks away, Central Park was alive with pedestrians, bicyclists, and joggers as they coursed through the park's major arteries to their destinations in New York City, where the drone of urban traffic awaited them. George enjoyed walking the neighborhood. He'd lose himself in the bustling sights and sounds of the city. And this day was no different.

Walking from the neighborhood Food Emporium, he looked forward to spending the late morning with Mary-Louise. Quiet breakfasts were how their relationship had moved from platonic to romantic, and they especially appreciated those moments. Plus, George was anxious to prepare for an afternoon meeting with his son, William, who was acting as mediator to nail down an agreeable divorce settlement with George's estranged wife, Barbara, and bring to a conclusion the marriage that in essence had ended two years earlier.

As George headed home that morning, William telephoned his father's apartment to confirm their afternoon appointment. Mary-Louise told him she'd have George return the call when he arrived home from the store. George was optimistic about the settlement and finally getting the lengthy divorce behind him, so he and Mary-Louise could move on with their life together. Also uppermost in George's mind was settling the divorce to help repair the damaged relationship he'd had with William, who had sided with his mother after his parents' separation.

As George continued his walk home, the usual cast of characters were out and about—nannies pushing babies in strollers, residents leaving their high-rises to walk their dogs, business people hurrying to the subway entrance just steps away. George, distracted with the nagging thought of the afternoon meeting, quickened his pace when his limestone building came into view.

He lived in the heart of Manhattan's Upper East Side, once called the Silk Stocking District, so named for the attire worn by the rich people who had once lived there. Long gone was the 19th-century farmland, as well as the market and garden districts that had peppered the area. Left were skyscrapers, rows of stylish townhouses, mansions, and the occasional walk-up apartment building.

For a millionaire antiques and art dealer who had once had interests in a casino and several properties in Puerto

Rico and New York, George lived a surprisingly modest life on New York's well-to-do Upper East Side—broadly defined as the area from Fifty-ninth to Ninety-sixth Streets, east of Central Park. His living quarters with Mary-Louise Hawkins were definitely nice, although small, with just one bedroom and a marbled-bath washroom. And while the apartment had a prestigious address with the coveted 10021 zip code in a luxurious high-rise complex, it was not quite up to the elite level of Fifth Avenue, which serves as *the* symbol of wealthy New York, where George once lived with his now-estranged wife Barbara. Still, he admired the high-end building that housed his current apartment.

The Upper East Side has a legacy of outstanding eclectic architecture, including George's pre-war apartment. The façade of his co-op, a mix of limestone and beige brick, created a grand entrance with its surround and above-the-door stone molding, with tall arched relief details and shallow columns on either side and carved renaissance-style capitals. Above that was a heavy, stately ornamental stone molding. The variety of styles added a touch of grace and grandeur from a bygone era. As a connoisseur of fine antiques, George appreciated the artistry that went into the face of the building and enjoyed walking through the double-glass doorway, framed in oak, with its etched Art Deco design. What George could not know was that he would never again walk through that entryway, and the anticipated meeting with his son and his soon-to-be ex-wife to finalize the divorce was not to be. What happened next, he never saw coming.

As he neared the entrance to his Sixty-ninth Street apartment, his face flushed from the damp morning air, what he heard next was startling. It sounded like an explosion, most probably coming from the construction site across the street.

"What the—?" George cried out a nanosecond later, when it dawned on him what the noise *really* was. It was the distinct sound of gunfire.

No, no, no! he said to himself, and then, *Mary-Louise!*

The force of the bullets entering George's back thrust him into a forward dive and catapulted him into the air; he landed in a skid on the rain-soaked concrete. He was face down just yards from his apartment lobby. Seconds felt like minutes.

Coins, bills, and groceries—a carton of eggs, a slab of cheese, a bottle of milk, pieces of fresh fruit—tumbled to the ground, along with George.

Sprawled on the sidewalk next to the wall, with his arms stretched out in front of him amidst the scattered groceries and money, George lifted his head and cried out, "Help me!"

The gunman stood a few feet from George. Out of the corner of his eye, the shooter, who showed no emotion, saw someone move. He quickly turned his attention from George toward a woman stepping out of a car parked at the curb. The two locked eyes, and then the assailant, with a cold, determined confidence, turned and hurried away on foot. He looked down and returned the black revolver, still in his left hand, to his waistband, hiding it under his jacket. Then he hurried up the sidewalk.

The shooter fled the scene as quickly as he had entered it. He headed a half-block west on East Sixty-ninth Street to Third Avenue before rounding the corner, turning right, and disappearing into a stream of pedestrians on the crowded sidewalk as he headed north. When the gunman was a safe distance away, he stepped toward the next pay phone he came across and placed a local call.

"It's done," the assassin said into the receiver. He hung up the phone and again disappeared into the morning pedestrian traffic.

Back at Sixty-ninth, lying flat on the concrete, his face ashen and his body alarmingly still, George called out once more. He tried to get up, but it felt as if an irresistible force held him down. He tried shifting his weight, but that didn't work either. Immobilized except for his head and neck, George Kogan rested the side of his face on the cold, wet sidewalk. He felt the light wind against his forehead.

Dark water stains below the air conditioners at each apartment window in George's building marred the exterior marble walls and portions of the concrete sidewalk below, where George lay bleeding.

He was alone. But not for long.

He tried once again to lift his head when he heard footsteps approach. Bystanders stood over him. He was confused. Just then, George heard a familiar voice.

"George! What is it? What happened? Why are you—" trailed Moses Crespo's voice as he viewed with horror the gunshot wounds on George's back and the blood seeping through his red T-shirt. Moses, who worked as a door attendant at Kogan's building, knelt next to George, stretched out on the damp concrete. He asked what had happened.

"I've been shot," George said.

To Moses, George seemed calm. Almost too calm. He was in obvious shock.

"Who did this?" Moses asked.

"I don't—I don't know. I didn't see anyone."

"Relax. Don't worry, George. I'll be right back," Moses said, adding, "Is there anything else?"

"Can you get Mary-Louise? I want—I want to speak to her," George told him.

"Okay," Moses said, then, "You will be all right. We are going to get help."

"I'm dying," George said as Moses hurried away, first to call 911 and then to summon George's girlfriend, Mary-Louise Hawkins.

Within a few long minutes, Mary-Louise walked through the lobby door expecting, per Moses' request, to talk to George. Instead, she found her boyfriend lying on the damp sidewalk in a pool of blood. As she stood under the canopy taking in the scene a few feet away from her, Mary-Louise became unglued. "She went hysterical, screaming and jumping," Moses said. "People had to restrain her." That awful sight, George lying helpless, was what would stay with Mary-Louise, plus the fact that she and George did not get to say good-bye to each other. In the short time that had elapsed since Moses found him, her boyfriend of two years was already slipping in and out of unconsciousness.

Moses would be the last person to speak with George Kogan. At that moment, Moses's mind was racing. He did not know what to think. He remembered George, a few months earlier, asking him not to accept any deliveries for him and not to confirm with anyone that he lived in the building.

Moses also wracked his brain trying to figure out why he had not heard the shots. Even though he had been in the lobby at the time of the shooting, he had not heard the gunfire. He had not known anything was amiss until a few minutes later, when a housekeeper ran to the door and, frightened by the gruesome scene playing out on the sidewalk, pounded on it to be let in. Then Moses realized why he hadn't immediately noticed the shots: Across the street, at 200 East Sixtyninth Street, construction workers pounded away, literally, on the Trump Palace, a luxury condominium complex that, at fifty-five stories, was the tallest building at the time in Upper Manhattan. Each weekday during construction, workers used air-powered nail guns to build the high-rise.

But the *pop, pop, pop* Moses thought was from the construction site was in reality the sound of gunfire as an executioner opened fire on George Kogan's back.

CHAPTER 2

George Kogan's Beginnings

New Yorkers awakened the next morning, on Wednesday, October 24, to the startling headlines that the day before an unidentified gunman had brazenly cut down wealthy businessman George Kogan in broad daylight and in cold blood as he walked from a neighborhood market to his girlfriend's Upper East Side apartment. It was frightful news.

George's apartment on East Sixty-ninth sat between Central Park and the East River in Lenox Hill, an ocean away from his beginnings in San Juan. As founding and prominent members of the Caribbean island's Jewish community, the Kogan clan had proudly started and operated a lucrative chain of home-furnishing stores and made real estate investments that became the Kogan empire. George grew up as a privileged member of unofficial Puerto Rican royalty.

George H. Kogan was born on September 25, 1941, a Thursday, to Solomon Kaganovitch, a Jewish émigré from Russia, and his wife Ida, a Canadian from Toronto. On the day in September 1941 when George was born, rain and snow fell in Russia, transforming the landscape to mud. The most noteworthy thing about that dark fall day was the fact that Jews were ordered to wear the yellow Star of David. For Jews in Europe, it was a frightening time. The Kaganovitch family was from Minsk, the capital and largest city in Belarus, Russia,

which is on the Svisloch and Niamiha rivers. Minsk had been
a battlefront city, and by the early 1930s, many residents,
including the large Kaganovitch family, had evacuated to the
West. George's father, Solomon, was one of nine children born
before the Bolshevik Revolution. After the conflict, members
of the Kaganovitch clan fled to Cuba, then to New York.
Solomon was among those who went to Cuba first, eventually passing through the Ellis Island Immigration Center's
portal—dubbed the "New World's Golden Door"—as they
arrived in America. At Ellis Island, most family members
listed their occupations as "trader," because, while in Minsk,
many had labored as today's equivalent of retail merchants.
As was common at the time for European arrivals, those
family members in the States Americanized their name,
changing it from Kaganovitch to Kogan.

The Kogans wanted to stay together, so they sought a ter-
ritory that would allow all of them in, one where they didn't
surpass the refugee quota, per the 1921 Emergency Quota
Act limiting admission of each nationality. Puerto Rico, even
though a commonwealth and a part of the United States,
wasn't overwhelmed with foreign immigrants seeking ad-
mittance. The San Juan area—a major port and tourist resort of the West Indies and the oldest city under the US
flag—was the only location where all fifty of the Kogans
could go to live. So, Solomon traveled to Puerto Rico, on
behalf of the family. "He was the one who went to Puerto
Rico to see if it was a good place to live," said one of
George's cousins, who grew up with him on the island.

Solomon reported back to the rest of the family that they
could buy a decent-sized piece of farmland in San Juan, not
far from a growing tourist area, and everyone could be there
together. Not to mention, there were ample job opportunities. And the port city's growing population of immigrant
Jews would make them feel welcome and at home.

While still on the US mainland, Solomon and other
members of the Kogan family began shipping wholesale
merchandise, through a partner in New York, to Puerto Rico
to sell for retail on the island. And "that's how the family

business got started," said Dr. Robert Goldstein, whose wife was a cousin of George's; Goldstein is considered the historian of the family he married into. They named their enterprise the New York Department Stores de Puerto Rico. "It was a tightly knit community on the island," another cousin said, "and a more tightly knit family." From that early start, the chain of stores that would sustain three generations was born, and the Kogans had a new homeland.

While in New York, Solomon had met, fallen in love with, and married a Canadian woman named Ida. Then the Kogan clan made their pilgrimmage to Puerto Rico, converging and reuniting in San Juan.

After Solomon and his siblings opened their first department store, the business flourished, as, one by one, the family built New York Department Stores into a lucrative chain of nine stores. The Kogans expanded the business and invested in property. According to a mention in the *Puerto Rico Daily Sun*, "The family had several major real estate holdings on the island." It was clearly a family enterprise, and many profited from it. "All of these siblings ended up owning the chain of department stores in Puerto Rico, and George's father was one of the founders," said a second cousin to George, who also eventually moved to New York. "Solomon's kids were well taken care of growing up. There were a lot of stores."

Solomon and Ida bought a rural property as a second home near the pastoral setting of Cayey, about thirty miles south of San Juan on the Central Mountain range. For many years, Solomon's homestead served as the Kogan family gathering place. Each Sunday without fail, all would gather for a picnic at what they nicknamed "Solomon's farm." It was the perfect place to escape the touristy city, even for brief respites. Back then, "It was pre-Castro, and you had Anglos who were mostly families who either were sent to Puerto Rico to run factories, or it was more that they ended up in Puerto Rico," said a cousin of George who grew up with him in San Juan. But the Kogan family, an enterprising bunch, made the most of it as entrepreneurs and never fell into factory work.

George was one of three siblings, including an older brother, Lawrence, and a younger sister, Myrna. Even though they lived in Puerto Rico, after grade schoool the children attended private preparatory and military schools on the East Coast. Their parents wanted them to have the best educations possible, which only the mainland, not the island, could provide.

George had a head for economics and learned the retail business from the bottom up by helping out at the stores, including working in the warehouse and unloading new shipped-in merchandise. Once he reached high school age, George was sent to an East Coast military school. But when he returned during the holidays and summers, he worked at the family stores. The next year, his sister was sent to a private boarding school in upstate New York, not far from the boys' academy George attended, and they regularly got together. In military school, George learned discipline that would help him later on in business. Retail ended up being the only trade he would learn, carrying on in his father's footsteps.

After high school, George enrolled at New York University. Since he'd gotten the hands-on background in running a store, George's decision to leave Puerto Rico and expand his business knowledge was embraced by the family. George felt he was evolving and growing as a businessman, and striking out on his own as an entrepreneur was his next step. Studying at university, he felt, would help him accomplish that goal. Eventually, George wanted to become his own boss, like his father. It was during George's years in college that he met Barbara, his future wife.

CHAPTER 3

Barbara Susan Siegel

Emanuel and Rose Siegel each grew up in New Jersey, just after the turn of the century. It also was where, after the couple was married, they chose to raise a family. In June of 1940, their first child, Elaine, was born. Then, a little less than three years later, they had a second daughter, Barbara Susan Siegel, born February 25, 1943, a Thursday.

Barbara grew up in the modest but comfortable suburb of Morristown, New Jersey, just three square miles and home to the Rabbinical College of America and surrounding synagogues. There, in the cocoon of a 1950s' middle-class community, the Siegels lived a simple lifestyle, attending temple as a family on the Sabbath and going to school and synagogue events together. The Siegels were solid members of the conservative neighborhood as the couple raised their daughters in the cozy 'burbs of New Jersey.

The town's neighborhoods were sprinkled with a variety of architecture: stately colonial, English Tudor, and Victorian. The Siegels' small home, on a well-manicured street, was sparsely but nicely furnished. While from all accounts the family was not wealthy, Emanuel earned an honest, decent living working at a small jewelry store he owned and free-lancing in the marketing field for local publications. The girls' parents worked hard and provided well for their daughters, dressing them modestly while keeping up with most of the latest fashions; Barbara came to prefer trendy yet understated clothes and tasteful home furnishings.

At Morristown High School, where Barbara attended school, she was active in the dance club. She loved performing, and whatever Barbara wanted, her parents supported. If Barbara chose to perform, then her parents were behind her 100 percent. They trusted her judgment. That unwavering parental loyalty toward Barbara would be challenged years later.

In 1959, when Barbara was just sixteen, she won a talent contest, which, for a teenager from New Jersey, had an amazing grand prize: a recording contract with Capitol Records. The deal, however, fell through, and Barbara never cut the record. But that did not stop her from pursuing her dream. She loved entertaining, loved being on stage and the center of attention. She continued performing after high school at Barnard College, a women's liberal arts school situated on the Columbia University campus, where she majored in art history. In 1961, while still a college student, she landed a dancing gig in an off-Broadway show in New York City. Everything was going as planned for Barbara. She still performed while working toward her college degree.

The component missing in Barbara's well-choreographed life was romance and the companionship of a man. She had dated a few classmates, but no one had caught her eye. Then, the day came that forever changed her life: She met a young college student named George Kogan. He had moved to New York in the late 1950s to enroll at New York University. George attended a theater production in which Barbara performed, then went backstage and introduced himself.

At their first meeting they chatted a bit, and Barbara, who'd been studying the arts and literature, learned that George was a business major. But George too was interested in the arts, and each realized that they had many other interests in common. On the spot, George asked Barbara out on a date.

A few days later, he took her to dinner in the city. She was flattered that George, who was a couple years older, was interested. He was taken by her appearance—pretty, five foot five, with thick brown hair, strikingly large, dark greenish-brown eyes, and a curvy figure. Plus, she was soft-spoken with a seemingly gentle nature and carried herself with a certain confidence. George particularly liked Barbara's easy smile and calm manner. Her quiet and sensible demeanor made her seem like she would be a life partner he could trust. Barbara, however, was not one to carry her heart on her sleeve, and the quietness about her at times was a cover for how she really felt inside. As part of a relatively new couple, George did not yet know that about Barbara.

George, an avuncular man with a shy but charming side, had a pleasant, boyish face. His likeable manner attracted Barbara. Best of all, George seemed to know what he wanted in life. She liked that about him. He seemed worldly to the somewhat sheltered Barbara. His business background impressed her as well. George, as a descendant of a notable, hard-working family, had since adolescence been exposed to the working world. His skill sets and business acumen, learned at his family's department-store chain, would serve him well in the future. He'd learned from his father how to become a moneymaker. By the early 1960s, the family business was worth $40 million.

Barbara had no idea just how wealthy the family was, but she could tell by George's gifts to her—pricey jewelry and expensive dinners—that he had money to spend. What Barbara also would not know until years later was that when she met George, he had been on a military deferment. As soon as he left school, the deferment would end, and he would automatically be eligible for the draft—unless he married. So, while George had not actively been looking to marry, it was at the back of his mind.

Soon, George and Barbara began spending more time together. Between classes, George would often meet Barbara on Barnard's campus, located in the neighborhood of Morningside Heights along the west side of Broadway. They were comfortable with each other. During their courtship, they took in some of the city's famous museums, including the Metropolitan Museum of Art. They shared a love of the arts and would eventually go on to sell paintings and other works together in their shops and galleries in both San Juan and New York City.

Besides art, they had other similar interests. Barbara had a knack when it came to business, thanks to the time she had spent helping out in her father's jewelry store. They also shared a love of fine furnishings and the history surrounding those pieces. George had grown up in the opulent surrounds of Old San Juan, a small island connected to the rest of the city, and, while Barbara had more modest beginnings, she too learned to appreciate the finer things in life. It was the early sixties, several years before flower power, free love, antiwar activities, or political activism became a cultural force. Barbara's desires were clear: a college education, a husband, and a family—in that order. Since Barbara was adamant about earning her bachelor's degree, the couple remained in New York until she graduated. George, however, wasn't as keen on his education as he was when he'd first entered college. He dropped out before finishing.

In 1964, three years after their chance meeting backstage at a Times Square theater, George and Barbara eloped to Virginia. Whether by design or not, by marrying, George had successfully dodged the draft. Barbara glowed and George beamed on their wedding day as they each repeated their vows to the justice of the peace who married them. They were excited about and focused on their future together, including building a family and a business. Both felt secure that their partnership as man and wife was off to an excellent start. After all, they wanted the same things. What could possibly go wrong?

CHAPTER 4

Mr. and Mrs. George Kogan

George was a dream come true for Barbara, the kind of man she'd always hoped to meet—educated, already successful, and from a wealthy, influential family, not to mention pleasant looking. One of George's most endearing qualities, however, was his deep affection and love for his family. He described for Barbara what it was like living in Puerto Rico in the thriving tourist area of San Juan, its port, the harbor, and his family's rural farm. His taste for living a posh lifestyle came through loud and clear to Barbara when he flew her first class to Puerto Rico to meet his extended family. She could hardly wait to move there permanently.

George eventually relocated with Barbara to the island. She had only lived in New Jersey, except for her time in New York City while she was in college, so she was excited about building a life somewhere new. Barbara and George settled in a nice apartment in the Condado district, a middle- to upper-class area just east of Old San Juan that offered a broad selection of accommodations and facilities in all price ranges. Luxurious homes nestled between high-rise condominiums and the shops, inns, restaurants, seaside parks, and museums that, as a whole, made up the Condado. Originally developed in the 1950s as San Juan's first tourist zone, the Condado district was created in the likeness of Miami Beach.

In the eastern area of the district was Ocean Park, a mile-wide beach encompassing residential homes and beach retreats.

George Kogan would soon have his own hotel on Ocean Park, which would make it possible for the Kogans to purchase an oceanfront penthouse on the Ashford Avenue strip, across the street from one of George's cousins. Located on the top floor of the Mirador del Condado condominiums, it came replete with a swimming pool and a white-sand beach in its backyard, plus an incredible view of the Atlantic Ocean.

"Oh, George, it's so beautiful," Barbara said as she stood in their four-bedroom apartment for the first time and looked out the bay window at the ocean below. It even included quarters for a live-in nanny.

"It's for you and our future children," he said.

Very much in love, the Kogans wanted to share their good fortune by having a family of their own. They tried to have a baby. When they were unsuccessful, they decided to pursue private adoption. Their much longed-for baby boy, born in Passaic, New Jersey, arrived in Puerto Rico a week after his birth in 1966. George and Barbara named him Scott. A month later, without the pressure on the couple to conceive, Barbara became pregnant with their second son, William Stewart, or Billy, as his family took to calling him. San Juan, a metropolis on the north coast facing the Atlantic, offered miles of swimming beaches, and it was a healthy place to raise a family. The Kogan boys, just ten months apart, thrived.

Condado was also the location of the University of Puerto Rico campus, making it convenient for Barbara while she pursued her graduate degree. Barbara cared for the children and, with the help of a housekeeper and nanny, eventually went back to work as her husband's business partner. For grade school, their sons attended public school, then went on to the Academia del Perpetuo Socorro, a Catholic preparatory school on the island.

The Kogan boys had a slew of cousins to play with, especially during family gatherings at the expansive Kogan farm. A main two-story home sat on the property, along with a smaller wooden house where farmhands lived. "It was a fabulous property. Absolutely beautiful," said one cousin, "with lemon trees, orange trees, chickens, horses. Some of the family rode the horses. I just loved going to Uncle Solomon's farm. It was a lot of fun, and there was so much to do." Joining in on the fun now were George and Barbara. Another cousin, a woman a few years younger than George, would sometimes see Barbara at parties hosted by Ida. "I saw Barbara occasionally when my grandmother would have Sunday brunches and everyone would come over," she said. "The gatherings were memorable and a Kogan tradition."

In January 1968, when Scott and Billy were young, their grandfather Solomon passed away. He was just sixty years old. Solomon was not only the Kogan family's father, uncle, and grandfather, he was the boss and the brains behind New York Department Stores de Puerto Rico. The patriarch of the Kogan clan was buried at the Jewish cemetery in San Juan, which the Orthodox Shaare Zion congregation oversees and keeps up through the International Jewish Cemetery Project. After her husband's death, Ida continued with the weekend gatherings at the family farm.

For George and Barbara, San Juan was a comfortable, upbeat, family-oriented environment. Over the course of the next twenty years, George and Barbara lived the good life in San Juan, raising their sons, traveling, investing in real estate, running a variety of retail businesses, and dabbling in the casino industry. George continued working in his family's business, albeit not full-time because of his busy schedule. The couple also owned and operated London House, a high-end jewelry store. Barbara's teenage years in her father's jewelry shop had come in handy. And George, like his father before him, had a vision, always thinking of ways to expand the couple's enterprises. Theirs was more than a marriage; Barbara and George were a team. She thrived in that environment, in a tropical and trendy resort area, raising a family while working side by side with her husband. Together, they built a good life for themselves and their family. Barbara was living her dream: comfortable surroundings with a husband, two children, and profitable, growing businesses. Barbara felt as if she were living a charmed existence.

By all appearances, the Kogans were happy, as a couple, as a family, and as business partners. If they disagreed on something, they made a point of never arguing in front of their sons. Barbara had a day nanny for the boys but was still involved in their lives. When they traveled, they'd take along a nanny and the boys and mix business with family vacations, including trips to Florida and New York. As the boys got older, they accompanied their parents to Europe on buying trips.

Barbara and George were among the affluent in Puerto Rico. As a couple, they were part of San Juan's high-society life. According to a cousin who'd worked with George and who asked not to be named, "George's wife was always mentioned as one of the ten best-dressed women on the island. She was always in the newspaper. I knew her on a superficial basis. I saw them around San Juan. It was mostly at family gatherings."

Unlike Barbara, George never dressed the part of a wealthy Puerto Rican. "I knew George from the store," the cousin continued. "The whole family was in the department store business. George was not a sharp dresser like Barbara. He wore just slacks and a shirt. I never saw him in a suit, even at the store—except I did see him in a suit at my wedding in 1970."

Barbara owned and operated a dress shop called Vog inside the Condado Beach Hotel. George, while working some in the family business, also continued to expand his own ventures. Soon, he opened Antiquarium, an antiques store. Shortly after, Barbara opened her own store and named it Ambiance, which the *Puerto Rico Daily Sun* once described as an "exclusive home furnishings shop." The businesses opened "one after the other," the cousin said.

George also ran the International Gem Enterprises, a company for which his wife served as vice president and secretary. In addition, he was president of the Magna Development Corporation, a nonresidential real estate group still operating today in San Juan.

As a sideline venture in the 1970s and '80s, George managed prizefighters and boxers. "He owned their contracts. It was like a hobby for him," said George's cousin.

In addition, in 1979, George made an offer of $350,000 to purchase from the Federal Deposit Insurance Corporation, or FDIC, Le Petit Hotel, which had previously gone out of business with control taken over by Banco Credito y Ahorro Ponceno, a local bank. Located in San Juan's Condado section, Le Petit Hotel had been abandoned by its operators in 1971, a year after it opened. Because the building had been vacant for some time, it was collapsing and needed repairs. George was the only one who formally bid on it, according to court documents, and his cash offer to the bank was accepted. But a potential buyer sued the FDIC a year later for selling the hotel to George, who was mentioned but not named as a defendant in the civil suit. The plaintiffs asked that the sale to be reversed, explaining that they'd tried to buy the hotel but the FDIC instead sold it to George Kogan. The plaintiffs' original offer to the bank had been $400,000, with financing. Bank representatives said in a reply to the suit that the bank had wanted no less than $490,000. Still, a month later, the bank turned around and sold it to George for a discounted cash arrangement of $350,000, which was why the plaintiffs sued.

According to the May 1982 decision by the United States Court of Appeals, First Circuit, however, the court sided with the FDIC that it was a sound sale and let the deal stand. "There are no allegations nor any indications in the record that the sale to Kogan was collusive or that the negotiations with the plaintiffs were a mere sham," the court ruled. "There is no indication in the record that the decision to accept the $350,000 offer was the result of anything but the exercise of the FDIC's discretion to sell the asset for those terms and conditions it deemed acceptable." In 1981, George bought a second hotel, the ninety-six-room Ramada San Juan Hotel and Casino, just a block from the Kogans' apartment.

Eventually, Barbara's parents followed her to San Juan to live, as did her sister, Elaine, and they also went into business.

Barbara's father, Manny Siegel, for many years operated a few tourism magazines on the island, including the *Caribbean Sun*, a publication that Barbara and George owned but Manny Siegel ran. Barbara's sister went to work in the couple's casino, ultimately becoming a floor supervisor.

As the Kogans' sons grew up, it was understood they would go on to college. Barbara believed in education and, even though George hadn't finished his degree, he, too, pushed his sons to further their educations. After Scott graduated the twelfth grade, he enrolled in a Boston, Massachusetts prep school to improve his English. His brother, Scott, wanted to attend, too. With both boys out of the house, the Kogans found themselves adjusting to life with just the two of them.

After private high school, Scott studied accounting and finance at Sacred Heart University in San Juan, while Bill enrolled at Connecticut College to work on his undergraduate degree before transferring to law school. With their boys grown, Barbara suggested to George that they return to New York, near her New Jersey roots.

"The first 25 years of our marriage, I have lived in Puerto Rico with you. Now, let's try the next 25 years in New York," Barbara told her husband.

George agreed, and, in preparation for the move, they sold their controlling interests in the Ramada Hotel and Casino to a group of New York investors in Brooklyn's Hasidic community. They then sold their four-bedroom penthouse apartment and purchased a smaller unit, also on Ashford Avenue in the Condado, which they kept for visits to the island and for their sons to use. Before the move, the couple also sold Ambiance, one of their stores in San Juan, for $1.85 million. Also, in 1985, in preparation for relocating to New York, the Kogans purchased an apartment at 61 East Seventy-seventh Street in Manhattan for $240,000.

George also sold off his interest in some of his other Puerto Rican businesses before he and Barbara moved back to New York. The farm property, where the family gatherings had taken place for years, was still a working farm and stayed in the family. George shared the land with other family members, who all were regularly paid out of profits from the farm, according to estate documents.

Then, George and Barbara returned to New York, the city where they had first met. Barbara's parents and sister remained on the island, living in the same Condado apartment building, but in separate units.

In 1988, a year after George and Barbara moved back to New York, the Kogan clan sold the family's chain of nine New York Department Stores de Puerto Rico. As one of Solomon's sons, George received a hefty share of the proceeds. After the sale, "Everybody went their own way," a cousin said.

But another reason George decided to return to New York and leave the Kogan clan behind in Puerto Rico was to be near his sister, Myrna Borus, who had moved from the island to New Jersey years earlier, after she married.

Despite the distance between them, Myrna had maintained a close relationship with her brother with regular phone calls to Puerto Rico and visits when business trips took George to the East Coast. But she did not know Barbara well. To her, Barbara was not a warm person. Myrna witnessed her brother slowly grow apart from his wife as George immersed himself in his various ventures and Barbara worked in her boutiques and attended high-society luncheons with the wives of successful businessmen in the San Juan area. Barbara, seemingly unaware of her husband's growing distance, loved being mentioned on the society pages of the local newspapers. George, on the other hand, was content to keep a low profile as he worked hard to keep his businesses successful.

Myrna first met her sister-in-law not long after Barbara and George's wedding in Virginia. "I think the reason they got married so quickly is that [George] didn't want to go into the service, and, at that time, if you were married, you didn't have to go into the service. Mostly, [Barbara] did her own thing and went her own way," Myrna would say, pointing out that she and Barbara never formed a strong relationship.

Barbara viewed the Kogans' move back to New York City as a new chapter in their life as a couple. Because their lives were busy, they'd been cohabiting more as friends than as a romantic couple, and Barbara looked at the relocation as an opportunity to rekindle the spark in their marriage. George, for his part, was looking forward to living near his sister. And as Barbara was soon to learn, he was about to make even bigger changes in his life than the move back to the States.

The Kogans settled down on the Upper East Side of Manhattan, living off the money they had made from the San Juan properties and businesses they'd sold. In June 1988, they began searching for a viable property in which to open a high-end antiques, art, and jewelry store. They found a prime location in the Madison Avenue area on East Seventy-sixth Street, a perfect spot for accommodating the rich and famous, and, in September of that year, they bought commercial space on the second floor. Madison Avenue, often referred to as "the fashionable road," is considered a premier shopping boulevard, starting at Fifty-seventh Street and spanning up to Eighty-fifth. The 30 East Seventy-sixth Street site, known for its boutiques, was the same location as New York City's then-famous Dining Room Table Shop. The Kogans were optimistic that *location, location, location* would pay off. After all, they each had extensive experience in retail, plus their shop would be a draw for Madison Avenue clientele, so they purchased the space for $600,000. The red brick, pitched-roof structure, built in 1925, was directly across the street from the Carlyle Hotel, so not only did it have potential neighborhood customers, but tourists as well. The antiques business was a natural fit for George, with his family's history of running a chain of high-end department stores for as long as George could remember. They called their new store Kogan & Company, fashioned after James II

Galleries, a popular high-end New York City antiques and retail store.

With the location set, Barbara began looking for a public-relations specialist to get out the word about the shop. She settled on Matthew Evins, owner of Evins Communications. Matthew appointed an employee, Mary-Louise Hawkins, as the lead publicist, along with a couple of other employees to work with Mary-Louise and handle PR for Kogan & Company.

Mary-Louise was well qualified for the job. She had gotten her history degree, with a focus on art, in 1985 from the private Ivy League Brown University in Providence, Rhode Island. Barbara instantly liked her and was impressed that Mary-Louise, the daughter of a wealthy owner of an oil re-tailing business, had studied ballet and attended the pricey and highly regarded Trinity School, a fixture on the Upper West Side since the late 1800s, as well as The Hotchkiss School, a boarding school located in Connecticut, two hours from New York. Mary-Louise was a socialite from the hamlet town of Manhasset, bordering the affluent North Shore on Long Island. Growing up, she'd lived in a beachfront home on an acre and a half with her sister and their parents, whom Mary-Louise once described as "country-club types."

Hawkins was blonde, pretty, sophisticated, confident, and energetic, which impressed Barbara, as did the junior year of college Mary-Louise spent studying in Paris. One of Mary-Louise's first jobs after graduating was at Sotheby's, setting up exhibits. She then worked at Tiffany & Co., a premier jeweler, which influenced Barbara's high opinion even more. Mary-Louise was raised in affluence and opulence. Barbara felt she had the exact touch the store needed.

Before her job with Evins Communications, Mary-Louise had worked for Matthew's mother, Mary Evins, who ran in high-society circles in New York. Mary-Louise spearheaded publicity for Mary Evins's projects. At Kogan & Company, Mary-Louise's job was to raise awareness of the business, getting mentions and blurbs in newspapers and magazines, including gossip columns. She soon became familiar with the shop's merchandise, which offered something for everyone, ranging from tables for $10,000 to coasters for $10, as well as pricey art and jewelry. Just Barbara, not George, had been working with Mary-Louise, although George and Mary-Louise had spoken once or twice on the phone.

To help even more with their new shop before it opened, the Kogans hired a store manager. They set up a meeting with Lia Fernandez, a manager from James II, which at the time specialized in nineteenth-century English porcelain and other high-end merchandise. The Kogans wanted someone with expertise in that area to manage their shop. The new manager was excited at the prospect of working in the Kogans' new store and accepted the offer. George and Barbara talked about their plans for the store's inventory and invited Lia on a purchasing trip they had planned for that August. During one of two meetings, they discussed a need for an additional person familiar with inventory and control systems. Fernandez suggested a woman she knew from James II whom she thought would be perfect for the job, so Barbara and George gave their new manager the green light to hire her. In addition, Fernandez hired four sales clerks, all of whom had worked for her in the past at James II. As the shop was about to open its doors for business, the Kogans felt everything was coming together nicely.

For the November 3, 1988, grand opening, they invited neighboring shop owners and residents, as well as the media, to their store. It was an exciting day for the Kogans and the store was abuzz with activity. That evening, at the opening-day party, Mary-Louise, looking luminous in a dressy suit, greeted visitors at the store's entrance. During the party, Barbara approached Mary-Louise, pointed out George, who was across the room, and said, "You have to meet my husband. He tells me he thinks you're attractive." Mary-Louise at the time thought it an odd comment, but she brushed it aside. Even so, when she was introduced to George at the end of the evening, she thanked him for the compliment.

"I meant it," he said to Mary-Louise. She in turn told him she was flattered. That first meeting was the spark that ignited their romance.

From the start, Kogan & Company, open seven days a week, catered to well-heeled clientele, tourists, and New York's rich and famous. George and Barbara were pleased that the shop was off to a wonderful start. But it was short lived. Just ten days after the grand opening, on the morning of November 13, a Sunday, Barbara asked her store manager Lia to report to the Kogans' apartment instead of to the shop. Once at their apartment, Barbara let Lia go, because she had disagreed with Barbara about the store's rules. George blamed Barbara for the debacle. After all, it was Barbara to whom the manager complained that the rules, which included asking clerks to use a basement bathroom, were a "wrong decision, discriminatory, and would embarrass and dispirit the employees." But Barbara put the rules into place anyway, and then decided to fire Fernandez. Barbara also informed the manager that she was firing the sales clerks, too. Thus, Barbara and George began running the store themselves.

A short time later, two of the employees, who were minorities, and the manager filed a discrimination lawsuit in US Federal Court against the Kogans that cited seven violations, including breach of an oral contract. The complaint named both Barbara and George. However, the employees singled out Barbara for asking them not to appear in public areas of the store when customers were present and to use the restroom in the basement instead of the one inside the shop. The Kogans argued bitterly over the suit. George hired attorney Martin I. Saperstein, with the law offices of Goodman & Saperstein. On the Kogans' behalf, Saperstein countersued, asking that the court dismiss the case. The wheels of justice in federal court, however, often move slowly, and no decision would come for a couple of years.

Later, it would become clear that not just New York City employees had been displeased with Barbara as a boss. A former San Juan employee chimed in as well, via a *New York*

Daily News online discussion forum on NYDailyNews.com. Identified only as the online name "Yoyo139," the employee wrote: "I worked for the Kogans when they lived in Puerto Rico. . . . She was a real piece of work . . . She was extremely used to the lavish living—a real 'princess' in every sense of the word, and a drama queen to boot."

Things did begin to settle down as George and Barbara put their energies into the shop. Barbara was pleased that George had taken such an interest in the store's daily operation, including the public-relations part, which she had handled in the past. She felt as much a partner in the couple's new business as she had in their earlier years in Puerto Rico. New York had been a good move for them, in Barbara's mind. Mary-Louise, for her part, had occasion to meet with George in those early days to hammer out publicity strategies for the shop. From the outside, all looked well.

Meanwhile, the Kogans relocated their living quarters to the famed Volney Hotel (which had since been converted into a co-op) at 34 East Seventy-fourth Street between Madison and Fifth, just blocks from their antique store. But after living there a short five months, they realized they no longer needed a two-story apartment. Jazz singer Lena Horne bought it for $525,000—$285,000 more than they'd paid. Horne, who lived nearby, was one of the Kogans' regular store customers. The couple had also bought a smaller, three-bedroom unit inside the Volney before their move from San Juan to New York, so their son Scott could use it while on break from college. After they sold their apartment to Horne, they bought yet another Volney apartment, this one smaller, to be near Scott.

Around the same time, Lena Horne, known for collecting antiques, was browsing inside Kogan & Company when a robber held up the store. Because the singer had been present, the media played up the story. With the bad press, despite the store's prime location, the Kogans' business floundered. They had been optimistic about the shop, but the New York market had turned out to be different from the resort clientele they had been accustomed to in San Juan. There, the Kogans' businesses had thrived. However, their Madison Avenue shop suffered, and the Kogans were unprepared for that. They had poured money into the store's inventory, not to mention investing in expensive improvements on the interior of the shop, plus the cost of hiring a public-relations firm.

It was Mary-Louise's task, as the lead publicist for Evins Communications, to counter the bad press by garnering positive write-ups for the store. She was able to get mentions in the *New York Post*'s "Page Six" column and other tabloid gossip sections. Business increased and things were back on track—or so Barbara thought. Mary-Louise regularly stopped by the shop, and both Barbara and George enjoyed having her there. George said as much to his wife, going so far as to describe Mary-Louise as "vivacious" and "attractive." Barbara did not think twice about George's comments. In fact, she passed on the compliments to Mary-Louise, just as she had at the store's grand opening.

Barbara even thought that Mary-Louise, twenty-six at the time, might be a good match for her oldest son, Scott, who was also single, twenty-two, and in college. She suggested to Mary-Louise that the two meet.

"Wouldn't it be nice to set them up on a date?" Barbara asked George and a couple of friends. Scott and Mary-Louise met for a coffee, but there was no chemistry between the two, and they did not go on a second date.

Around the same time, George and Mary-Louise began spending more time together to work on strategies to give Kogan & Company a larger public presence. Barbara hadn't given it a second thought, because she'd had no reason to distrust her husband in the past. She continued maintaining the store's day-to-day operations, while George worked behind the scenes, purchasing merchandise and overseeing PR. The frequency of George and Mary-Louise's meetings increased, and they began catching lunches together after their meetings. "In the course of our conversations," Mary-Louise said, "he would ask me questions about where I grew up, what my background was, where I was educated, what my family was like. He asked me personal questions." During one of their first lunch dates, at the upscale Plaza Hotel, their relationship became even more personal.

"He was friendly and sweet," Mary-Louise later said. George confided in Mary-Louise that he had been unhappy in his marriage for some time. He'd grown—evolved, even— and, for him, the marriage had changed as he and Barbara grew apart, despite working together in their New York business. He'd done some soul searching about his marriage, but he didn't want to try to salvage it. He told Mary-Louise he'd like to get to know her better and wondered if she'd be interested. Over the course of that lunch, George told Mary-Louise once again that he found her attractive. She didn't refuse George's overtures, despite the age difference, George's marriage, and the betrayal of Barbara such a relationship would entail. Instead, Mary-Louise was flattered, just as she had been when Barbara had unwittingly relayed George's compliment about her after the store's grand opening party. That's how trusting and secure Barbara had been in her relationship with her husband and how unaware she was that there was trouble in her marriage.

Soon, lunches at the Plaza graduated to breakfasts before work at Mary-Louise's co-op apartment. "He often, when I was on my way to work, would come up behind me on the street and say, 'Do you want to have breakfast before you go to work?' I lived on Sixty-ninth and Third and his business was on Madison, so he'd have breakfast at my place on his way down [to work]," Mary-Louise would later explain.

The relationship turned even more personal in mid-November 1988 when George invited Mary-Louise to join him on a business trip to Puerto Rico. She hadn't been there before, and she looked forward to having George show her around his home turf. They checked into the Caribe Hilton, an oceanfront resort on an exclusive seventeen-acre tropical peninsula near Old San Juan with a private balcony and a view of the lagoon. It could not have been a more romantic setting.

George was smitten, and Mary-Louise was impressed by the time she spent with the worldly older man. They soaked up the sun, enjoyed long walks on the beach, and indulged in the local culture and food. It was there, on his old stomping grounds, that George swept Mary-Louise off her feet. Old San Juan was also where, during their four-day stay, the two-some's relationship turned from business-friendly to sexually charged. That romantic getaway would be one of the things that would rankle Barbara the most, once she learned of the adulterous relationship.

When George and Mary-Louise returned home, the relationship continued stronger than ever, unbeknownst to Barbara. Then, about a week after they returned from their trip, George reserved a room at the Plaza Hotel for Mary-Louise, took her to it, and told her, "If I come back tonight, it's because I've left [Barbara] and I'm coming to you."

"And if I don't come back," he added, "it's because I can't go through with it."

That evening, George did return to the Plaza Hotel, with its old-world luxury and elegance. And he returned to Mary-Louise. Officially, George and Mary-Louise were now a couple; Barbara and George were no more.

That night was when Barbara learned the awful truth that her husband had been having an affair with Mary-Louise.

"I'm moving out," George told her as he packed a bag.

"What are you saying, George?" she asked, stunned.

"Our marriage isn't working," he said. "I'm in love with Mary-Louise."

Barbara did not take the news well. She felt betrayed, not only by her trusted husband of twenty-four years, but by Mary-Louise too. George was twenty years Mary-Louise's senior, and, more hurtful to Barbara, Mary-Louise was two decades younger than she was. George didn't want to discuss it. He had made up his mind. And there was no changing it. George could hardly wait to get back to the Plaza, where Mary-Louise was waiting for him.

Before he left the apartment, he told his son Bill, who had been staying with George and Barbara while he finished college, that he would call him. But Bill did not appreciate that his father had cheated on his mother. A bitterness toward George formed that evening, and it would last the next eighteen months.

While Mary-Louise and George celebrated his newfound freedom, Barbara and Bill remained at home, devastated by news of the affair and by George's abrupt move out of the apartment he had shared with Barbara. Bill tried to comfort his mother, but he was at a loss for words. Like his mother, he didn't understand what had just transpired. It all had happened so fast.

George had quickly become infatuated with Mary-Louise, and the feeling was mutual. Despite what was going on back home, Mary-Louise became his focus. Two weeks later, Mary-Louise and George took another trip, to St. Bartholomew Island in the West Indies, where they acknowledged they were falling in love with each other. Although George, in his mid-40s, was not strikingly handsome, his hair had held its dark color and he still had that boyish, friendly charm, coupled with a slight shyness that had attracted Barbara two and a half decades earlier. Despite the years, George's demeanor was still endearing and appealing. For her part, Mary-Louise made George feel like a new man. He felt alive. He felt young. And, for the first time in many years, he was in love.

Though Jewish, he celebrated Christmas day with Mary-Louise's family on Long Island and, the same month, he moved into Mary-Louise's East Sixty-ninth Street co-op, a brown-brick, eleven-story apartment building that was erected in 1928 and converted to a co-op in 1982. It was just steps from the subway, a convenient location for George.

But having lost George so abruptly, especially to a woman entrusted to do work for the Kogans' store, was more than Barbara could bear. So, on the day after Christmas, on Friday, December 26, Barbara picked up the phone and called Matthew Evins, Mary-Louise's boss.

"Do you know that your employee is having an affair with my husband?" she asked the startled Evins.

Caught off guard, he told Barbara he would look into it

and get back to her. That same day, Matthew summoned Mary-Louise to his office to confront her and get her side of the story. He felt partially responsible, because he'd been the one to assign Mary-Louise to the Kogan & Company account. Evins was all business, so this type of behavior shocked him.

"Do you have anything to tell me about you and George?" Matthew asked Mary-Louise after she stepped into his office.

"No," Mary-Louise answered. She appeared surprised by the question.

"Are you having an affair with George Kogan?"

"No," she told him.

"You're sure? Are you intimate?"

"No," Mary-Louise answered.

But, after they talked longer, Mary-Louise admitted that her relationship with George was more than just business.

Without hesitation, Matthew told Mary-Louise, "I'm going to have to fire you. You cannot consort with a client. It is unacceptable for you to see Mr. Kogan." Mary-Louise had crossed the line, and Matthew felt he had no choice but to let her go.

That same afternoon, after learning about Mary-Louise's firing, Matthew received a phone call from George.

"Look," George told Matthew, "you've got to hire her back. It's my fault. It is not her fault. Please, hire her back."

"No way," Matthew said.

George asked Matthew to meet him for a drink at a local pub to talk about it further, and Matthew agreed.

Once there, George again pleaded with Matthew, saying, "Please hire her back."

"I can't do that," Evins said, telling George the same thing he had told Mary-Louise.

A couple days later, Matthew got another call from Barbara Kogan. She'd had a surprising change of heart.

"Please hire Mary-Louise back," Barbara asked. "George is going to take this out on me. There are going to be recriminations. There is going to be retaliation. You have to hire her back."

But Matthew again refused. He could not rehire Mary-Louise, he said, because she had violated the rules. It was unacceptable business behavior, and Matthew said he had no choice. He no longer felt confident in her. He also terminated his firm's contract with Kogan & Company.

Shortly after, to ring in the New Year and to help Mary-Louise through the disappointment of losing her job, George took her to Anguilla, in the West Indies, where they spent five days. To George, it seemed like a fitting refuge, even though his wife and younger son were left at home, crushed by the unraveling of the Kogans' marriage and trying to digest the recent turn of events.

Then, during three weekends in January, George and Mary-Louise also traveled to Miami Beach, Florida, and stayed at the Pritikin Longevity Center & Spa for a couple of days. After that, they rented a nearby apartment, on Palm Bay Court, for an additional twelve days. They were head over heels in love.

Barbara, however, was receiving the bills in the mail and was very much aware of all the places George and Mary-Louise traveled, causing her intense emotional distress. She felt betrayed by both George and Mary-Louise, and even at times blamed herself, because she'd been the one to hire Mary-Louise. In February 1989, using attorney Norman Perlman, Barbara filed for divorce against George for dumping her for the younger woman. Officially, adultery was the reason given for the divorce. Barbara had papers served on her husband, once he arrived home from vacationing with Mary-Louise, as he sat at a coffee shop around the corner from Mary-Louise's East Sixty-ninth Street apartment. The day before, Barbara had packed up George's clothes in suitcases and had them delivered to Mary-Louise's apartment lobby.

Then, Mary-Louise was served a court summons as well, a few days later, as she sat inside the same coffee shop. Barbara wanted Mary-Louise's statement about sharing rent with George, because Barbara was convinced that joint funds, shared by the Kogans, were being used to pay for apartment costs. But Mary-Louise, it would later be determined, lived rent-free in the apartment, which her father owned.

Barbara had not only lost her husband, but she'd also lost the store. Per George's request, she stopped working at the shop, and George took over running it, eventually closing it down temporarily. Once his personal life settled down, he reopened it. But for Barbara, life as she knew it had ceased to exist. She was hurt. The hurt would gradually turn to anger as the divorce proceedings grew "acrimonious," a tabloid would later report.

Amid the bad feelings during the divorce, there was some relief. In June 1990, Barbara and George each received the good news from the US Federal Court. A judge had dismissed the discrimination lawsuit filed against them two years earlier by some of their former Kogan & Company employees. Jurists ruled on the side of the Kogans, dismissing two of the claims and tossing out the remaining five allegations because of a "lack of subject-matter jurisdiction." Besides recommending filing it as a civil suit, the court ruled there were no written employment contracts outlining the store's rules and no witnesses who overheard Barbara telling the manager those rules; it was a matter of the manager's word against the Kogans. The case lacked evidence to warrant a discrimination suit—thus the dismissal. It was a welcome relief to Barbara and George, especially while in the throes of their nasty divorce.

Once George had separated from Barbara, he underwent a transformation that was immediately noticeable to his friends and family. A friend, interviewed by the *New York Post* after George's murder, said he was "happy. George and Mary-Louise were adorable," the friend told the paper. "They told us they planned to get married. He always introduced her as his fiancée." One of George's cousins, raised in Puerto Rico with him, was pleasantly surprised with the positive change in George's demeanor. He and his wife had seen George walking in the city one evening with Mary-Louise, holding her hand. It was about two months before the murder. George's cousin and wife were on their way to Greenwich Village for dinner. "We were driving down Third Avenue on our way to the Village," said his cousin's wife, who asked that their names not be used. " 'There's George!' my husband said, pointing him out on the sidewalk. We rolled down the window and called to him. My husband stopped the car and George came over. He seemed so happy and full of life. They were going out for drinks. He invited us to go with them, and we said we were famished, coming back from one of our children's events and heading to dinner, but said we would get together with them later. He wanted us to meet his girlfriend. He looked at Mary-Louise and told her, 'These are my cousins.' He was beaming and seemed pleased to have run into us."

Also, the cousin said, "He seemed happy and smiling about extending his evening to us. That is something that would not have happened with Barbara. You never knew how she would be toward you. Sometimes she would be standoffish, not smiling and not friendly, and then the next time she would hug you and smile."

They told George and Mary-Louise, "We'll catch you the next time we're in the city."

"The next thing we knew, he was gone," his cousin's wife continued. "At that time, when we ran into him, he was the George I'd never before seen, unconcerned with material things and just happy."

Another relative, who also did not want to be named, agreed. "He did come to life after Barbara. He completely adored Mary-Louise, as did she completely and wholly adore him."

George's sister, Myrna Borus, said she visited the couple in their East Sixty-ninth Street apartment. Borus also noted that her brother seemed happier once he left Barbara and moved in with Mary-Louise: "It was a wonderful relationship. [Mary-Louise] taught him how to live."

But was his new life with Mary-Louise *really* a bed of roses? She and George were regularly cash-strapped, because, as Mary-Louise later explained it, George owed many people money, and many people owed him. On top of that, the court froze George and Barbara's joint assets until the finalization of their divorce. Even so, George and Mary-Louise vacationed together in the Caribbean and Miami, staying at resorts. By all outward signs and despite the financial stress, they appeared to be happy.

CHAPTER 5

"Lifestyle to Maintain"

Included in Barbara Kogan's divorce papers was a separate section titled "Lifestyle." Barbara, who had hired pricey attorney Norman Perlman to represent her interests, had a lifestyle to maintain, the divorce documents contended. Boldly and unabashedly, as stated in the divorce complaint, it was an expensive lifestyle. The reason for the Kogans' divorce was cited as "adultery," which, in New York in 1989, was grounds for dissolution of marriage. The divorce complaint read: "That the defendant did commit an act or acts of adultery with a woman known as Mary-Louise Hawkins at the following times and places," and then the paperwork listed the data, based on credit card receipts Barbara had gathered for restaurants, hotels, and resorts George and Mary-Louise had visited.

After the Kogans separated, Barbara wanted a change, so she moved out of the Volney apartment house and rented a two-bedroom condominium in the stylish Olympic Tower at 641 Fifth Avenue in Midtown, near St. Patrick's Cathedral and Rockefeller Center. It was the same building where billionaire Adnan Khashoggi had had his two-floor condominium in the fifty-two-story, mostly glass, modern complex with its elegant stainless steel detailing surrounding the bottom two stories. The building was erected in 1976 in a joint construction venture that included Greek shipping tycoon Aristotle Onassis. For Barbara, it was a prime, posh location. It was also convenient to the city's most famous boutiques and cultural institutions. Each day, she entered the building's atrium with its thirty-foot-high ceiling, then could take an escalator to the concourse retail level to merchants that included Italian handbag dealer Roberta di Camerino, leather goods purveyor Mark Cross, and jeweler H. Stern. Barbara's ego had been dealt a tough blow with the breakup. Even though her financial future had not yet been decided, Barbara took up the high-rise life of style and comfort in apartment 32-C.

Because it was a pricey place to live, in February of 1989, Barbara, through her attorney, filed court papers asking for $5,000 a week in temporary alimony. Perlman cited, in the "Lifestyle" section of the divorce papers, Barbara's $5,000 monthly American Express bill as supporting evidence that she required that sum per week to live. In the last half of 1988 and early 1989 alone, Perlman contended, Barbara and George's American Express bill totaled $250,000. The hefty alimony, her attorney wrote in the paperwork, was so she could continue living the lifestyle to which she had become accustomed during her marriage. The attorney also asked that Barbara be given child support of $250 a week for their son William, who was still in college and living in the couple's former apartment. In addition, she asked for $100,000 for current and future legal fees for her attorneys and $25,000 for her accountants.

Included on the inventory list, besides real property the couple owned together, was their share of the Kogan family farm in Puerto Rico. Also listed was inventory inside the Kogan & Company shop with an estimated value of more than $1 million. Then there was high-end jewelry, also listed, left over from the London House shop the couple once owned in San Juan.

Explaining the reason for the large alimony request, Barbara wrote the following in a sworn affidavit:

For better or for worse, we have lived in this lifestyle for many years. I would certainly not want to live a

> *different way while my husband continues to live such*
> *a style with his girlfriend replacing me.*
>   *It is not my purpose to justify such an existence*
> *with this affidavit but to merely offer proof as to the*
> *economics of my marriage.*

After the separation, Barbara traveled several times to
San Juan to remove belongings from the couple's three-
bedroom San Juan apartment, where Scott had been living
with roommate Omar Quinones, a muscular, large man who
practiced judo. She'd gone to the apartment so many times
and removed joint belongings that a judge had ordered her to
either return the merchandise, or, if she had sold it as her
husband had suspected, to provide an accounting to the
court. The judge then ordered the couple not to sell any of
their property until after their divorce, which tied up their
assets and put them each in a financial bind.

"Every little piece of jewelry owned by the Kogans became a bone of contention in this legal action," a prosecutor
would later say about the Kogans' divorce.

Barbara, for her part, was still emotional and bitter about
the divorce, as evidenced by her affidavit:

> *My husband, 47 years old, after twenty-four years*
> *of marriage, has taken up with a 27-year-old par-*
> *amour.*
>   *Instead of being discreet about his actions and move-*
> *ments, he has openly and notoriously conducted an*
> *affair with her, embarrassing me before my family*
> *and friends and business associates.*
>   *My husband has seen fit to travel to various exotic*
> *places with his paramour, Mary-Louise Hawkins, and*
> *has purchased numerous items, including lingerie,*
> *gifts, clothing, and the like. He has seen fit I believe*
> *deliberately to have the checks and charges sent back*
> *to my home so that I'm advised of this.*
>   *I do believe that he is a coward who wants me to be*
> *the one who brings the action for divorce.*

I believe for reasons of his own, he chooses not to sue for divorce and has caused me to do that, which, as an apparently dissatisfied mate, he should be doing.

Barbara also complained in the divorce affidavit that her estranged husband had sent her flowers for her birthday:

My 46th birthday was on Friday, February 10. I received flowers from my husband, who is living with his paramour, with a card, which said, "Dear Barbara. Happy birthday. I will always be with you. George."

Can you imagine? He's living with a paramour, twenty-four years old, twenty-five years old, and he sends me flowers and he doesn't even sign it "love," and why he would send me flowers when he's living with someone is beyond me. The word "love" is absent from the note and it is just confusing to me why he would even send me flowers in the first place.

This simple act, I suppose, recognition on my husband's part, has, in and of itself, sent me into a tailspin.

He would have been better off simply avoiding the entire gesture.

This note and flowers come after weeks of being abused verbally and being kept in a constant state of confusion.

Then, Barbara wrote:

It is possible that he had affairs while we lived in Puerto Rico, but I certainly never knew about them. And if he did have affairs, at least he had the decency and the common sense to be discreet about his activities.

It is because of the timing of what has recently occurred that I am absolutely knocked off my feet by his cruelty and seeming indifference to my own efforts and problems.

*I have always considered myself a strong woman
emotionally and capable of handling many problems
at once. However, having one's own child come home
to describe what he saw—that he saw my husband with
a girlfriend walking and acting in a particular fashion
on the sidewalk, was enough to prove to me that I am
certainly not as strong emotionally as I thought.*

*Oddly enough, I am not filled with anger. I am more
numb than anything else.*

Barbara clearly was, as she put it, in an emotional tail-spin, and seemingly out for blood. She and George had been partners, Barbara repeated to her lawyer, and she expected the estate to be split evenly: "We own the businesses together." In the meantime, as her divorce papers requested, she wanted to be paid handily.

Barbara's request for alimony did not go over well with the court. The first request was denied. After a long line of attorneys represented Barbara, high-profile lawyer Aaron Richard Golub later took over her case; he re-filed her wishes for alimony. Golub's request, like Perlman's before it, was summarily denied. It was a difficult blow for Barbara. First, the court froze the couple's assets. Then Barbara's request for alimony was twice denied. She was becoming even more distressed.

To represent George's interests, he, too, hired a high-powered divorce attorney. Mary-Louise, at her recommendation, accompanied George to attorney Frank Bonem's office, where George signed an agreement for Bonem to represent him in the dissolution of his marriage to Barbara. Bonem was later put in charge of matrimonial law at Proskauer Rose, where Bonem was a partner, eventually becoming a member of the City of New York's Committee on Matrimonial Law and sitting for five years as a member of the Judicial Committee on Women in the Courts. Through Bonem, a former federal prosecutor, George successfully got Barbara cut out of their previously joint bank accounts. It was another blow to Barbara.

One thing the court did not address was the insurance policies the couple had taken out on George's life. Family court Judge Walter Schackman didn't believe either party would pay the premiums, which, with their assets frozen by the court, they could not afford. It would turn out to be a fatal flaw in a chain of events surrounding the divorce.

Fast-forward eighteen months to 1990. The Kogans' divorce was still bitterly winding its way through the court system. By then, Barbara had gone through four more attorneys, including rehiring Norman Perlman, then retaining Bernard Post, Richard Zalk, and, finally, Richard Golub. In a hearing, Judge Walter Schackman had ordered George to redo his answers to a motion filed by Barbara, which asked for financial disclosures of all of George's assets.

Hiring high-profile lawyer Richard Golub as her final divorce counsel was an interesting—albeit an expensive—choice. After graduating from the University of North Carolina's law school in 1967, Golub relocated to New York, first working on Wall Street, then as a trial lawyer specializing in entertainment, business, and commercial litigation. Two of his most famous cases included Denise Rich and Donald Trump. He also once successfully represented actor William Hurt in a palimony suit brought against Hurt by his ballerina girlfriend. In Germany, TV station GBH aired a one-hour television special based on Golub's life. His legal career had segued into filmmaking with the production of a documentary, and then moved to the big-screen movie *Factory Girl*, a biopic about Edie Sedgwick and Andy Warhol's infamous Factory studio. Golub also became a novelist.

Attorney Golub may have been successful in other pursuits, but when it came to Kogan versus Kogan, Barbara wasn't getting what she wanted. The final blow came in September 1990 when George's attorney, Frank Bonem, filed a contempt-of-court motion against Barbara for violating the judge's orders, looting the couple's business, and continuing to sell the couple's joint property, much of which she'd gotten during her trips to the couple's former apartment in Puerto Rico while visiting her son Scott. If she violated the order again, the judge would hold her in contempt and fine her or send her to jail—or both. Barbara's nerves were frazzled. She was beside herself with the position she found herself in, and she was reaching the end of her rope. Barbara responded to the court's order with a September 28, 1990, response:

> *George Kogan stole $800,000 worth of property and jewelry from the London House Hotel in San Juan and $17,000 worth of china and cloth, linen tablecloths, and linen napkins from our apartment in San Juan, Puerto Rico.*

Two weeks later, on October 10, Scott Kogan, who lived in his parents' former home, was nonplussed when told about his mother's letter calling his father a thief. To counter the allegation, Scott filed an affidavit with the court, on behalf of his father, which read:

> *Dad did not steal property from the London House. I went into the London House. I examined the property. There was only $3,500 worth of jewelry. He didn't steal anything nor did he steal any china or linens from the apartment.*

It came around the same time as Judge Schackman's final order to not provide Barbara temporary alimony. At the hearing to discuss the Kogans' finances, the judge told Barbara and George, "Both parties deny having any income, yet you both are living well." He then officially denied payment of alimony. "If you want support in terms of alimony, your remedy is a quick trial, and the trial will determine what alimony you get after the trial. During this pre-trial period, you are not to get anything," the judge said. Barbara and George continued to be banned by the court from selling any of their real estate, owned jointly, until after the divorce. Barbara was crushed and complained to friends and family that she was "penniless." Until the financial dispute was settled and the divorce was final, Barbara, her friends said, depended on her mother, Rose Siegel, to send her money.

George's divorce attorney, Frank Bonem, eventually filed a statement with the court, telling the judge that George's net worth was somewhere between $2 to $3 million on the low side and $10 to $12 million on the high side, and that most of his real estate holdings were in Puerto Rico, with a few in New York. Any money was tied up in real estate holdings and businesses, his statement said.

Despite the release to the court of George's worth, Barbara still believed her husband was hiding assets and continued to feel she needed a lawyer in Puerto Rico to help her find those missing assets. So, Barbara retained attorney Manuel Martinez, originally from Puerto Rico, a minor-league lawyer with a small general-law practice, where he mostly handled housing eviction cases. Barbara had been looking for a divorce attorney on the island, and because Martinez was from Puerto Rico and had once practiced law there, Barbara thought he was the one to help her.

So, on a weekday, Martinez would later say, Barbara Kogan walked into his office, on Broadway in the downtown area of Manhattan, seeking assistance. She had already started a list of the couple's assets, which included the life-insurance policies they'd taken out years earlier. The couple had believed during happier times that purchasing the policies was a sound decision to protect their businesses and to ensure that Barbara and their sons were taken care of, should anything happen to George.

In an effort to acquire proof of those assets, on October 15, 1990, Barbara telephoned State Mutual Companies asking if the three life-insurance policies on her husband's life were still in force and, if so, who the beneficiaries were. Barbara's attorney contended that Barbara had needed the information, because the main policy on George's life—for $2 million—had built up equity and was considered an asset. A copy of the policy was the proof Barbara needed for the divorce court, the attorney said. The other two policies were worth $1 million each. Barbara had asked that a copy of each be overnighted to her via Federal Express. Barbara also immediately paid a $2,000 premium through a real estate escrow account to keep the policies in force.

Eight days later, George Kogan was dead.

CHAPTER 6

Scene of the Crime

"Good morning, Moses," George said to the doorman as he walked through the lobby of 205 East Sixty-ninth, George and Mary-Louise's tony high-rise apartment. As he stepped outside, a light, crisp, morning rain was falling, invigorating George as he walked the block to a neighborhood market.

It was just after 9:30 as he made his way in the fall drizzle. George wasn't in a hurry to get to work at his Fifth Avenue antiques shop. But the rain—and the sixty-degree temperature—speeded up his step as he hurried to the Third Avenue market to pick up groceries for a late breakfast with Mary-Louise. George, dressed in sweat pants and a T-shirt, carried two bags from the Food Emporium back to his apartment.

On his way back, as the signal light turned red, he hastily crossed Third Avenue, navigating traffic in concert with other pedestrians, as he turned the corner onto Sixty-ninth Street toward home, while skirting cars that zipped by. Waiting for him inside his ground-floor apartment was Mary-Louise. Their home, where he'd lived with her for the last two years, represented a new beginning for George, and he relished every moment they shared together. He slowed, then veered left on the sidewalk as he got closer to the entrance of the residential co-op. Flanking the canvas-canopied doorway were extra-large stone Victorian urn planters holding juniper trees. He passed the door to a private doctor's office just twenty feet before the entrance to the first floor of his building. Across the sidewalk from the office was a cypress tree large enough for someone to move behind and not be noticed. But George wasn't thinking about any of that. He just wanted to get out of the cool morning air and into the apartment. He didn't pay attention to the noise of the construction workers just across the street as he passed them on his way home.

George enjoyed living in Lenox Hill. He and Mary-Louise had redecorated the interior of their apartment with high-end antiques, most of which were from George's shop. The couple's furnishings made for an elegant yet warm environment. The passion of their relationship had not died down after two years. George still felt like a teenager in love for the first time.

That morning was a typical weekday. Third Avenue, where George and Mary-Louise regularly walked, was abustle as usual with traffic. Five foot ten and carrying a few extra pounds, including the beginnings of jowls, George was trying to get in better shape, and the walks helped him with that. Still, physically he felt good.

Like many New Yorkers, George was a creature of habit. On this day, he simply walked to the market, then retraced his steps and quickly made his way home, as he had so many times before. He was light on his feet as a gunman suddenly came up from behind, stepping out from the shadows. With pistol drawn, the killer brazenly rushed toward George. No words were exchanged as the gunman pumped three .44-caliber bullets into George's back at close range. George didn't stand a chance.

Catapulted off the ground, George landed face down with his head toward Second Avenue and his body parallel to the building wall a few feet from the entrance to the doctor's office.

George could hear his heart beating and feel a huge force inside, like a hand reaching in, squeezing his chest.

Doorman Moses Crespo had been working at the elegant

pre-war building for more than twenty years when the shooting occurred. This particular morning, Moses had been sorting the mail, readying it to put into tenants' mailboxes, while a coworker stood by to watch the door. "It was a busy morning," Moses said. "This is a busy street." He and the coworker heard the shots, but didn't realize it was gunfire. When Moses finished sorting the mail, he walked to the front of the lobby toward the desk, which is when he heard the loud noise. "I heard some *pop* sound, you know, like shots." It was the same sound he'd heard day after day as construction workers used power nail guns across the street. He didn't think twice about the noise—until his coworker called out to him.

"What's that in the mirror?" he asked Moses. Just inside the canopy, two large security mirrors were placed at each end, so that the person on duty could see who came and went. "Someone's lying on the sidewalk." The coworker looked closer into the mirrors to see who had fallen. "Moses!" the coworker said, alarmed. "It's George Kogan!"

Just then, a housekeeper pounded on the oak-framed, heavy glass door, yelling, "Let me in!" She'd been walking toward George and was about to step under the canopy when the gunman, hot on George's heels, caught up to him. As the housekeeper watched in horror, the suspect pulled a revolver from his belt, aimed straight for George's back, and opened fire at close range, hitting his mark fast and furiously. One shot wasn't enough. He pumped off two more rounds. The gunman made certain the bullets hit home.

The horrific scene unfolding before her eyes left the cleaning woman terrified and in a panic. "One of the ladies who works in the building rushed the door, saying, 'Please! Hurry up! Open the *door*!'" Crespo said. She continued yelling out to Crespo until he unlocked the door and let her in. She would be the only eyewitness to see the entire shooting, from start to finish.

Inside the lobby, she was barely consolable.

That's when Crespo ran outside to where George lay on the sidewalk. Moses, stunned by the events, bent down and talked to George while he was still conscious. Then, George rested the side of his face on the rain-soaked concrete and thought about death. His final request, made to Moses, was to summon Mary-Louise to his side. As Moses hurried away for help, George spoke his last words before slipping into unconsciousness: "I'm dying."

Doing what George had requested—getting help and sending Mary-Louise outside to be with George—Moses hurried to just inside the building's entrance and, using the lobby wall phone at his security post, called emergency 911, where a dispatch operator at the New York Police Communications office answered.

"911," the operator said. "What is your emergency?"

"There's been a shooting," Moses said.

"What is the exact location of your emergency?"

"Two-oh-five East Sixty-ninth Street. A man has been shot. He's on the sidewalk," Moses told the dispatcher.

"What is your last name?"

"Crespo. C-R-E-S-P-O."

"What is your first name?"

"Moses."

"Who was shot?" the dispatch operator asked.

"George Kogan," Moses said, before being asked to spell the name. "He lives here, at two-oh-five East Sixty-ninth. He's outside."

"Is he breathing?"

"Yes."

"Okay. An ambulance is on the way and police are en route, sir."

"Thank you."

"Help is on the way," the dispatcher assured him.

Moses hung up and rushed toward the back of the building, where George lived in Apartment 1D with Mary-Louise. He knocked on the door.

Inside, Mary-Louise thought to herself, *George must have forgotten his key.*

She'd been expecting her boyfriend to arrive home from the market. A minute later, Mary-Louise answered and appeared surprised to instead see Moses standing at the door. She could tell by the look on the doorman's face that something wasn't right.

"Is everything okay?"

"George wants to talk to you," Moses said, without telling her the reason he was there. Moses did not want to be the one to break the news to Mary-Louise that her boyfriend had been gunned down and was on the ground, badly injured. Still, by Moses's alarmed demeanor, she felt a foreboding as she hurried with Moses the short distance from her ground-floor apartment to the lobby.

Moses opened the street door for Mary-Louise, and she hurried outside. Just then, the sound of an ambulance's siren filled the air as paramedics raced to the building. "They were here fast. An ambulance was already in the area when George was shot," Crespo said.

Mary-Louise was in utter shock to find George sprawled on the sidewalk lying in a pool of blood. Groceries and cash were strewn all around him. Mary-Louise didn't run to George. She stood frozen under the canopy about ten feet away, immobilized by fear. Her next reaction as she stood in front of the building was to cry out.

On the sidewalk next to George, "Loose change and bills were everywhere," Crespo said. "I don't know how the money got there. George was lying in the middle of it. Mary-Louise saw George and started screaming." Witnesses picked up the money and handed the bills to Moses.

Other witnesses stood in stunned shock as the aftermath of the crime played itself out, unfolding like the scene in a murder mystery it was. Soon, a fleet of cop cars and emergency vehicles swarmed the street, and the squawk of police radio traffic punctuated the sounds of the city.

Moses stationed himself at the doorway of 205 East Sixty-ninth, making sure to keep the door locked. NYPD Officer Joseph Girimonte, a patrol cop, heard the dispatch call and hurried from the 19th Precinct, which covers the Upper East Side from Fifty-ninth to Ninety-sixth and from Fifth Avenue to the East River. "I was the first officer to arrive. I got to the scene. There was a fat person—a fat man—laying on the floor in front of that address," Girimonte said.

Then, shortly after that, police officers Medina and Costleigh with the Emergency Service Unit heard a call come in at 10:10 a.m. "A person shot at 205 East Sixty-ninth Street," it said. They headed out in the unit's Truck 2 and arrived screeching to the curb.

The majority of officers and detectives on the scene were from the 19th Precinct, which was considered "ultra chic," a primo assignment, and different from the nearby 20th. "Under the watchful eyes of the NYPD's 19th Precinct, the Upper East Side is a conglomerate of tree-lined streets with million-dollar brownstones, multi-million-dollar apartments on Fifth and Park Avenues, and stores and bars on Madison and Lexington Avenues so swank that one needn't even think of entering to buy something unless they can produce an American Express platinum card for inspection," wrote Samuel M. Katz in his 1997 book *Anytime, Anywhere* about NYPD's Emergency Services Unit. "The city's Who's Who live on the Upper East Side, from Mayor Rudolph Guliani and Police Commissioner Howard Safir, to diplomats, dukes and duchesses, playboys (and some bunnies), high rollers, and captains of industry."

At the scene of the crime, word quickly spread in the neighborhood that there had been a shooting, and a growing crowd of onlookers gathered. Mary-Louise, in the meantime, stood shocked, still crying and recoiling in horror before a doorman and a couple of residents, in fear that she too might be shot, ushered Mary-Louise back inside the lobby. But before they led her back inside, Mary-Louise shouted, "It was the wife! His wife did it!"

That single, spontaneous statement, uttered in a moment of intense emotion and heard loud and clear by two witnesses, set the course for what would become a nearly twenty-year police investigation of "the wife," Barbara Kogan.

CHAPTER 7
The Hospital

On the sidewalk, an ambulance arrived with three paramedics, who knelt down to help George Kogan. Just a few minutes had passed since George had been gunned down, yet the street was already packed.

To get to the victim, paramedics had to break through the crowd and clear a path so they could begin working on George. They immediately checked the forty-nine-year-old for vital signs. They then covered him with a blanket to keep him warm. Within minutes, they called the physician on duty at New York Hospital's emergency room.

"He's breathing and semiconscious," a medic said. They put an oxygen mask, which covered George's nose and mouth, on his face as they prepared him for the short trip to the hospital. They didn't see any spent bullets on the sidewalk. While medics could not fully assess the damage of the gunshot wounds because of all the blood, they assumed the injuries were massive, especially since the bullets and fragments no doubt remained in his body. They knew they needed to get George to the hospital, and stat. Paramedics prepared to transport him to the hospital, where a team headed by a surgeon would spend the next four hours trying to save him.

While George wasn't completely unconscious, he could no longer speak, and his skin was ashen. He was slipping into a coma. "The ambulance medics picked him up on a gurney and took him away," Crespo said. "That was the end of it."

At least that was the end of it at 205 East Sixty-ninth Street. Meanwhile, one medic carried the oxygen tank while the other wheeled George on a gurney to the rear of the ambulance. One stayed by George's side inside the ambulance, to monitor his vital signs, as the door closed. The driver flipped on the sirens and lights and rushed the five-block, two-minute route to New York Hospital at 525 East Sixty-eighth Street. The driver pulled up next to the curb, and waiting emergency personnel rushed outside to the ambulance as the medics rolled George Kogan's gurney into the emergency room. George had lapsed into unconsciousness during the short ride to the hospital. But he was still alive.

Inside the emergency room a team of attendants assessed him. Then, with a physician, they prepared George for surgery. Dr. Michael Marano needed to stop the bleeding and see if he could remove the bullets and fragments. George's wounds were life-threatening, and he was placed on the critical list.

For the next four hours, Marano and the medical team operated on George. One of the high-caliber slugs had gone straight through his body, entering his back and exiting his chest. Doctors were able to remove one of the bullets lodged in his chest. But one remained. He suffered from penetrating injuries and ballistic trauma with massive blood loss. Once they went into surgery, doctors discovered that one of the bullets had punched a hole in George's heart.

As word of the shooting spread, friends and family gathered at the hospital. A woman at the scene, in the apartment lobby, asked Mary-Louise for her parents' phone number and then called her mom for her.

With George on the way to the hospital, Mary-Louise returned to her apartment to call George's sister, Myrna Borus. "She was hysterical, screaming, and I couldn't understand a word she was saying, and I had to slow her down, because I didn't know what she was talking about," Borus would say. But she did pick out from that conversation that

Mary-Louise was about to leave for the hospital. "She told me which hospital, and I ran over," Borus noted.

Mary-Louise acknowledged that after seeing George on the sidewalk, she "panicked, screamed, ran. I was grabbed back into the building, because everybody was sort of unsure what was happening and didn't know if I was going to be next, or what, so I just panicked." Mary-Louise had no recollection of what she'd said that morning. "There were people sort of gawking, and there were a couple of people who worked in the building, but I don't remember anything else," she said.

Mary-Louise, accompanied by a doorman, took a cab to the hospital. Once there, she called George's sons, Billy and Scott. She told police that she also called George's lawyers. One by one, family arrived at the hospital: Myrna and her daughter, along with Mary-Louise's parents and Billy.

Once at the hospital, Billy called his mother. But Barbara didn't pick up the phone in her Fifth Avenue apartment.

"Mom, Dad's been shot. He's in the hospital. They're going to operate," said a tearful Billy in his voice message to his mother. Then he assured her he would keep her informed and asked her to meet him at the hospital. He also told her that Mary-Louise was there.

Billy, beside himself, tried calling his mother again later, but still her answering machine picked up. Barbara eventually returned his call, but she remained at home. "She never came to the hospital," Billy's aunt, Myrna Borus, said, "but she kept calling."

"Mom, maybe you should come," Billy told his mother.

"I don't think I should go, what with Mary-Louise there, Billy," she said. "It might be uncomfortable."

The decision not to visit her dying husband would come back to haunt Barbara. She would later tell a newspaper reporter she'd been at home and in distress, telling *The Post* she was in her apartment "screaming and in shock" and then "fell asleep." Many did not believe her, especially since Barbara's phone records later revealed she'd spent a good part of that time on phone calls.

Her divorce attorney, Richard Golub, when reached by a newspaper, said that for safety reasons, Barbara couldn't go to the hospital; she was in fear for her life because a gunman was still on the loose and she too could be a target. "She wanted to be there at the end. Just because you are divorcing someone doesn't mean you don't still have feelings for them," the attorney told the *Post*. But police wouldn't provide Barbara armed protection at the hospital, "So I told her she shouldn't leave the apartment," Golub said. "She was very upset that she couldn't be there. I'm very worried about her safety and the safety of the family. We don't know who did this or where they could be."

Hospital officials would later say they'd contacted Barbara several times, pleading with her to visit the hospital, because George wasn't doing well and it could be the last time she'd be able to see him. Despite their pleas, Barbara stayed home.

Thus, prominently missing from George's bedside was his estranged wife, who lived in the Olympic Tower at 641 Fifth Avenue, just a mile and three quarters from the hospital in Midtown Center. She could have easily caught a cab and been there in a matter of minutes.

At 11:38 a.m., about an hour and a half after the shooting, Barbara called her parents, Rose and Emanuel Siegel, at their home in Puerto Rico. The phone records showed it was a short conversation.

Barbara also called an unnamed friend who visited her at her apartment. Barbara had asked her friend to comb out her hair, in preparation for a trip to the hospital, should Barbara decide to go. The friend, it turned out, was a hairdresser.

At the hospital, a couple hours after arriving, Mary-Louise left briefly to go home, take a shower, change her clothes, and return to the waiting-room vigil, anticipating with George's family word from doctors about his condition.

In the late afternoon, the hospital phoned Barbara a final time. The news was grave. Her husband had passed away just after 4 p.m., a hospital official told her. Doctors tried to revive him, but they were unsuccessful. They did what they could, but with injuries and damage to his liver, lungs, and heart, George had bled internally, and doctors could not stop the hemorrhaging.

Six hours after the shooting on October 23, doctors in the ICU's recovery room officially pronounced George H. Kogan dead. As soon as George died, police elevated their investigation to a homicide instead of an attempted murder.

Family members at the hospital, unaware that George had died, waited for word about his condition. George's sister, Myrna, later remembered in detail the distrubing turn of events: "They told us to sit somewhere and wait and that they would tell us. And by the time I went screaming to ask what was going on, it had been an hour that he had passed away and they didn't tell me anything."

Instead, it was Barbara, still officially George's wife and the immediate next of kin, who was the first to be told. The news drifted out to George's other family members, as well as to Mary-Louise, but only after it was obvious, from the doctors' and nurses' demeanor toward the family, that George's status had gravely changed. His family members and Mary-Louise Hawkins, at the hospital together in the waiting room, were stunned not only that he'd been shot, but, now, that he was dead. They turned to one another for comfort.

George's son Scott, in the meantime, had arrived at his part-time job at Sacred Heart University's business administration department in San Juan, Puerto Rico, when a co-worker shouted out to him from across a room, "Hey, Scott, the boss wants to see you." Scott walked to the department director's office and she told him there'd been an accident involving his father. His aunt Elaine, Barbara's sister, made flight arrangements for the two of them and, later that day, they flew together to New York. At the airport to meet them was Scott's brother, Billy, who gave them the grave news that their father had died.

About an hour and a half after her husband's death, at 5:30 p.m., Barbara dialed her good friend Dawna Cole, who at the time lived in Norwich, New York. Barbara, Dawna said, was hysterical and wasn't making sense. Dawna was surpised when Barbara asked if she knew the name of the attorney who represented their mutual friend, LuAnn Fratt, after Fratt killed her husband and was prosecuted for the crime. Fratt, whose attorney used a self-defense strategy, was later acquitted.

"Do you know who her lawyer was, in case I need one?" Barbara asked Dawna.

"I think it was Michael Dowd," Dawna answered.

George Kogan's body was taken to the New York City Medical Examiner's Office, which looks into suspicious and violent deaths.

The next morning, Myrna Borus drove from her New Jersey home to Manhattan to meet Officer Joseph Girimonte, the first officer at the crime scene, at the medical examiner's office. Girimonte, who could not reach Barbara, needed Myrna to positively identify her brother's body before the autopsy could be performed.

Staff gave Girimonte, who had been on the NYPD force since 1985, a photo of the newly deceased George's face. Once Myrna arrived, Girimonte showed her the photo. George's face was ghostly pale.

"Is this your brother, George Kogan?"

"Yes, that's George," said Myrna, through tears and overcome by the events of the day before. She, of course, recognized her brother. What she did not recognize was the death mask that his face had become. Girimonte extended his condolences. "I'm very sorry for your loss, ma'am," he told her. "I know it's not easy."

It was true. And, for Myrna, unthinkable. George was gone. Never again would she be able to chat on the phone with her favorite brother, closer in age to her than their brother Lawrence, or travel with him, as they'd done over the years. She thought back to when her daughter had passed away and how she'd leaned on George during those sad days. And she thought about the good times nine years earlier, in 1981, when she'd taken a two-week vacation to Europe with George and Barbara, on a buying trip for their San

Juan stores. Her brother "wanted me to learn the jewelry business," Myrna later explained.

"We went to London, to Paris, and to Rome," she recalled. While in Italy, "We went to Oscar's in Milan." George preferred staying at "only the top hotels, and always with a fancy car. Nothing but the best."

Myrna was still processing the reality of losing George, especially the violent way he'd died, which made the loss even more difficult. She still couldn't believe it. Myrna, along with the rest of the family, would never fully recover from the heartbreak of that misty fall morning when they lost George.

The same day Myrna positively identified her brother's lifeless body, Dr. Aglae Charlot, an associate New York City medical examiner, prepared for the autopsy, number M909837. Twenty-four hours after the murder, the team of detectives on the Kogan case went to the city's main morgue and, as the lead investigators, observed Doctor Charlot perform the autopsy on George Kogan's body. Officer Joseph Girimonte was there as well.

George's body had been refrigerated overnight at the morgue, located at First Avenue near Thirtieth Street, between two major city hospitals, Bellevue and NYU Medical Center. The body was cold as Dr. Charlot began her examination. She noted the height as five foot ten inches and the weight as 265 pounds. The body had "incised wounds" in the chest and torso that were made during surgery, and tubes were still in his nose and inside his mouth from when ER surgeons had worked on him the day before. The tubes were also visible in the photo Myrna had viewed at the medical examiner's office. Three entrance wounds were in the back, and one had tiny abrasions consistent with injuries caused by gunpowder, from a muzzle that was about twelve to eighteen inches from the back when fired, according to notes written by Dr. Charlot. The bullets had stopped George Kogan in his tracks.

Charlot pulled the remaining bullet from George's back. The first had been removed by a hospital surgeon the day before: the second went into George's back and exited from his chest, but it was not recovered at the scene. Thus, the two pulled slugs, both deformed from entering his body, became the only physical evidence to help detectives in their hunt for the killer.

After completing the autopsy, Dr. Charlot filled out the death certificate and indicated the cause (multiple gunshot wounds) and manner (homicidal). With that, George Kogan's death officially became the 673rd homicide in 1990 in New York City.

Detective John Kraljic, a ballistic and forensic firearms examiner with the NYPD's Firearms Analysis Section, performed laboratory tests on the .44-caliber deformed slugs removed during the autopsy and surgery. What he learned was striking. One of the unforgiving bullets George was shot with was a copper-jacketed, hollow-point .44 caliber. Because it was a little larger than, say, a .38, Kraljic said in his report, "It has the potential to cause more damage." The hollow point is "supposed to create more damage to the target that it hits. It also slows it down, so it doesn't over-penetrate and go through the target." Once inside the body, hollow points expand, or mushroom, and cause more damage. The other slug removed from his body was the same, except this one wasn't a hollow-point round. "A man-stopper" is the nickname for the powerful .44-caliber bullet. According to a 2006 Strategypage.com article, "American troops prefer the century-old .44 caliber pistol, considered an accurate, high-velocity weapon, to lighter 9mm models."

A Los Angeles Police SWAT-team member, who asked that his name not be used, said, "It is all about 'stopping power.' A forty-four will stop a grizzly bear."

Don White, who was with the Bexar County Sheriff's Department's homicide investigation division in San Antonio for eighteen years, analyzed the circumstances surrounding the Kogan shooting. If this was a contract hit, he said, the goal "is two shots to the body, one to the head." But as George flew forward, that was not possible. The final shot appeared to have been fired when George was on the ground, which could explain why two bullets did not exit his body, because the ground may have prevented them from doing so. At close range, there would be very little bullet expansion inside the body, White said: "No expansion, no large hole."

That also explained why door attendant Moses Crespo did not immediately notice the wounds on George's back. "At first, I didn't know what was wrong with George," Crespo said. "I asked him, 'What is it? What's wrong?' He told me he was shot. Then I looked at his back and saw the blood start to seep through his shirt. But I did not see that at first."

According to White, "The forty-four is a big bullet, and it travels fairly fast. What you can get is a sudden increase in blood pressure, from the pressure of the bullets, and this will turn out the lights, so to speak, very quickly." And it did. George, within minutes of being shot, lost consciousness after talking to Moses. "The shooter may have even used a three-alloy metal that is very hard," White explained. "You'd expect the bullets to go all the way through and exit. The bullets, if found, are hard enough that the lands and grooves don't show up. Ballistics would have a hard time with that." As it turned out, ballistics tests were inconclusive—other than identifying the type of gun used to fire the bullets—because there was no murder weapon with which to compare the bullet fragments. The unusual manufacturing process of the snub-nosed barrel, Don White said, leaves distinctive marks on each slug. But without the gun, ballistic and forensic firearms examiner John Kraljic, along with homicide detectives, reached a dead end.

At that early stage in the case, detectives did not yet have a suspect. But this much they knew: The gunman was either a professional hit man or someone with a grudge against George Kogan. The shooting, they said, was not random. And whoever shot George wanted him dead.

Investigators hit the Lenox Hill neighborhood, combing the area to search for clues to help them learn the identity of the shooter. Cops began piecing together a timeline surrounding George's murder.

Officer Henry Medina, a twenty-nine-year veteran at that point, was with NYPD's Emergency Squad Unit 2 and arrived at the scene to set up perimeters and help in the investigation. Each member of this unit was trained to serve as an emergency medical technician and to assist police officers. When Medina received the call that a person was shot in front of 205 East Sixty-ninth, his unit headed out and arrived three minutes later. "I observed a white male on the sidewalk with three gunshot wounds to him. We took out our medical equipment and we were going to start CPR on him, and then the New York City emergency ambulance arrived on the scene, and we assisted them in putting him onto the ambulance and they took him to the hospital," Medina said. "We tried to give him oxygen. After he was put in the ambulance, we roped off the area of the address and we searched for evidence."

Medina, who went on to receive his department's Medal of Valor in 2004, walked a zigzag path across the wide sidewalk in search of evidence. But police were unable to spot any tangible evidence at the scene. "We were looking for a weapon that was used, spent cartridges, or spent rounds," he said. Because the gunman had used a revolver, it would not have left behind spent shell casings. Instead, the casings remained inside the gun. But police did not know that was the case until bullets were removed from George during emergency surgery and during the autopsy.

Officer Girimonte, as a patrol officer, finished stringing yellow police tape to clearly define the perimeter around the spot where George was shot and to keep curious onlookers from walking all over the crime scene, contaminating possible evidence.

At 10:20 a.m., NYPD Sergeant Joe Fornabaio arrived to help with interviews. He interviewed Beverly Kantor, who had stepped out of her parked car to walk to a nearby market, only to see the shooting just after it happened. "I looked up and saw a white male holding a gun," she told police detectives, "and I ducked down, because I didn't want to be shot at."

Shortly after Sergeant Fornabaio arrived on the scene, homicide detectives Mike Sheehan and Anthony Vasquez also responded to the call at 10:25 a.m. They were there fifteen minutes later to interview more witnesses, including Moses Crespo, who relayed what he had seen.

The detectives and their investigative team spent the day at the scene, diagramming it, marking the evidence, including the coins, bills, and groceries scattered about the sidewalk, gathering what little evidence there was. The rain-soaked sidewalk hindered them; there were no fingerprints or footprints to dust.

Also arriving on the scene was Deputy District Attorney Joel Seidemann, with the Manhattan DA's murder unit. He was on homicide call that day, so Seidemann too headed to the scene of the crime soon after notification.

In the meantime, Sheehan and Vasquez spoke with witness Roger Wideman, a Federal Express delivery person who happened to be at the scene. Wideman had just driven up and jumped out of his delivery truck; he stood at the service entrance at 205 East Sixty-ninth. Suddenly, "three or four" shots rang out, he explained. He immediately looked up and saw a thin white man, about five foot ten inches tall, hurrying up Sixty-ninth, then turning north onto Third Avenue. Wideman told NYPD detectives that the gunman wore a dark-colored trench coat and a neon-colored cap, and that his hands were near his waist area. Wideman walked toward the victim and saw that George was shot, but since others were starting to approach him, too, he left the scene and continued on his route. Near Sixty-eighth Street and Lexington Avenue, Wideman "saw a man, possibly the perp, running and looking back," he told police. The man headed toward Madison Avenue, where Wideman got a closer look and a better description. The suspect was in his forties, about five foot eleven inches tall, weighed about 165 pounds, had the beginnings of a gray-and-brown beard, wore dark glasses, and had not yet ditched the trench coat and bright-colored cap. Wideman was sure it was the same man he had seen standing near the victim a few minutes earlier.

As detectives Sheehan and Vasquez continued their interviews, Officer Joseph Hamilton with NYPD's Crime Scene Unit got a call at 11:20 a.m. to respond to 205 East Sixty-ninth. From the Bronx, at Third Avenue and Fordham Road, the unit headed to the Upper East Side. They arrived thirty-five minutes later to "a taped-off area in front of the building, detectives, and not much else," Hamilton said. "I made a physical examination of the scene, tried to make note of anything of importance at the scene, and took seven photographs." He, too, found no tangible evidence after spending about thirty to forty-five minutes at the scene.

Meanwhile, Sheehan and Vasquez interviewed another eyewitness, Terence Grau, who was at a pay phone on the southwest corner of Sixty-ninth and Third Avenue when he heard what he called "four shots." Grau looked down Sixty-ninth and saw a white man, thirty-five to forty years old, five foot ten with glasses, wearing a red lumberjack-type shirt underneath a nondescript outer garment. The suspect ran as he turned north onto Third Avenue, turning his head and looking back as he fled. According to the police report from Grau's interview: "Before the male got to the corner of Sixty-ninth and Third Avenue, [Grau] sees the male attempting to put something into his [jacket] pocket and having trouble doing so. Before he gets to the corner, the male secrets the object around his waist area. He thinks the male had the gun in his left hand. Asked how he would know it was a gun, he stated it was the way the man held it."

Detectives Sheehan and Vasquez also questioned Hector Agstini, who had been working as a repairperson two doors up at The Fairfax luxury residences at 201 East Sixty-ninth. He'd been on break, standing just inside the lobby doors, when he heard what he told investigators were "four shots." Then, he saw a partially bearded man, about forty to forty-five years old and wearing glasses, a bright green day-glo baseball cap, and a dark gray vest with light gray sleeves. The man was "walking fast toward Third," according to his statement to police. "He further observed this male place what appeared to be a handgun in his waistband. Hector didn't observe where this male headed after hitting Third Avenue," according to the police report.

Later in the day, Officer Girimonte—still on duty and wearing his navy blue uniform—went to the hospital to check on the status of George Kogan. "I remember seeing the gentleman that I had seen in the street on the operating table with his chest open, and he was deceased. He had died," he would later say. The first officer to arrive at the scene immediately after the crime, it was his job to keep in contact with the family and do the follow-up with the victim, checking on his condition. As a second-generation cop, he'd been exposed plenty of times to a variety of situations involving families of victims. It was Officer Girimonte's job to remain unemotional and professional, especially since this attempted homicide would now become a full-blown murder investigation.

At 5 p.m., Charles Hage, twenty-seven years old and in New York City visiting his brother, telephoned NYPD's 19th Precinct to tell police what he had seen earlier in the day. Officer Steve Melluso, who had been at the scene that morning, took the call. Hage told Officer Melluso that he'd happened to be standing on the northwest corner of Sixty-ninth and Third just after ten o'clock when he heard what sounded like three gunshots. Hage then saw a man running on Third Avenue, away from the scene. Hage also mentioned that the suspect had a reddish-gray beard and looked like he was carrying a Walkman.

One of the first questions a homicide detective asks is who might benefit from the murder. The answer in the Kogan case came two days after the murder, when a cursory look by investigators into George Kogan's insurance papers showed that his estranged wife, Barbara, was the main beneficiary of Kogan's $4.8 million insurance policies. For detectives, it served as potential circumstantial evidence and a possible motive for murder.

The killing was called the worst murder in New York City in recent history. The front-page headlines the next morning screamed "MURDER." The front page of *The New York Post* read, "Millionaire Slain on East Side." *Newsday*'s headline said, "Daylight 'Hit' On Upper East Side." United Press International's headline story, which ran across the wire, read, "Police say real estate tycoon was target of a 'hit.' "

Almost immediately, media interest shifted from focusing on the shooting to the details of the investigation. *Newsday* assigned newspaper reporter Mitch Gelman the story. "I worked in police headquarters for *Newsday*. Whenever there was a homicide in New York City, the police department precinct would be recorded, and, handwritten on a white sheet of paper, the address, male, white, the age, a name if they had it, and what had transpired. And depending upon the case, we decided at the paper who was in the best position of covering it." As it happened, the George Kogan murder occurred when Gelman was on duty. "I have a general recollection of the case when it happened," he said. "There weren't a lot of murders at the time on that side of Manhattan." Gelman also remembered the funeral service, because he'd gotten a parking ticket outside the chapel on the busy Upper East Side.

Gelman wrote what he called a "second-day story" that appeared two days after the murder, on page 6 of *Newsday*, with a headline that read, "Love, Money Focus Of East Side Murder Probe." The article began, "Real estate developer George Kogan was gunned down on an Upper East Side street Tuesday for either love or money."

"Detectives yesterday probed the gambling connections of a luxury resort and casino that Kogan developed in San Juan and recently sold to a group of Brooklyn investors and Kogan's other real estate dealings," the article continued. Police told Gelman, "Kogan had spent a good part of his life in San Juan." The article also said police interviewed acquaintances "about Kogan's personal life and his pending divorce, which was bitterly contested, according to friends and others involved in the proceedings."

That same day, police tried unsuccessfully to speak with Barbara. "The girlfriend has been very cooperative," a police detective told Gelman about Mary-Louise. "We still want to talk to the wife."

Attorney Aaron Golub explained Barbara's decision not to immediately speak with officers: "I don't think she's being uncooperative. [Police officers'] expectations of interviewing someone immediately after a tragedy like this are unrealistic."

Just a day after the murder, investigators were already building a profile of the killer, based upon information they'd gathered. According to police, the gunman, based on witness accounts, was a white man about five foot ten inches tall, weighing roughly 165 pounds. He fired the three shots from a high-caliber handgun—specifically, a Bulldog .44. "This was a pure hit. There was no robbery involved," one investigator familiar with the case told *Newsday*.

The Bulldog revolver is a high-powered, five-shot handgun that uses a .44 special high-caliber bullet. It was a top-selling gun in the 1980s for manufacturer Charter Arms. It was also the weapon of choice for serial killer David Berkowitz, nicknamed the "Son of Sam" and "The .44-Caliber Killer," who went on a murder spree in 1976 and '77 in New York City. "There are only about ten guns that will shoot a .44," said a Los Angeles Police Department undercover detective, "and they are big handguns to be able to handle the pressure created by firing that beast." The Bulldog, meant for use at close range, fit the bill for George Kogan's killer. It told police that the killing was not random, that the shooter had planned how and when he was going to hit George, and, particularly, that he was planning to hit his victim at close range. Also, the shooter was able to easily conceal the snub-nosed revolver by tucking it into his waistband. The gunman needed to be an experienced shooter, White said, because of the powerful recoil of the Bulldog, which requires expert, hands-on experience. With that type of weapon used in a brazen, daylight shooting in a public setting, NYPD investigators knew from the start that the killer was a professional hired gun.

Detectives from the Manhattan North Homicide Squad—a prestigious unit of veterans—tried to make sense of the case as they pieced together the details of George's life. The team interviewed his friends, family, and international business associates. Investigators admitted that they "had little to go on" from witnesses. Even so, from the little evidence they had and the circumstances under which George was killed, they continued to believe the killer was a hired gun. They also said they hoped leads to a suspect would emerge as they looked closer at George's complex web of finances, which stretched from the Caribbean to the East Coast.

Early in the probe, quoting unnamed sources, *Newsday*, in an October 26, 1990, article, reported that George Kogan had "ties to Puerto Rican gamblers and reputedly to Brooklyn mobsters" that could have led to his death. Reporter Mitch Gelman cited police as saying that George had been living beyond his means and owed money to "many people." Investigators probed the nuances of his bitter divorce and looked into reports that he was "living off the wealth of a woman he moved in with two years earlier," Gelman reported. Detectives, the article said, were ruling out nothing in their probe. Also, an unidentified friend of George told the *New York Post* that the shooting didn't surprise him. "I'm not shocked by this because there was another side to George," he told the newspaper.

Investigators emphatically said Kogan was the target of a "hit" and they were looking to question Kogan's estranged wife, Barbara, and others about the killing.

Years later, Barbara Kogan's attorney would suggest a reason for Kogan's murder. "[George] dealt with underworld characters on a daily basis, and, most importantly, he stiffed everybody he ever did business with, not just his wife," defense lawyer Barry Levin said.

Captain Stephen Davis, who at the time was a New York City Police Department spokesperson, broke the news to the press that the murder was a hitman's doing, noting that George had not been robbed of money. But that did not explain witness accounts that cash was scattered all over the sidewalk near where George had been gunned down. The police had not yet interviewed Barbara Kogan, the captain said, because she was "under sedation," according to her lawyer. Detectives had already interviewed Mary-Louise Hawkins. Captain Davis told reporters that he was unable to confirm a report in the *New York Post* about the Kogans and their "messy divorce battle" in which George had attempted to freeze his estranged wife's bank accounts and other assets.

Two days after the murder, an investigator, identified only as a "city detective," told reporter Mitch Gelman, "The next step [in the investigation], after we talk to the rest of the cutthroat real estate people and women in Kogan's life here in New York, will be to bring in the authorities in San Juan (Puerto Rico). Right now, there is no telling where this will go."

Police learned that George owned real estate in New York with a total fair market value of $1.85 million, assets considered community property in the Kogans' divorce proceeding. This was in addition to the hefty life insurance policies taken out on George's life and left to Barbara, making her a prime suspect.

CHAPTER 8

Early Investigation

Before his father was buried, Scott Kogan tried to talk to Barbara about funeral arrangements for his father. But, he would later say, she wanted only to talk about his father's will and not his burial. To Scott, his mother seemed too pre-occupied with finances.

"There are more pressing issues. We have to bury him," Scott told his mother. So, he and his brother Billy, as well as George's siblings, helped plan their father's service and burial. On October 26, 1990, a Friday morning, a traditional Jewish funeral service, with a visitation immediately before, was held for George H. Kogan. It was hosted by the historic Riverside Memorial Chapel on Manhattan's Upper West Side, which has provided services for New York's Jewish community for more than a century.

Attending George's service and burial three days after his murder were two homicide cops from NYPD's Manhattan North Homicide Squad. At that stage in the police investigation, detectives had already started probing George's personal life and financial records, looking deeper for clues into who might have wanted him dead.

The funeral service was part of the homicide team's investigation. It's not at all unusual—common, even—for police to attend funerals to see who is there, who is not, and to watch for unusual behavior by mourners, including those who appear to be genuinely mourning and those who look like they're faking it. So detectives were there when George H. Kogan was laid to rest "beneath overcast skies," as a *Newsday* article titled "Slain Businessman's Final Farewell" described it.

"My father would have been pleased that you came," Scott Kogan told 150 friends and relatives who filled the chapel's pews during the morning service. "He provided a sound education, both religious and secular, for his children, and left memories for all of us."

Barbara Kogan sat front and center, between the couple's grown sons, Scott, twenty-four, and Billy, twenty-three. In the pew behind were George's brother Lawrence, sister Myrna, and mother Ida, as well as George's distraught twelve-year-old niece, Taryn Kogan, who wept throughout the service.

Missing from the service was George's live-in girlfriend of two years, Mary-Louise Hawkins. She had been by George's side at the hospital and at his deathbed, but out of fear of a media frenzy, Mary-Louise stayed away from the funeral and burial, paying her respects in her own way. George's family understood her absence, especially considering the Kogans' nasty divorce and the animosity Barbara held toward Mary-Louise, whom she felt had stolen her husband from her.

Barbara's parents, Emanuel and Rose, also did not attend.

Divorce attorney Aaron Richard Golub attended the funeral, as did Barbara's estate attorney Norman H. Donald III. Scott's roommate in Puerto Rico, Omar Quinones, was there as well.

Also in attendance to show his respects was John Lyons, who had been Barbara's recent male companion and friend. Lyons attended the service with lawyer Manuel Martinez, whom Barbara had retained a couple months earlier to help her find a Puerto Rican divorce attorney.

Lyons, tall and slim, with skin marred by acne scars, was in his early forties and two or three years younger than Barbara. He had a calm and quiet demeanor with a gentlemanly air about him. His apartment, on East Fifty-sixth Street near Madison Avenue, wasn't far from Barbara's Olympic Tower suite. Lyons was a companion for Barbara, a woman still lonely two years after the sudden end of her lengthy marriage to George.

During the service, even the rabbi who presided over Kogan's funeral acknowledged trouble between Barbara and George. "This marriage had its problems, as all marriages do," Rabbi Robert Graubart said during his eulogy. "But Barbara has fond memories of their early years together in Puerto Rico. And if you measure this marriage by its legacy—two young men of good character—it was among the most successful."

Afterward, *Newsday* photographer Ozier Muhammad captured Barbara as she left the chapel with her sons and friends and headed out in a limousine for the twenty-five-mile drive to Beth David Cemetery in Elmont, on Long Island, for George Kogan's interment.

At the burial, once George's body was placed in the ground, each person poured a shovelful of dirt onto the casket. After groundskeepers finished filling his grave, each attendee chose a rock to place at the head of the grave site. Rocks, unlike perishable flowers, remain for years atop the tombstone, leaving an enduring record of all who paid their respects to George Kogan that day.

For George's extended family, his murder was not only horrifyingly shocking but also a tremendous loss. "He was a personality who was charming," said one cousin, who asked not to be named. "There was always something interesting going on in his life. He joked around quite a bit. He didn't so much talk about his business. He was just colorful." At family gatherings after George's death, the conversation eventually turned to the topic of George's murder. "We talked about it and explored possibilities about who could have done it," the cousin said. "They're sorrowful conversations. He didn't deserve it. He was a nice man. He was always good to us."

A family stone, engraved with the letters KOGAN, now sits at the head of George's plot, at grave number three in the upper row of section four. His plot also has a footstone with his name, date of birth, and date of death. His final resting place, next to a path at Beth David Cemetery, is surrounded by trees. George is the only member of the Kogan family buried there.

Deputy District Attorney Joel Seidemann, some years later, mocked Barbara's presence at her estranged husband's funeral. "She played up the role of the grieving widow at the funeral," he said, "showing up in sunglasses, claiming to be grateful for the good years she had with George." It wasn't the first time authorities thought they'd caught Barbara play-acting, as also evidenced in the hours following the shooting when she told police she cried and screamed.

With the passage of time, however, Barbara increasingly had difficulties keeping up the façade of the grieving wife.

CHAPTER 9

Life After George

By 1990, Barbara no longer worked at Kogan & Company, because of her acrimonious separation from George. She found work helping manage a Madison Avenue art gallery. But after George's death, she took charge once again of the New York shop they had opened together.

Barbara would not have to worry about earning a living for long. Two years after George Kogan's death, her financial woes ended, or so it seemed, when she received the first of two life-insurance payments from George's policies. Also, in George's will, he had left his estranged wife the legal minimum amount of money, one-third of his estate, including interest, paid out in installments for the rest of her life. A portion went to George's brother Lawrence, according to estate records, because he was a partner with George in some of his investments. The balance—roughly half a million dollars—was left to be split between his two sons. But it was Barbara alone who was the beneficiary of the three life-insurance policies, worth a total of $4,831,431.

In October 1991, while the SMA Insurance Company underwent its own investigation into the death of George Kogan, the company reached an agreement with Barbara's attorney to make a partial payment of $2 million to the cash-strapped Mrs. Kogan.

With the payout, George, who had fought to keep his

assets from Barbara, inadvertently, after death, made his estranged wife a rich woman.

And so it was that life without George moved forward. In 1994, their oldest son, Billy, was admitted to the New York Bar Association after graduating with a juris doctorate from the Benjamin N. Cardozo School of Law at Yeshiva University in New York. His father, no doubt, would have been proud. That same year, in November, the Kogans' oldest son, Scott, was married.

By all outward appearances, life was going well for Barbara and her family. But money appeared to still be a motivating factor for her. To that end, she had not given up trying to find property she and George had owned jointly, as evidenced in 1995 when she penned a letter to Mary-Louise Hawkins, dated March 3. But Barbara no longer knew where Mary-Louise lived or where to send the note.

That was because life after George had changed drastically for Mary Louis as well. Even though she'd been fired from her public relations job at Evins Communications after the owner learned of her affair with George, Mary-Louise knew her former boss to be a fair man. She swallowed her pride and contacted him. She asked for the opportunity to make amends and to work for his firm again, and he rehired her. "People make mistakes," Evins later said. "People are entitled to a second chance. And she was also younger, and I felt she was entitled to a second chance, and that's what I gave her."

After living at the East Sixty-ninth Street co-op for two years with George, Mary-Louise moved out of the apartment owned by her father and relocated to The Horizon high-rise at 415 East Thirty-seventh Street in the Tudor City neighborhood of Manhattan, where she had purchased a condominium. She eventually married and moved to the United Kingdom with her new husband. Authorities in New York stayed in touch, keeping her abreast of the murder investigation. It was, detectives told Mary-Louise at the time, "an active investigation."

In hopes that her note would reach Mary-Louise, Barbara

sent it in care of her mother on Long Island. Mary-Louise's mother, in turn, faxed the note to her daughter. In it, Barbara indicated to Mary-Louise that it was her belief that Mary-Louise had kept 245 pieces of jewelry that were removed from the Kogan & Company store. Barbara asked Mary-Louise to return the pieces.

"Most of the inventory of jewelry from our business which George had in his possession was never recovered," Barbara wrote to Mary-Louise. "You were very kind to mention that to my lawyer a few years ago and ask him where to bring the jewelry." Mary-Louise handed over the note to police, and, according to legal documents, denied ever saying such a thing to Barbara's attorney.

While running the business, Barbara stayed in touch with friends and family. She maintained a solid relationship with her youngest son, Billy. And during trips to Puerto Rico to see her parents and sister, she'd occasionally visit her oldest son, Scott, although their relationship had become strained during his parents' separation.

Then, on June 11, 1995, Barbara lost her father, Emanuel Siegel, who passed away in San Juan, Puerto Rico. He had been through a lot, watching his daughter lose her husband, only to be held under a cloud of suspicion by police. The Kogan sons had lost their father, then, five years later, their maternal grandfather, who had been a strong figure in their formative years in San Juan. For Barbara, who had encouraged her parents to follow her to the island, losing her father was a devastating blow, and she grew increasingly lonely.

The next year, in 1996, the remaining half of the insurance money, held back during SMA Insurance Company's investigation, was released to Barbara. It marked the end of the insurance case, which was formally closed, according to Richard Lutz, the company's attorney, because an investigator was unable to determine who was responsible for George's death. It was a high point for Barbara, boosting her confidence that the police investigation would end the same way.

That same year, nearly a decade after opening the New York store with her husband, now with insurance money to live on, Barbara no longer needed the store. She closed Kogan & Company's doors for good.

Then, on Sunday, May 12, 1996, Billy married. A wedding announcement appeared on the front page of the *New York Times*' "Style" section. It read, in part:

> *Emily Jane Feffer, the daughter of Mr. and Mrs. Paul Feffer of New York, was married last evening to William Stewart Kogan, a son of Barbara Kogan of New York and the late George Kogan. Rabbi David Greenberg officiated at the United Nations Plaza Hyatt Hotel.*

Barbara was proud of her son and happy to see his wedding make the society pages of *The New York Times*. The irony, however, of the ceremony being held at the Plaza Hotel, where George had once courted Mary-Louise Hawkins, was not lost on Barbara. It seemed that everywhere she turned she was reminded of George's affair. She kept a stiff upper lip and, as the mother of the groom, paid for the rehearsal dinner, on the eve of the wedding, using the insurance money.

But Barbara's status as a wealthy widow who'd inherited a large payout did not last long. In 1998, just two years after Barbara collected the final installment on the life-insurance policies, she filed for bankruptcy relief. That was when personal financial details, provided in the public bankruptcy file, were revealed about her lavish lifestyle following her husband's murder.

The bankruptcy court also investigated Barbara, because it was well known that Barbara had inherited a large sum of money, and it seemed odd to the court, even suspect, that in just a few years she'd found herself broke. The court ultimately learned that Barbara had gone through the money quickly because of extravagant spending habits.

Those habits, according to the bankruptcy court records, included two plastic surgeries that totaled $105,000, psychotherapy for $84,000, apartment renovations for $160,000, travel costs of $83,000, fancy health and beauty spa visits totaling $100,000, and thousands more for sundry items, including a Hamptons summer rental.

While both the police and bankruptcy investigations continued, Barbara was sued for nonpayment of a New York City lease she'd entered into for apartment 8G at the Parc Vendome luxury condominiums. The dispute was over the two-bedroom, one-bath suite Barbara had leased at a monthly cost of $3,000, beginning February 1, 1998, and ending January 31, 2000. Located in Midtown West at 340 West Fifty-seventh Street, the Parc Vendome was advertised as "world-class residential living" and "a return to the pre-war elegance of the 1920s and 1930s with all the amenities and security of [today]."

Before she moved in to the apartment, accompanying her application and $200 fee were three glowing letters of recommendation, including one from her accountant and another from Paolo Raboletta, general manager of the Ramada San Juan, a beachfront boutique hotel located in trendy Condado. Raboletta wrote in the letter that, as co-owner of the hotel, Barbara continued to receive income from the hotel. Here is a portion of the letter:

> *This letter is to verify that Barbara Kogan is the co-owner of the Ramada San Juan in the prestigious Condado section of San Juan, Puerto Rico.*
>
> *As co-owner, Mrs. Kogan is entitled to receive as current income the majority of the net income of the hotel each year. Per her instructions, please find a copy of the latest year-end income statement of the hotel, which shows net income in excess of $1.5 million in 1997.*

It was a startling revelation, a statement about "high income," especially in light of Barbara filing in 1998 for bankruptcy protection against creditors. But it wasn't true that Barbara received income from the hotel, because George had sold that hotel in 1986 for $11 million.

A second letter of recommendation, dated January 1, 1998,

was from Barbara's accountant, Jerry Persampieri with Barash, Friedman, Friedberg & Adasko certified public accountants. They stated that they had been her accountants for five years and she had a net worth of over $850,000.

Another letter was from Shirley Anne Mueller, a friend of Barbara who was an attorney. A paragraph in her letter, dated January 21, 1998, read:

> *I have known Ms. Kogan for more than 10 years and I assure you that she would be a wonderful addition to your building. Ms. Kogan is conscientious, polite, helpful, and friendly. In addition, she is involved with the community in supporting various charitable organizations and has been a very successful entrepreneur and businesswoman.*

Barbara was approved for the two-year lease, with a $6,000 security deposit and a fifteen-percent fee of $5,400 paid in advance through McDonagh Real Estate, which had brokered the deal on Barbara's behalf. The monthly sublease payment the first year was $3,000, and the second year it was $3,100 per month. Barbara, on the application, had written that she needed to move into the apartment "ASAP."

It was while Barbara was living at the pricey Parc Vendome that, on July 27, 1998, she filed a voluntary petition under Chapter 7 of the Bankruptcy Code. A court-appointed trustee discovered, during a September meeting, that Barbara had "failed to accurately disclose all of her assets in her bankruptcy petition." Then, three months later in December 1998, Barbara, by letter, asked to amend her bankruptcy petition to include a $1.5 million claim against her husband's estate. But a red flag was raised at a January 1999 examination meeting with the trustee, when, according to the court record, "[Barbara] revealed several glaring errors and omissions in her original bankruptcy petition, including, but not limited to, her sole ownership of two corporations, a farm in Puerto Rico, substantial interests in both foreign and domestic corporations, as well as several domestic and foreign bank accounts." Barbara didn't explain her failure to "disclose her complete financial status and provide sufficient documentation."

"Nearly five months after these discrepancies were uncovered at her examination," the trustee said, "the Debtor filed an amended petition. Even the amended petition, however, failed to set forth full and complete truthful disclosure."

In other words, Barbara had lied, and it did not go over well with the court.

Barbara's troubles were far from over. Her mother, Rose, a day before her ninety-third birthday and nearly five years after her husband Emanuel's death, passed away in Puerto Rico.

That spring, two months after the expiration of Barbara's lease at the Parc Vendome, the apartment owner sued her for not paying her rent as agreed. At 3:45 p.m. on Wednesday, April 5, 2000, a process server walked into the lobby of the Parc Vendome at the West Fifty-seventh Street entrance. William Reilly, the door attendant on duty, told the document server that Barbara wasn't at home at that time of day and that he was not permitted to sign for her. Reilly then referred the server to Parc Vendome's management office and called the office to let them know. Reilly was told on the phone that he could not be served in place of Barbara. When the door attendant informed the server that he could not accept the papers, the server tossed the documents on the doorman's desk and said, "You just did." With that, the process server walked out the door.

Afterward, Sonia Nunez, assistant management supervisor at the Parc Vendome, delivered the documents to Barbara's mailbox, with a written explanation about how they were left at the Parc Vendome.

The legal claim left with the doorman was on behalf of Dr. Benjamin Jagendorf, the Brooklyn owner of Barbara's Parc Vendome apartment. The suit asked for the accrued back rent of $30,000, plus $200,000 for use and occupancy for Barbara, who had stopped paying rent but continued living there after the lease had expired.

The court summons served to illustrate that ten years after Barbara had received the more than $4 million from her husband's insurance payout, she was in financial ruin. According to US Bankruptcy Court records, she had spent the money fast and furiously.

During a deposition before the court made its decision, a bankruptcy attorney asked Barbara tough questions and pointed out discrepancies in her financial records. Barbara was so distraught, she threatened suicide. "I am killing myself, and you can be the executor of the estate of Barbara Kogan," Barbara said to her attorney during the deposition. It was obvious to Barbara what direction the bankruptcy decision was headed, and she wasn't holding up well under the strain.

She was right. The court denied Barbara's bankruptcy request, tossing out the case because she had omitted millions of dollars in assets. US Bankruptcy Judge Burton R. Lifland, in his decision dated March 26, 2001, cited Remington Investment Corporation, which, as a collector of the bad debt against Barbara, had filed with the court objecting to Barbara's bankruptcy application. "Remington asserts that Barbara Kogan is the poster child for the denial of a discharge," because of those assets, the judge wrote.

Ultimately, Judge Lifland sided with Remington Investment, stating: "Indeed, the Debtor's false statements and omissions on her original petition, the continuing discrepancies contained in her amended petition, her evasive deposition testimony, and her belated attempts to explain the loss of her assets reveal her complete disregard for the accuracy and thoroughness in accounting for her one-time possession of millions of dollars in insurance benefit proceeds, real estate holdings, and other monies." With that, Judge Lifland denied Barbara Kogan's bankruptcy application.

The same month, Barbara was dealt another blow when George's brother Lawrence took his former sister-in-law to court to recoup money he'd invested in the couple's businesses. Had Barbara's bankruptcy filing been approved, it would have protected her from creditors, including Lawrence.

In his suit, Lawrence stated that Barbara owed him several hundred thousand dollars from business deals Lawrence had had with George, as well as with Barbara.

"He believes she has millions of dollars in assets. He believes she is trying to hide the assets and defraud the court and her creditors," Raymond A. Bragar, Lawrence's lawyer, wrote in the lawsuit.

Lawrence Kogan's suit, filed in Manhattan's State Supreme Court, stated that his sister-in-law had received more than $4 million in insurance money, as well as hundreds of thousands of dollars in jewelry from her late husband's safe-deposit boxes. Lawrence's filing also said that the Kogan & Company store had had an inventory worth more than $1 million, and that Barbara Kogan had failed to account for this inventory. Lawrence requested that the Manhattan district attorney's office unseal the Kogans' divorce file, which was included as part of the police investigation because of the murder. Lawrence was looking for financial data to back up his claim, and he believed it was in the divorce paperwork. The district attorney's office, however, took no position on the sealed materials. Ultimately, as the criminal investigation into George Kogan's homicide progressed, the records would eventually become public, but not before Barbara had spent most of the insurance payout and wouldn't have enough money left for Lawrence to collect, if he obtained a judgment.

To cover her living expenses, Barbara worked a variety of jobs, all in sales, including representing a cosmetics brand on a luxury cruise line.

Her friend, Clarissa Barth, a merchandise manager at the time for Starboard Cruise Services, signed up Barbara as a cosmetics vendor on several trips. So, in 2002, Barbara invited her son Billy and his family on a trip out to sea with her. "It was a Christmas cruise out of the Caribbean," Clarissa said. "She never told me her family was going. They went on board too and stayed in cabins."

As a vendor, Barbara did not have to pay for her own

cruise, but her family had to pay their costs. Having her family with her turned out fine work-wise, Clarissa said, even though Barbara was on the ship to sell. "She always did well on cruises. She was a very good salesperson. She worked hard, like a person who was starting out," Clarissa said.

Then, the following year, in 2003, Barbara met and married a new husband. "Barbara was Internet savvy and joined online dating groups to meet men," Clarissa said. By then in her sixties, Barbara was in a hurry to meet her match. She'd met Arthur William "Bill" Bodine and mistakenly thought he had money. He'd previously been married to Elana Jan McBurney, with whom he'd had one child, Bradford Sterling Bodine. Barbara knew very little about Bodine, other than him telling her he was an investment adviser. She didn't know that Bill had been on probation when she met him. He had been sentenced in 1994 to twenty-one months in a federal prison, according to federal documents, for taking money from a high-ranking Libyan official.

Bill and Barbara, as newlyweds, rented a two-bedroom house on Pondfield Road in the village of Bronxville in New York's Lower Hudson Valley. It was convenient for both and just a dozen miles from Midtown Manhattan. During their marriage, Barbara continued working as a sales rep, selling merchandise from jewelry, perfume, and cosmetics lines. In October 2003, Grimoldi Milano, manufacturer of luxury timepieces, appointed Barbara Bodine, who was going by the last name of her second husband, to managing director. In an announcement about a variety of promotions, including Barbara's, a blurb in *JCK Magazine* said, "Kogan-Bodine previously was director of International Sales at Gori & Zucchi Inc. and Liz Claiborne." In addition, Barbara worked as regional sales manager for Waterford Crystal in the Caribbean, splitting her time between New York City and San Juan. She was also selling pricey watches and perfumes for Bergdorf Goodman, a luxury goods company.

By 2004, Barbara and Bill returned to Manhattan, this time moving into a rental at 65 West Ninety-fifth Street, where they stayed until mid-2005. But by that time, just two years into the marriage, their relationship had soured and they began divorce proceedings.

Clarissa Barth described Barbara as having spoken longingly about her first husband, but with regret about the second. "[Her second husband was] a guy who said he was going to do well. His ship never came in. She really missed her first husband. She called him the 'love of my life.' Barbara regretted remarrying. She said she was getting a divorce and asked where she should live."

That seemed to be one of the toughest questions for Barbara—where to live. According to a residency timeline compiled by NYPD investigators, Barbara lived in no less than a dozen homes after her husband's murder.

Around that time, when she spoke with Clarissa, Barbara had moved to 316 East Fifty-fifth Street in Midtown Manhattan between First and Second Avenues, and to 59 Kensington Road, in Bronxville. She also rented an apartment in San Juan, Puerto Rico, again in Condado. The leases meant that Barbara was simultaneously maintaining three apartments.

The main thoroughfare of Condado was Avenida Ashford, long considered the Park Avenue of San Juan, where Barbara Kogan rented an apartment not long after she and her second husband, Bill, separated. She signed the lease with the name of Barbara S. Bodine.

Barbara continued selling cosmetics through a company associated with her friend Clarissa Barth. They'd go shopping together or out to eat, when Barbara visited Clarissa in Florida on several occasions. To Clarissa, contrary to how news reports had portrayed her, Barbara did not seem focused on money.

"She wasn't materialistic," Clarissa said. "She wasn't like that. I went shopping with her many times. Once, I bought Pradas. Barbara said, 'Wow.' She knew where the sales and bargains were. She sent me to a Ferragamo [shoes] super sale."

The Barbara who Clarissa knew was generous. "She was here one Christmas, and my son wanted something, and his father hadn't bought it for him. So Barbara got it for him," Clarissa said. "She ran in circles and knew all these big people, but she wasn't a name dropper. She, truthfully, was an average person."

To Clarissa, Barbara appeared vulnerable. "She was just a sweet lady, but she was really lonely," she said. "She was probably mentally broken. She's easily manipulated. She was very knowledgeable, educated, and she was fun."

Barbara, she said, had had her astrological chart done. "It was after nine-eleven, and the woman said Barbara had to wear yellow, so Barbara wore nothing but yellow for a while," Clarissa said.

In the sales industry, Barth noted, "Out of all the people who have helped me, it was Barbara. She taught me a lot." Besides helping her navigate the Internet, Barbara helped Clarissa find a lawyer. "She told me how to look up attorneys," she said. "I asked her how she knew to do that. She said, 'My son is an attorney.' Barbara talked about her children a lot. They meant the world to her."

Barbara's sons' paternal grandmother, Ida Kogan, passed away in October 2006, two days after her ninety-second birthday. She'd lived the last years of her life with George's brother, Lawrence, in Bal Harbour, Florida, a high-end village in Miami-Dade County. "Ida had a lot of physical problems," said Richard Goldstein, George's cousin by marriage, who saw Ida as his patient whenever she visited family on the East Coast. "She had bad knees and other things wrong with her." Ida was buried at the Jewish cemetery in San Juan, Puerto Rico, alongside her husband, Solomon's, grave.

In 2008, when Clarissa Barth had not heard from Barbara for several months, she sent her an e-mail. It didn't bounce back, which, to Clarissa, meant that Barbara's e-mail account was still open. When more time passed without Clarissa hearing from Barbara, she Googled her name. And that's when Clarissa learned the distressing news that authorities suspected her friend in the death of her husband, George. "They've painted an awful picture of Barbara," Clarissa said. "It breaks my heart. Never, never, never in a million years did I see that in her. It's a very sad story."

Life for Barbara had not gone nearly as smoothly as she had expected. The divorce debacle was behind her, but her husband's murder was not. She had gotten the insurance money, but then there was the lengthy in-house insurance probe, plus the police investigation that targeted her as the main person of interest. Years later, the murder case had not yet been closed, because, Barbara learned, there is no statute of limitations when it comes to homicide. The probe into her husband's slaying was like a continual weight bearing down on Barbara, and the insurance money had not eased that burden.

CHAPTER 10

"Ex-Lawyer of the Day"

While Barbara attempted to move on, a grand jury quietly indicted her one-time lawyer, Manuel Serafin Martinez, for the murder of George Kogan. On Wednesday, June 26, 1996, a sealed, one-page, two-count indictment, number 5073-96, was signed by District Attorney Robert Morgenthau, charging Martinez with murder and criminal solicitation, both in the second degree. However, on that June day, Martinez, at this point unaware of the indictment, sat in a Mexican prison serving out a jail term in an unrelated case.

With the murder charge, New York City investigators, along with the determined Assistant District Attorney Joel Seidemann, had won their first indictment in the slaying of George Kogan eight years after his murder. No one officially knew it at the time, although it had been rumored. It would be eleven more years before Martinez would be brought to the United States to face the allegations against him.

That is not how Manuel Martinez, attorney at law, had planned out his life. In fact, he had not intended to become a lawyer at all. That had been his mother's wish. Manuel had set his sights higher. From the time he was a young boy, he'd wanted to join the priesthood. Instead, his mother pushed him to enroll in law school.

Even so, becoming an attorney was a big deal in Manuel's life and seen by his family as a major accomplishment, in large part because Manuel's paternal grandfather had practiced law in Puerto Rico. Manuel's father had planned to become an attorney like his father before him, but when he applied to Columbia University's law school, he was told he was too old to attend.

Manuel, born in Miami, Florida, on Thursday, August 18, 1949, and his sister, Nilda Martinez Ortiz, were named after their parents. When the children were born, their father was in his forties and their mother was in her thirties. Their mother was a stay-at-home wife, and their father did advertising work, including acting as the voice in Puerto Rico for Cerveza Corona advertisements. Manuel's father also was the creator of a cartoon character named "Cantalicio," described as a Puerto Rican "average guy" in old-fashioned cartoons that today can be viewed on YouTube. "[My dad] did all the sketches for the spots, and it gave him a sort of fame," Nilda said. In addition, their father managed a longtime show called *Los Jíbaros de la Radio*.

Though Manuel was born in Miami, when he was just a year old the family relocated to the metropolitan area of Bayamón in Puerto Rico's northern coastal valley. Puerto Rico became Manuel's homeland.

Their mother insisted her children learn proper English, so she regularly took them to bookstores and to a public library. "My mom used to take us to San Juan to buy books, because Mom was a tremendous reader," Nilda said. "She found out that she could go to the Pan-American Bookstore in Old San Juan to buy books printed in English. She bought Manuel and me books so we could also read in English." Manny, as he was called, spoke "slowly and meticulously," even as a child, his sister said. His voice wasn't deep, but it was commanding. Later, as a bilingual American, he had no accent.

Manny, who attended the St. Rose School and Convent, skipped the fourth grade and was an "A" student from grade school through high school. "Our parents were so concerned about our educations and the correct way of speaking and behaving," Nilda said. "I have to admit that they were very strict, especially with Manuel. He had to get better grades, and he really was a good student. He always got A's and honors in school, ever since he was very young. Manny was the nerd type, always studying. He was always pushed by our father."

Their father continually urged Manny to "be better," Nilda explained.

"My parents were very strict with him, because he was a boy. I remember, when Manuel was very young, he used to work at supermarkets helping people carry their bags. Then he sold shoes in a department store, and men's clothes. But I was never allowed to work."

Manuel also went to church each morning before school to perform his duties as an altar boy. In classes, he was proud to wear the school uniform: a white shirt with a black tie and black pants. He suffered from asthma, but he still rode bikes and roller-skated with his sister in their neighborhood, even though, his sister said, "Manuel always fell and he always had bruises."

Manuel followed his grandfather's example and enrolled at the University of Puerto Rico, graduating with his juris doctorate from the university's law school, the oldest in Puerto Rico. In 1973, Manny passed Puerto Rico's bar examination, and the next year, at age twenty-five, he moved to New York to begin his law career there. He had to work as a legal aide instead of as an attorney, because he had not yet taken that state's bar exam. It would not be until 1985, after first failing the exam, that he was admitted to the New York State Bar Association.

Life was finally going Manny's way. He enjoyed his work and dressed the part of a New York lawyer, wearing tailor-made suits and, when he dressed casually, slacks and polo shirts. "I never saw him wear jeans," his sister said. Manuel had found his niche in New York and was ready to settle down with a family. He had met Beatriz Oller, a woman his age, and asked her to marry him. Manuel flew Beatriz to Mexico City in the summer of 1988 to meet his sister and their father. While there, Manuel and Beatriz traveled to

Cuernavaca, the capital city of Morelos, Mexico, where Manuel's father, who suffered from Alzheimer's disease, was living. Manuel drove the fifty-five miles south on the D-95 freeway to Cuernavaca, to what Nilda called "an old-age home," to introduce their father to Manuel's future wife. The family did not take well to Beatriz, who acted standoffish toward them, but Manuel explained away his fiancée's behavior as "eccentricities."

On August 1, 1989, in a civil ceremony at City Hall in New York City, Manuel Martinez and Beatriz Oller were married.

A year later, Barbara Kogan hired Martinez to help her find a divorce attorney in Puerto Rico. Martinez had a rough edge about him, often speaking in crude terms about women, including his wife. It seemed an odd partnership for Barbara, a woman who carried herself with a quiet dignity and had once helped run high-end home furnishings, women's fashions, and antique stores, and whose husband ran a hotel and casino. Even so, Barbara felt that Martinez, because he had attended law school in Puerto Rico, could help with her divorce. Then, just two months after Barbara hired Manuel, her husband was killed, rendering the pending divorce moot.

But Martinez, an accountant as well as an attorney, assisted Barbara and her parents with financial papers, and on August 11, 1991, ten months after her husband's death, Barbara wrote out a check to Martinez for $3,008. On two other occasions, she wrote checks to Martinez for $1,000 each, making for a grand total paid out to him of $5,008, spanning a year. The checks, Barbara's attorney would later explain, were payments for legal and CPA services, for notarizing documents for Barbara's parents, and for helping to find Barbara a divorce attorney in Puerto Rico.

While Manuel and Beatriz's son, Manelita "Manel" Ignacio Martinez-Oller, who was born in the summer of 1991, was still a baby, the couple separated in an acrimonious divorce.

Trouble seemed to follow Martinez. He was such a braggart that Carlos Piovanetti, a realtor renting space from

Martinez, snitched to authorities based on comments Martinez made during a casual meeting. Piovanetti's testimony was later used as evidence against Martinez in the Kogan murder trial. The meeting took place in July 1992, when Martinez went out for drinks with Piovanetti. Piovanetti was in the office before and after George Kogan was killed, and he saw Martinez's reaction firsthand.

Manuel trusted Carlos, a fellow Puerto Rican, and had become friendly enough to go for after-work drinks at the Spaghetti Western Italian café in the Tribeca neighorhood. It was at that restaurant, Piovanetti would later say, that Martinez made an astounding confession—an admission that would become a *coup de grace* for the DA's office. That fortuitous meeting marked the first new lead in the George Kogan murder investigation in nearly two years, and ultimately it would lead to what the state prosecutor later called "the big break" in the cold case. It happened after Martinez and Piovanetti drank shots of tequila, chased with beer. Carlos would later say he pressed Manuel for details about the Kogan case. For two years, Carlos had suspected Manuel of having knowledge about the case, especially when Manuel had several times in the office imitated the way George fell to the ground and held his hands to chest, saying, "God save me." Carlos had always wondered how Martinez knew that.

"Tell me the truth," Piovanetti told Martinez at the restaurant. "You've got to level with me. You've got to learn to trust me. I'm the only one you have left. Tell me, were you or were you not involved in the George Kogan murder?"

"If we talk about it," Martinez told him, "I don't ever want to discuss this with you again. You have to give me your word on that."

"And I gave him my word and I also swore that I would never reveal what he said to anyone else," Piovanetti later explained. "So, he told me that Mrs. Kogan came to him and told him that her husband had left her for a much younger woman, that the woman was the publicist, that he had left her with no money, that she had arranged for a hit [with a man named] Paulie Prosano [who] charged fifty thousand dollars.

And at that moment I stopped him and I said, 'Wait a second. You told me she had no money. Where is she going to get fifty thousand dollars from?' And [Manny] said, 'Remember my trip to Puerto Rico? Well, [Barbara] borrowed the money from her mother.'"

Martinez, as Piovanetti told it, had talked Barbara Kogan into the murder, convincing her it was "the right thing to do," because her husband wasn't giving her any money. The alleged hit man was someone Piovanetti referred to as Paul "Tony Pro" Prosano, an acquaintance of Martinez's. Carlos Piovanetti also said Martinez told him, "Remember the morning [at the office] that you got that call from Paulie? He called me and said, 'It's done.'"

Piovanetti didn't think about that restaurant conversation again for a couple of months, until September 15, 1992. Manuel beeped him while Carlos was being questioned by Westchester County Police about a seemingly unrelated fraud case, where checks were stolen from the county and Carlos was one of the players in the scheme. So, the beep came at an opportune time for Carlos. He told police he had information about the George Kogan murder. Carlos returned the page by telephoning Martinez, and, unbeknownst to Manuel, the conversation was tape-recorded by authorities as Carlos sat inside the Westchester District Attorney's office. It was Carlos's only opportunity to negotiate a "Queen for a Day" agreement between himself and the District Attorney's office. In return, Carlos facilitated the taped conversation that directly linked Manuel Martinez to Prosano, paving the way for a murder indictment against Martinez.

In the ensuing affidavit, Assistant District Attorney Seidemann described the recorded conversation as the break in the Kogan case he'd been waiting for. The probe had stalled because of uncooperative witnesses and jurisdictional roadblocks that thwarted the investigation—until the Westchester County District Attorney's office's stolen checks investigation led them to Piovanetti and Martinez. In the course of this investigation, detectives discovered that one of the fraudulent checks had been made out to a "Joaquin

Rios." Then, detectives learned that Martinez, a notary public, had notarized a power-of-attorney document giving Carlos Piovanetti the right to cash checks endorsed by Joaquin Rios. There was also a fiduciary agreement between Piovanetti and Rios.

There was, however, a major problem with Rios's endorsement. The laundering accusation against Piovanetti was because investigators learned that Joaquin Rios was a fictitious identity set up to cash the stolen checks anonymously. A stolen check made out to one Joaquin Rios for $50,000 was traced back to a Westchester County bank account, leading investigators to suspect Ted Garofolo, a director in the county's department of finance, of stealing checks from the inside and passing them on to office worker Carmine Molisse, who dropped them off at Carlos Piovanetti's office, rented from Martinez.

Detective Dennis Zack, in a police affidavit, explained the latest evidence against Martinez: "We received a call that there were seven checks missing from the Westchester County Department of Finance, and that one of the checks had been deposited and attempted to be used. . . . These checks could be deposited, negotiated, the funds could be drawn on these accounts, and everybody was making money."

Piovanetti was an obvious suspect, and he was worried. As investigators closed in, he knew he was doomed. His fears were realized when he was arrested and "the shit hit the fan," as Piovanetti later put it.

Around the same time, Westchester County office worker Carmine Molisse was also looking to make a plea deal. Ultimately, she was convicted and given six months in jail and, following her release, five years probation. She also was ordered to pay restitution for the money she stole from the county. Through the Manhattan DA's office, she'd struck a deal, in exchange for her testimony against Martinez, which lessened what she had to pay back to the state. Garofolo and Molisse were arrested, and Molisse, in an agreement to turn state's evidence, went before a grand jury that was looking into Manuel Martinez's possible role in the George Kogan murder. Ted Garofolo, for his part, would be tried, convicted, and sentenced to a year and a half in prison.

As for Carlos Piovanetti, the only way for him to lighten the hefty fifteen-year sentence he faced for the charge of fraud against a government body would be to cross the line and become a confidential informant—also known as a C.I.—for authorities.

With the stroke of a pen, Carlos Piovanetti, by signing the Queen-for-a-Day agreement, became a snitch against Manuel Martinez. But he would not do it without the explicit promise of protection. He was afraid of retaliation should Martinez find out about the deal. Assistant DA Seidemann was prepared to do that for Piovanetti. Also, Carlos wouldn't sign the agreement without the promise that his real estate license wouldn't be revoked. The state agreed. It was a sweet deal for Carlos, especially given that DEA agents familiar with him had warned Detective Dennis Zack that Piovanetti was not a reliable informant, let alone a material witness in a trial. But the Manhattan DA's office needed the information against Martinez and entered into the Queen-for-a-Day deal with Piovanetti anyway. And while the DA's office got its big break through him, Piovanetti, too, got the break he needed, which was to keep his sentence for fraud charges to a minimum.

The name of the agreement with Piovanetti, Queen-for-a-Day, comes from the vintage television show of the same title. The contestant told the host her problems, and the audience rang an applause meter. The contestant then got the relief she requested. A legal Queen-for-a-Day agreement, also known as a proffer, is set up when a defendant is hoping to get a favorable plea agreement from an assistant district attorney in exchange for providing information.

Detective Dennis Zack, who was present during the Queen-for-a-Day meeting with Piovanetti, described it as "an agreement between the prosecutor and a witness, or a defendant, to provide information that could be useful in our investigation." In exchange, the advantage for Piovanetti was that "as long as it was truthful, it would not be used against [Piovanetti]," Zack said.

Statements on the audiotape, Joel Seidemann later wrote in an affidavit, pointed to Martinez's scheme to murder Lenny Cherry, a plumber hired to do maintenance work in Martinez's office building. The audiotape evidence, Seidemann wrote, also pointed to relevant information that would help with a separate case against Barbara Kogan.

Manuel, in the meantime, was not holding up well emotionally. He had "a nervous breakdown," according to his sister Nilda, and, from September 1992 to June 1996, he went on state disability. It was also during that time that Manuel grew what he called his "Vandyke beard." "It was a product of my severe depression," he later explained.

In the midst of that nervous breakdown, on November 26, 1993, police went to Martinez's house after receiving a report about a gun being fired in a New Jersey residential section. Officers entered the three-story brownstone and confiscated two guns, a 12-gauge Mossberg shotgun and a .25-caliber Beretta, both registered in Martinez's name in Dutchess County. "I used them at the firing range," Martinez explained. Police did not charge him with a crime, but they confiscated the guns. In February 1996, Martinez, while still on state disability in New York, relocated to Mexico City to live near his sister. From media reports, he also knew that law enforcement and the DA in New York were closing in on him, so he quietly left America. The distance didn't seem to matter; during Manuel's lengthy stay in Mexico, Assistant District Attorney Joel Seidemann continued pursuing him in connection with George's murder. Seidemann wanted justice for George.

Meanwhile, in 1996, the DA's office had been working with a second informant. His name was Steven Cerenzio, identified as a police informant and a long-time associate of Paul Prosano. Cerenzio had helped with the Kogan investigation in exchange for decreasing his prison term for an unconnected 1995 robbery, where Cerenzio had used a toy gun to stick up a Payless shoe store. His punishment was shaved down from the maximum fifteen years in prison to less than five. Manuel Martinez's attorney, Jonathan Strauss, said that Cerenzio came forward "not out of a sense of civic duty or anything like that." Instead, Strauss explained, Cerenzio became an informant "because the government gave him a deal, and wait until you see this deal. . . . This is the kicker. 'We're going to house you in a facility that has trailers on the location, so you can have your conjugal visits right there.' That's in the agreement. . . . Pretty sweet deal."

In February 1996, Cerenzio spoke during taped conversations with Debra Serrano, another friend of Paul Prosano, in a bid to implicate the suspected hit man in the Kogan murder. Serrano, who, according to police documents, was intoxicated when she talked to Cerenzio, insisted she knew nothing about the Kogan killing, but she did say she witnessed Prosano ditch a revolver, describing it as "silver," which authorities said was similar to the missing one used to fatally wound George Kogan. The gun, she said, was tossed by Prosano from his houseboat into Sheepshead Bay, in Brooklyn. Police scuba divers searched the floor of the bay, but did not locate the weapon.

However, an eyewitness to the George Kogan shooting said the gunman had used a black-colored revolver, not a silver one. And while a snub-nosed pistol was used to kill George, no hard evidence tied the Sheepshead Bay revolver to the Kogan case.

The next break came after Detective Ernest Bugge interviewed Manuel's ex-wife, Beatriz Oller. Detectives Bugge and Joseph Buffolino had been assigned to the case in 1995. They began seriously pursuing Martinez as a suspect in George Kogan's murder, which led them to Martinez's former wife. She met with detectives Bugge and Buffolino in October 1995, with an attorney by her side. Beatriz Oller was visibly uncomfortable, so Bugge, who grew up on Staten Island and went on to graduate from Brooklyn's St. Joseph College, tried to put her at ease. But Beatriz was "mostly upset and nervous and fidgety and shaking," Bugge would later say. Her attorney told the detectives she was "fearful of her husband" and "did not want to speak to us," Bugge said.

It was not until Detective Bugge interviewed her again in March 1996 that Oller began offering useful information. The eleven-hour, two-session interview, which police said was not recorded, resulted in Oller telling Bugge that her husband had admitted to her while she was still married to him that he had been involved in the death of George Kogan. It was exactly what Assistant District Attorney Joel Seidemann had been seeking.

Back in Mexico, Irving Anolik, Martinez's attorney, sent Seidemann a letter on March 22, 1996, asking to meet with him and Martinez in Mexico to discuss the Kogan case. Seidemann received the letter on March 29. But the indictment handed down against Martinez two months later, in June 1996, stated that Seidemann had been unaware of Martinez's whereabouts. For the next eleven years, all systems pushed forward toward finding and arresting Martinez.

Martinez had no prior American criminal record, but that was not the case in Mexico. During his time living in Mexico, he'd been jailed in two different Mexican prisons after being convicted of drug-related charges. From June 15, 1996, until April 8, 2005, Martinez was at the Ciudad Reynosa prison in Tamaulipas, which holds about 2,000 inmates. Reynosa is across the border from McAllen, Texas. He was moved to the Altamira prison, also in Tamaulipas, after he "survived an attempt on my life," according to Martinez.

While imprisoned in Mexico, Martinez, not one to sit idle, stayed busy. He became a self-proclaimed informant to both the US and Mexican governments. While incarcerated inside the walls of Altamira, Martinez claimed that fellow inmate Raul Valladares, along with his jailed associates, carried on their underworld work. Martinez claimed that he "personally knew and partied with major drug lords" who he named in a letter he wrote to the Drug Enforcement Agency's Anthony Placido, an agent serving as special administrator for intelligence.

"All of them continued in the 'business' from the security and comfort of their cells via cellulars that could reach Colombia," Martinez wrote in a letter to the DEA. He also wrote that he was not seeking "money or appreciation or any letter of recommendation from anyone." Instead, he wanted information about a DEA agent, Fred Geiger, for whom he'd been looking ever since the agent stopped by Martinez's law office. Martinez had launched a negative campaign against his one-time office tenant and friend Carlos Piovanetti, after Martinez learned that Carlos had become a police informant, providing information against him in the Kogan murder. Martinez, in his attempt to fight back, retaliated with what he felt to be damaging information about a client of Piovanetti's. Agent Geiger had gone to Martinez's New York office, Martinez said, asking for information about a suspected Colombian drug dealer known as "El Mono," or "The Monkey," who happened to be a real estate client of Piovanetti's. Martinez seized the opportunity to help by copying El Mono's flight schedule from a file in Piovanetti's desk. He gave the agent a copy and sent him on his way. The flight schedule, Martinez explained, included dates of cocaine shipments purportedly going through JFK International Airport. It wasn't known if the information panned out, and Martinez was never able to find the agent or even confirm that the man in fact worked for the DEA.

Because of the incriminating comments made on tape by Martinez to Carlos Piovanetti, the case was sent to a grand jury, which charged Martinez with "aiding and abetting" Barbara Kogan in the slaying of her husband. That was how, as he sat behind bars in Mexico, Manuel Martinez was formally indicted as an accessory in the murder of George H. Kogan.

CHAPTER 11

Preparing for Trial

Just before Martinez's trial, after a witness list was provided to both sides, defense lawyer Jonathan Strauss petitioned the court requesting that "missing witness" instructions be given out and explained to the jury. Strauss felt the prosecution had failed by not calling Barbara Kogan and Paul Prosano as witnesses. Neither was a defendant, and they had not been indicted for George's murder, yet their names popped up throughout Manuel's trial—with Prosano as the possible hired gunman and Kogan as a co-conspirator in the murder plot with Martinez.

Prosecutor Seidemann, in an August 15, 2007, affidavit, briefly explained why he was not planning to call Barbara to the stand: "As for Barbara Kogan, given her interview with the NYPD in which she said she has no information on the Kogan murder, it is hard to see how she could assist this defendant in his defense." Outside the courtroom, Assistant DA Seidemann, according to Martinez, had told defense attorney Strauss that the prosecution left Barbara off the witness list because she had passed away.

Seidemann, in his answer to the missing witness report, called Strauss's request "laughable." The judge agreed and ruled against the defense. In making that ruling, Judge Michael Obus said, "There is no reason to believe that either of these potential witnesses is in control of the people in the sense of being likely to be favorable to them."

Another snag with potential witnesses was Aaron Richard Golub, who had represented Barbara in the divorce while her husband was still alive. Barbara's new attorney promised to block Golub from testifying, because of attorney-client confidentiality.

Further, police weren't allowed to use any of the initial information from their one eyewitness, the housekeeper who was in shock and quickly fled the scene. Moses Crespo explained that the woman the housekeeper had worked for had died, and the housekeeper "basically disappeared. Police tried to find her, but I think she left the country and went to live maybe in Mexico." Without her appearance in court, her original statement was considered hearsay. Because of that, no one would ever know if she saw the gunman try to take money from George—which could possibly have explained the cash on the sidewalk—or what else she may have seen.

With setbacks like this for the prosecution throughout the trial, Strauss reassured Martinez that all was going well, and that he was optimistic about the outcome. "Manny, I see no smoking gun," he told his client. Based on the prosecution's lack of direct evidence, Strauss was confident he could obtain an acquittal for Martinez.

A year earlier, in April of 2007, Seidemann had made a confusing statement about calling Barbara Kogan as a witness, which was included in the defense's motion to dismiss the case against Martinez. Martinez was accused of conspiring with Barbara in the murder of her husband, yet prosecutors did not include her as one of their witnesses.

The issue of whether Barbara Kogan was dead or alive was curious. As a step in discovery, Seidemann and the NYPD investigators assigned to the DA's unit obtained full listings of all apartments and homes Barbara had lived in since her husband's death, and those addresses were included in the court file. At that point, Barbara, in fact, had been splitting her time between an apartment in Manhattan and one in Puerto Rico. She did not appear to be hiding, though Seidemann had told Strauss and written in a court document that it was his belief that Barbara was dead.

On July 2, 2007, Strauss wrote to the court requesting that discovery materials be handed over to him, so he could better represent his client. In his letter, he told the judge, "As the court is aware, there exists extensive discovery materials, and it would be impossible for the defense to digest the voluminous amount of materials if they are supplied on the eve of trial. Additionally, because of the delay in prosecution in this case, our investigation has been unduly hampered and we simply could not follow up leads and interview potential witnesses if this discovery material was supplied only days before the trial was to commence."

And while Manuel Martinez was the only one headed for trial in the spring of 2008 for the Kogan shooting, it was still as if Barbara Kogan were about to be tried as well. Prosecutors admitted to trying unsuccessfully for years to get Martinez to testify against Barbara Kogan. Martinez was offered a plea agreement, but he refused and instead put his fate in the hands of a jury.

In another document addressed to the court dated August 16, 2007, Strauss put in writing that Barbara Kogan could not be a witness at Martinez's trial, because she had died. "One of the witnesses who would have cleared the defendant, Barbara Kogan, upon information and belief has died several years ago. After conversations with the People and my Investigator, I have been unable to confirm Mrs. Kogan's whereabouts or whether or not she is still alive. Mrs. Kogan was the wife of George Kogan. However, her testimony was never preserved and she is no longer available to testify for the defendant. Additionally, the defendant's alibi witness, Fernando Alvarez [a law clerk], who was with the defendant at the time of the murder, cannot be located. Similarly, Richard Golub, Esq., and Norman Donald, Esq., Mrs. Kogan's attorneys, cannot be located."

"The six-year delay between when the murder occurred and when the defendant was indicted," Strauss continued, "should be viewed as pre-indictment delay." Based on that argument, Strauss requested that all charges against his client be dropped.

Judge Michael Obus responded in a September 21, 2007, ruling, "Barbara Kogan is alive and well and living in Puerto Rico where the defense can locate her." That was news to Strauss, because the prosecutor had told him in April 2007 that Barbara was dead, which hampered the defense. It was frustrating for Strauss in an already complicated case.

Going forward to trial when they could not find witnesses was not a good scenario for the defense. Despite this, the case moved forward through the judicial system toward trial.

A week before Martinez's trial was to begin, Judge Obus ordered the prosecution to turn over all discovery materials to the defense. "This will give us an opportunity to more thoroughly prepare for trial," Strauss, in a letter to Martinez, said about the ruling. That opportunity did not come: By the second week of trial, the defense still did not have all of the discovery materials. Seidemann, for his part, said that he had provided the defense with "twenty-two boxes of information." Missing from those boxes was the transcript of the conversation between Martinez and Carlos Piovanetti, which was a result of the deal he'd cut to lessen the charges pending against him. The prosecution was instead saving the transcript for trial and planning to inform the defense just before Carlos was to take the stand.

Martinez's attorney, Jonathan Strauss, ridiculed the allegations lodged against his client as a "house of cards."

"The case is based on two main witnesses, a convincing liar . . . and an ex-wife who hates his guts," attorney Strauss said, referring to Beatriz Oller, Martinez's ex-wife. In exchange for his testimony, Piovanetti, described by Strauss as an "ex-con," was handed a plea deal for his cooperation against Martinez. As for Beatriz Oller's potential testimony, according to Strauss, it was a matter of a bitter ex-wife exacting revenge.

Prosecutors also attempted to make a deal with alleged

shooter Paul Prosano, asking him to make monitored phone calls to Martinez in exchange for lesser charges in Prosano's kidnapping case. Prosano was charged with kidnapping in a series of push-in robberies and ultimately convicted in 1998. But he was not charged as the trigger man, or even as an accessory, in George Kogan's killing. Prosano, as a person of interest in the case, refused to help the prosecution with its case. The man who was named, informally, as the shooter, was asked to help the DA convict Martinez, whom they said had hired Prosano as the hit man, yet Prosano, the alleged killer, was not charged with murder.

Martinez also was offered a deal by prosecutors on the condition that he turn state's evidence and testify against Barbara Kogan. Martinez came back with an impossible counteroffer: no jail time for himself. When Seidemann refused, Martinez in turn rejected the plea bargain and instead took his chances at trial. Had Martinez accepted Seidemann's offer, he would have spent just five years in prison, as opposed to the twenty-five-year sentence he faced if convicted.

One of Martinez's biggest problems was that two weeks before George's murder, Martinez, allegedly on Barbara Kogan's behalf, had offered a job to a man named Nelson Ramirez to tail George. Ramirez testified at a grand jury hearing that Martinez had asked him to follow "a person in a divorce suit." Ramirez, who went to Martinez's office to meet with him, also told the grand jury that when he met Martinez, he was offered $100 a day to follow Kogan. But Ramirez turned down the job. According to Ramirez's testimony, Martinez also asked him to make a pact that the two would never again speak about the job offer. Then, Ramirez left Martinez's office and stopped by his friend Wilmer Rodriguez's desk, and the two walked to the elevator bank. Wilmer, who worked for Martinez, asked Nelson, "How'd your meeting with Manny go?"

"He wants me to follow somebody in a divorce," Nelson said. "I'm not doing that shit."

Martinez would later explain his reasoning and desire to

hire someone untrained to follow George Kogan. He said it was because Barbara could not afford a private investigator to follow her husband to see if he was hiding money from her. In a letter, Martinez described Ramirez as "an unemployed friend":

Ramirez was not a licensed private investigator nor did Barbara Kogan need one for the work to be performed. I explained to [Ramirez] that I had a client—Barbara Kogan's name was not disclosed—who was getting a divorce, her husband of 24 years of marriage had discarded her for a younger woman, her husband was very wealthy, was strangling her emotionally, financially, my client could not afford a licensed private investigator and she had to know whether her husband was hiding marital assets, not reporting to the court all sources of income and essentially defrauding her. It's just like he customarily did when conducting business. He hid her legitimate share of the property accumulated during the marriage.

Ramirez's responsibilities, if he accepted the job offer, consisted of following George Kogan, the business places he was frequenting, any business associates he would meet and report to me. Any hiring and budget had to be approved by my client because she was in a very difficult financial position. I tentatively offered him $150 per day for eight to ten hours of work per day, seven days per week, for at least two weeks.

Ramirez did not accept this proposal. I never took it personally, and I did not get upset (as he subsequently falsely testified). Remember, Seidemann insisted Paul Prosano was the hit man I used. If that had been the case, why would I need anyone to follow George Kogan, his business associates, etc., when Prosano could have waited outside 205 East 69th Street for George Kogan to exit and kill him face to face? Note that Seidemann's theory of the murder that he fell in love with was provided by Mary-Louise Hawkins.

Barbara, through her previous attorney, Golub, could have asked the court to compel George to hand over his complete financial records to learn what she needed to know for the divorce proceedings. The court had already ordered a financial record at one point, compelling George to provide a complete financial picture to the court. Even so, according to Martinez, Barbara continued to feel she needed more than what the Manhattan courts could provide for her, so, through Martinez, she attempted to hire someone to tail her husband.

It was not the first time Manuel had hired a private eye. In August of 1992, not long after he had divorce papers served on his wife in Miami, Martinez hired private investigator Robert Dyer, who was based in Miami. A friend had referred Dyer to Martinez, who later explained that he'd hired the investigator to keep him updated on his wife and son during the divorce. It ended up being a lot more than that; the PI videotaped Martinez's wife kissing another man while Martinez's son was in the car.

Another problem for Martinez as he headed into trial was a brief interview he'd granted in October 1995 to *New York Post* reporter Al Guart.

An article about the Kogan murder ran in the *Post*'s October 17, 1995, edition, quoting anonymous sources, so the reporter called Martinez's New York telephone number seeking a comment for a follow-up story. Guart hit pay dirt: Martinez called him back. And while the telephone interview was short, the ensuing article, advertised on the front page of the *Post* as "exclusive" and titled "Lawyer Dares: Indict Me in Tycoon's Death," was packed with details. The reporter learned, when his call was returned, that Martinez was out of the country and living in Mexico City, a fact of which, up until that point, the district attorney's office and police had been unaware.

The article also said that a grand jury had met, but had not yet handed down an indictment against Martinez.

"Do you know Barbara Kogan?" Guart asked Martinez.

"No," Manuel answered.

It was a lie. And it was not a smart move on Martinez's part, especially since the denial was quoted in the *Post*, and because Martinez contradicted himself in the same article, telling the newspaper that, as his client, he had found Barbara a divorce attorney in Puerto Rico. In addition, the article named Paul Prosano as the man police believed to be the gunman.

Guart quoted Martinez, in his dare to the DA, "If the grand jury is going to indict me, they should go ahead with it. I don't get intimidated by any grand jury, and any newspaper, any shaky informant. I have nothing to be concerned about, nothing to fear."

Challenging authorities was also not a smart move on Martinez's part. It came at a time when law enforcement was trying to extradite him. In the meantime, Assistant DA Seidemann was still hoping Martinez would eventually testify against both Prosano and Barbara.

The *Post*'s Guart had called Barbara as well, asking if she had anything to do with her husband's murder. She told Guart she knew nothing. "I deny any knowledge of my husband's murder. I want everything fully investigated, and I hope they find the people responsible for this."

Martinez would later say it had been a mistake for him to return the message Al Guart left on his New York City answering machine, which Martinez had called to retrieve messages. "[The reporter] wanted to know if I knew Barbara Kogan and Paul Prosano," Martinez said. "I was under no legal obligation to talk to him, and I should have never returned his message. He caught me off guard."

Back in Mexico City, Martinez had hooked up with the wrong people, and, not long after moving there, he was arrested and incarcerated in the Reynosa prison.

In the meantime, unaware of Martinez's trouble with the law in Mexico, New York-area law enforcement, including the District Attorney's office, had lost track of Manuel Martinez. All they knew was that he had moved to somewhere in Mexico, which the *Post* article confirmed. Detective Ernie Bugge, hoping to locate Manuel, put out a request to the

FBI's Joint Fugitive Task Force asking for help in apprehending Martinez. Two months later, in December 1996, an FBI agent informed Bugge that Martinez had been charged in Mexico with crimes arising out of the embezzlement of 8 million pesos by two fraudulent electronic transfers from Bancomer. The Mexican government had brought two cases against Martinez, one in Tamaupilas and the other in Tuluxa, Mexico.

Back in the States, once they learned where Martinez was, officials attempted to extradite Manuel from Mexico to face charges in New York. The lengthy process began in May 2001, after the US Embassy in Mexico, through Mexico's attorney general office, filed a provisional detention petition. But at the end of the sixty-day period, embassy officials failed to file an extradition petition and the application expired. However, the US Department of Justice and Mexico's Procuraduria General de la Republica abruptly ended the deportation proceedings in January 2002 after Martinez was sentenced to thirteen years, eleven months in a Mexican prison in the second case against him in Mexico. New York investigators put their efforts on hold. Then, after Martinez's appeal led to the reversal of his conviction and the case against him was ultimately dismissed, US officials pursued him again.

On March 17, 2007, Martinez was released from the Penal del Altiplano federal maximum-security prison in Toluca, Mexico, forty miles southwest of Mexico City. He did not know he was at risk of being deported or extradited, because he was unaware of the indictment that had been handed down in 1996. And, as far as he knew, no recent extradition paperwork had been filed. Plus, Martinez later said, he had dual citizenship, in Mexico and in the US, and felt he was protected by Mexican law from being deported.

But in 2007, shortly after Martinez's release from the Mexican prison, a New York law enforcement officer, armed with the 1996 indictment for George Kogan's murder, arrived in Mexico. Days later, around 3:30 a.m. on March 22, Martinez, amid his strong protests, was taken into custody. In the case paperwork, he was classified a "violent felony offender" and "flight risk." With Martinez's sentence served out in Mexico, US feds escorted him back to New York, where he was jailed at Rikers Island. Martinez ultimately filed a motion to dismiss the US charges against him based upon an unreasonable delay in prosecuting him for murder and solicitation to have George Kogan killed. It would be the first of dozens of motions, letters and affidavits Martinez would file with the court.

On September 21, 2007, Martinez, still at Rikers, got his answer to the motion to dismiss when Judge Obus denied it. The judge contended in his ruling that the probe into George's murder was a "good-faith investigation and much of the delay was because Martinez had been incarcerated in Mexico."

Judge Obus also addressed the issue of Martinez's return to the States. Manuel maintained that he was removed from Mexico illegally. He contended that he was transported out of Mexico but not through a formal deportation. The feds went in, took him back to the States, and then charged him with murder. Those steps did not include extradition, defined as a formal process by which a fugitive found in one country is surrendered to another country.

The judge's ruling in that matter was clear.

> *In their response to defendant's motion to dismiss, the People include a fifty-paragraph, partial summary of their efforts to return defendant to New York. These efforts included attempts at deportation, extradition and prisoner exchange, and, contrary to defendant's argument, began when the People learned of defendant's actual whereabouts in December 1996. In the course of their attempts, the People—who, as state officials, were not permitted to directly contact Mexican authorities—negotiated with Mexican officials through FBI agents in Texas and Mexico, the Department of Justice, the State Department and the United States Consulate. The People chronicled the precise date of each letter, telephone call, and conversation, and established that, in the end, the Mexican government*

THE MILLIONAIRE'S WIFE 107

refused to release defendant until he completed his trials and prison sentences for various crimes he committed in that country. In addition, the People were advised by a Department of Justice official that the Mexican government would likely refuse extradition because defendant faced life imprisonment in New York, a sentence deemed cruel and unusual punishment by the Mexican supreme court. Ultimately, defendant completed his sentence and was deported to New York.

Meanwhile, as Martinez fought, after the fact, his forced movement from Mexico to the US, prosecutors seemed certain that if they moved toward criminally prosecuting Martinez, he would eventually turn state's evidence, and, instead of being tried for murder, he would testify against Barbara Kogan as his co-conspirator. Martinez, however, would not relent. He refused any talk about cooperating with prosecutors and let the case move forward to trial. It became clear to prosecutors that Martinez did not intend to cooperate with the state against his former client.

Jonathan Strauss, Martinez's defense attorney, balked at the charges. "I haven't seen a scintilla of physical evidence to support their theory," Strauss told reporters. "He's always maintained his innocence, and he's looking forward to being vindicated."

"I was not deported," Martinez wrote in a letter to his attorney. "I was kidnapped and my constitutional right of due process was trampled. . . . Can you appreciate my concern that I may be facing a Kangaroo Court with no integrity, no sense of justice, and no respect for the law?

"The FBI used five National Institute of Migration thugs to forcibly take me to Mexico City's International Airport where FBI agent Romero received me."

FBI Special Agent Robert Romero was at the Benito Juarez International Airport in Mexico City awaiting Martinez and his escorts' arrival. Then, with the handcuffed Martinez at his side, Romero, as well as a Mexican National Institute of Migration officer, boarded Aeromexico's Flight 408 for

New York City. "I was escorted to New York City's JFK Airport where FBI Agent Romero and a NIM thug handed me to the NYPD," Martinez said. After the plane was on American soil, Romero then identified himself to Martinez as Special Agent Romero.

The next morning, on Friday, March 23, Martinez, still wearing the jeans, sneakers, T-shirt, and light jacket he'd been transported in the day before, was booked, fingerprinted, and photographed by the NYPD, and a one-page profile was added into the department's computer system, alongside a mugshot and a full-body frontal photo:

New York City Police Department
Mugshot Pedigree

MARTINEZ MANUEL
NYSID# 2556964R
Arrest #: M07000668
Arrest date: 03-22-2007
Top charge: PL 1252501: MURDER 2ND: INTEN-
    TIONAL
Date of birth: 08-18-49
Age at offense: 57
PCT of Arrest: 005 PRECINCT
Source: LIVE

PHYSICAL DESCRIPTION
Race: WHITE HISPANIC
Sex: MALE
Height: 5'11"
Weight: 190
Hair Length: NORMAL
Hair Color: SALT AND PEPPER
Hair Type: CURLY / WAVY
Eye Color: GREEN

The same day, Martinez appeared before Judge Laura Ward in Part 70 of the Supreme Court of the State of New

York. The case was adjourned until April 5, 2007, to give Martinez an opportunity to have defense counsel represent him before the court.

Martinez's attorney friend in Mexico, Irving Analik, recommended that he hire New York–based defense attorney Jonothan Strauss. Martinez hired him privately rather than as court-appointed counsel, and Strauss was by his side at his April 5 arraignment. They both received a copy of the two-count indictment, Case Number 179/1996, which briefly outlined the state case against Martinez. It stated that two "incidents," as the DA called them, occurred, prompting the indictment.

Although Martinez had been indicted in 1996, his arrival in the US was the first time he had seen the formal charges that had been rendered against him. The one-page, once-sealed indictment, dated June 26, 1996, and filed by the 11th Special Grand Jury, May/June 1996 term, formally charged Martinez with one count of murder in the second degree for the death of George Kogan. Translated in this instance, the second-degree charge meant that Martinez didn't pull the trigger but was accused of being materially responsible. He was also charged with a single count of criminal solicitation in the second degree in connection with the taped September 15, 1992, conversation between Manuel and Carlos Piovanetti, in which police contended Martinez had incriminated himself by admitting to Carlos that he'd assisted in George Kogan's murder.

From Rikers Island, where he was newly incarcerated, Martinez quickly fired off a letter to US Attorney General Alberto Gonzalez to protest his arrest—or what he referred to as his "kidnapping"—by federal agents from Mexico to the United States. The letter read:

> *On March 22, 2007 I was kidnapped from Mexico City in violation of the above-referenced federal statute (The Federal Kidnapping Act, 18 USCS). . . . The law was ignored in my kidnap.*

Manuel ended his letter with a command:

> *I demand a Federal investigation, prosecution of all responsible parties for my kidnapping that still continues, my immediate release, just compensation for the damages sustained and full disclosure to the press. I am seriously concerned that certain employees of the U.S. Department of Justice may be acting like criminals blatantly violating Federal law and trying to disguise my kidnapping as a "deportation."*

In preparation for trial and because of the gravity of the recorded conversation, the state requested and was granted protective orders for Carlos Piovanetti and Beatriz Oller, asking that their names not be disclosed to the defendant and defense counsel until after they testified. When her husband confessed to having George Kogan killed, Beatriz said her husband "threatened to kill her and their child, Manelita, if she told anyone," Seidemann said in his written request for a protective order for Oller. The orders were signed a year before Martinez's trial.

Just before his trial commenced in downtown Manhattan, Manuel Martinez was transferred at 1 a.m. on March 18, 2008, from the C-95 Buiding on Rikers Island to the Manhattan House of Detention, which housed the city jail and Central Booking, also known as "The Tombs" because of some of its colonial-style buildings. Martinez's personal property, including his legal documents, notes, and grand jury minutes, all "mysteriously disappeared," he said.

He described the papers as "vital to my defense." He added, "How could I participate in any meaningful way and defend myself in my trial under those circumstances? All my work product of twelve months vanished in this move." During his trial, Jonathan Strauss, representing Martinez, would bring up that point several times to the judge. His legal materials were never recovered.

During voir dire, Jonathan Strauss had several questions for the panel of jurors before they were approved. One ques-

tion in particular—what Strauss called a "hard-ball question"—
was particularly important to defense counsel. "The charge
here is murder," he told the panel. "It's serious. Someone
didn't go home and you may see pictures of a dead body
here. My client has denied these allegations. The judge has
asked you, the government has asked you, now I have to ask
you, you know, if there is anything with respect to the charge
itself. You may see family members in the audience, you
know. No one is looking for legal vengeance or for a lynch
mob. We're looking for fair and impartial jurors that can
fairly look at evidence or lack of evidence in the case. So, for
the charge alone, is that going to prevent you from giving
my client a fair trial?"

One by one, each panelist answered "No."

During the selection process, prosecutor Joel Seidemann
asked each juror if they would require him to prove the guilt
of other participants, including Martinez, in order to reach a
guilty verdict. Because it was a circumstantial case, he also
asked them if they needed to see "CSI" evidence to convict.
"There is not going to be 'CSI'-type evidence in this case."

Seidemann also prepared the jury for possible inconsistencies in witness testimony, even after an objection by the
defense. "I anticipate that when witnesses try to recall
events, there will be inconsistencies," the prosecutor told
prospective jurors. "My question to you is can you listen to
the evidence and decide whether the inconsistencies are mi-
nor or are central to whether or not we proved our case?"

Jurors told Seidemann they'd still be able to render a
guilty verdict, despite inconsistencies in testimony. Then, he
said, "I tell you right now it's our theory that [the defendant]
did not pull the trigger, but that he set this in motion and had
a hand in hiring the hit man."

After Strauss objected and the judge sustained it, Seidemann reworded his question and was able to ask it without a
protest from Strauss: "Well, my question is, when you hear
different witnesses testify, or even the same witness, that are
trying to recall an event that occurred way in the past, I anticipate there will be inconsistencies in the testimony. My

question is if we satisfy you with evidence beyond a reasonable doubt, what will your verdict be even if there are inconsistencies?"

The next day, on Tuesday, March 19, eighteen years after an assassin's bullets cut down George Kogan in a public, apparent hit-for-hire, Manuel Martinez, by now fifty-seven years old, was taken to the New York Supreme Court, Part 51 courtroom, at 100 Centre Street in lower Manhattan. The same day, a jury panel of his peers—twelve jurors and four alternates—was selected.

The panel was a mostly educated group that included: an unemployed construction worker from Spanish Harlem; a mechanical engineer from the Upper East Side; a chemist from Inwood; a social worker from the Upper East Side; a book editor from Chelsea; a daycare director from Manhattan; a language interpreter from Murray Hill; an investment firm worker from Midtown Manhattan; a school principal from Union Square; a human resources employee from Midtown West; a retired computer technician from Manhattan; a retired nurse from the Lower East Side; a college instructor from Harlem; a biologist from Midtown West; a tax law firm legal aid from Hell's Kitchen; and a documentary filmmaker from Manhattan.

Then they stood before Judge Michael Obus with their right hands raised and were sworn in. Martinez was about to have his day in court.

CHAPTER 12

Opening Statements

Defendant Manuel S. Martinez, accused of murder in the second degree and criminal solicitation in the second degree, sat quietly at the defense table and listened as Judge Michael Obus instructed attorneys before allowing opening statements, which are vital for attorneys to lay out their side of the story for jurors. The judge reminded defense attorney Jonathan Strauss that the essence of the state's case was Martinez's "own admissions." Those admissions, jurors would soon learn, were statements allegedly given years earlier and revealed in open court as secondhand accounts. The judge appeared prepared to allow the statements as evidence.

Martinez intently listened, taking copious notes, as the lead prosecutor, Joel J. Seidemann, laid out for the jury the theory of the case as he saw it, and how, through a lengthy investigation, authorities had determined the murder to have taken place.

Prosecutor Seidemann pointed directly at defendant Manuel Martinez and called him a murderer. "May it please the court, Mr. Foreperson, ladies and gentlemen of the jury, this is a case about a lawyer who became a murderer," Seidemann said, "a lawyer who chose not to resolve this dispute that a client had with another by coming before a court and a jury but, rather, chose to hire a hit man who would then go and kill the client's adversary by shooting him in the back three times."

The prosecutor told jurors, while he pointed toward Martinez, "The evidence in this case will show that that attorney did not place his trust in front of a highly engaged and experienced judge, like Judge Obus, or fair-minded New Yorkers, a jury of fair-minded New Yorkers like yourself, but rather he chose to place his trust in the assassin's bullet."

Seidemann described Martinez as a heroin-addicted real estate lawyer (Martinez has denied the drug accusation) who was down on his luck and wanted George Kogan's money. To get that done, the prosecution contended, Martinez needed to convince Barbara Kogan to have her estranged husband killed. "He wanted to be a Mafia don," Seidemann told the jury, "living the fantasy world of *The Godfather* and going to the real world of hurting, killing, and destroying lives."

"Through this case," he told the jury, as he lifted his arm to point at Martinez, "you'll learn that the evidence will show that that lawyer who had his client's adversary killed is seated right over here, right in this seat over here with the tie and jacket. That's the lawyer who had George Kogan killed on October 23, 1990."

Seidemann accused Martinez of taking hit money from Barbara and using it to renovate apartments 2F and 2R in the brownstone building where Manuel and his wife, Beatriz Oller, lived.

Martinez's lawyer, Jonathan Strauss, then took his turn with his opening statement by talking about what the prosecution did and did not have. "So, let me fill you in on a couple of things that the government left out of their theory, okay?" Strauss said. "Barbara Kogan had no involvement whatsoever in this murder."

He also filled in the jury on the Queen-for-a-Day agreement the District Attorney's office had made with Carlos Piovanetti in exchange for testimony against Martinez, attempting to tear down the prosecution's strongest piece of evidence.

"You're going to find out about Carlos Piovanetti," Strauss

told them. "You are going to learn he is convicted of criminally engaging in fraud, in theft. . . . What is Mr. Piovanetti going to come in here and claim? Everything he's going to tell you has been in the newspapers for years," he said, explaining that Piovanetti didn't offer the prosecution anything that they didn't already know. "You are going to hear that Mr. Piovanetti was caught in a fraudulent scheme. He tried to steal thousands and thousands of dollars from the taxpayers of Westchester County. And you are going to hear that he initially, when the police came to him, he lied to them. He lied to the police. He has no problem lying.

"And you're going to learn that Mr. Piovanetti was looking at fifteen years in jail," Strauss continued, "for his fraudulent scheme up in Westchester. Now, you heard there was a cooperation agreement here. So, instead of fifteen years, he got a misdemeanor. No felony conviction. No jail time, and a relief of civil disabilities so he can go on with his life. He's going to come in here and tell all of you that Manny Martinez confessed to him. . . . They will not even tell you a date that this alleged confession took place." That alleged confession, Strauss explained, was in exchange for no incarceration for Piovanetti.

He also talked about the alleged gunman and an eyewitness. "You're going to hear that there is a witness—an eyewitness—to the event. A woman by the name of Beverly Kantor was there, feet away from the incident, when it happened. . . . You're going to hear that they took a picture of Paulie Prosano, stuck it in a photo array, and showed it to Mrs. Kantor.

"And guess what?" attorney Strauss continued. "Mrs. Kantor, the eyewitness who was there, who was real evidence, [with] no ax to grind, [with] no consent agreement with conjugal visits, you know what she says? 'I don't recognize him as the shooter.' He is not picked out of the photo array as the shooter of George Kogan."

Strauss also pointed out that the alleged shooter, Paul Prosano, was not officially named nor charged as an accomplice. "There is no gun linking him, Paulie Prosano, to this crime," Strauss told the jury. "There is nothing. So much for Paulie Prosano being the shooter."

Then, Strauss told jurors, "I don't like to speak ill of the dead, but the man abandoned his wife of twenty-four years and tried to cut her out of everything. The fact that this upset Mrs. Kogan, well, you could all understand that's all true, all right? But what's more interesting that you're going to hear [is] the way Mr. Kogan conducted his life, his business, is that he owed a lot of people a lot of money. And with his business in the casino business, he made a lot of enemies."

Then, Strauss summed up the prosecution's opening statement and his description, along with a slideshow, of the people who would be testifying for the prosecution and against Martinez. He ended his opening statement by reminding the jury that the case before them was based on circumstantial evidence: "This case has a lot. It has a murder of a man. It has an alleged solicitation of murder of another man. It has adultery allegations, sexual allegations, drugs. It has everything but evidence. That's the one thing this case doesn't have."

Then he ended his opening with a quote: "Mark Twain once wrote this: 'A lie can travel halfway around the world before the truth gets its shoes on.' And, on behalf of Manuel Martinez, the truth has its shoes on. They're laced up and they are going to stamp this lie out right now."

Before the trial started, Strauss and Martinez discussed Martinez's option to take the stand and testify in his own defense. Strauss cautioned him against doing so. "Manny, Seidemann is going to keep you two days on the stand." Martinez felt ill prepared for trial, due especially to the loss of his papers during his transfer from Rikers. Besides, "They don't have any evidence against you," Strauss told him. The lack of physical evidence was what Strauss relied on. But as the trial progressed, the circumstantial evidence against Manuel Martinez, which once seemed so skimpy, began taking on a life of its own.

CHAPTER 13

The Trial that Was

With few words, Judge Michael Obus introduced Manuel Martinez and his defense team to a jury of Martinez's peers. "I'm just going to introduce you to some of the participants here," the judge told the panel. "The name of the defendant, which you may have heard when the name of the case was called into the record, is Manuel Martinez. Seated next to Martinez is his attorney, Mr. Jonathan Strauss, and also seated at counsel table is Mr. [James] Coffey, who is just assisting Mr. Strauss in this matter.

"Seated at the other counsel table," Obus continued, "is Assistant District Attorney Joel Seidemann and his colleague, Ms. Soumya Dayananda."

Thus began the criminal trial in the State of New York versus Manuel Martinez.

The first witness called to the stand by the prosecution was Moses Crespo, the door attendant on duty that fateful morning. He was sworn in and the questioning began. Crespo, a soft-spoken man who stayed in shape by riding his mountain bike to and from his doorman job at the 205 East Sixty-ninth Street apartment building from his home in Queens, was asked to speak up. Then, he was asked to verify, including through crime-scene photos, what he had seen and heard that morning. On the stand, he confirmed what he had said to police years earlier on the day of the murder.

Years later, while standing outside 205 East Sixty-ninth Street, Moses said, "I've been interviewed many, many times for this case." As Moses stood on the sidewalk and described for a writer the scene from that October day and the events as they unfolded, he called George Kogan his friend: "He was my *paisano*, my countryman. We were both from Puerto Rico. He was a nice man, a friendly man. He was my brother."

Back in the courtroom, Moses explained to the jury their cordial relationship: "Basically, he was a friendly person to begin with, and, besides that, we came from the same country, Puerto Rico."

Moses also testified that in the two years he'd known George, while George lived at the apartment with Mary-Louise, he'd met George's two sons. But he'd only once met Barbara. "One morning, I was working and she showed up at the building asking for George Kogan," Moses testified. "She just turned around and walked away."

"And why was that?" the prosecutor asked.

"Because I did not allow her to go into the building," said Moses, who also testified that he saw George and Mary-Louise every day while on the job at 205 East Sixty-ninth Street.

When asked how he viewed George and Mary-Louise as a couple, Moses said, "They seemed very happy together."

Moses started to tell the jury how the housekeeper had pounded on the lobby door to be let in just after George was shot. But as Moses began providing details, the defense objected and the court did not allow Moses to continue.

When asked what he saw after he ran outside to where George lay on the sidewalk, when he looked at George's back, he said, "I could see some marks. It looked like bullet holes."

He then told the jury how he'd hurried back to the apartment building to first call 911, then to notify Mary-Louise. "I didn't mention anything was going on," he said. "I just told her to come out, and she went out." Moses described how, once outside, Mary-Louise lost her composure and was so distraught that she had to be restrained and led back into the apartment building. "After that," Moses testified, "I had

Scene of the crime at 205 East 69th Street

(Photo by author)

Barbara Kogan at arraignment, cuffed and remanded to custody
(Courtesy: *New York Daily News*)

Kogan death probe will extend to island

By GINO PONTI
Of The STAR Staff

New York police said Friday their investigation into the shooting death of millionaire George Kogan would extend to Puerto Rico, where Kogan had a number of business and real estate holdings.

"We are looking into all his business connections, including those in Puerto Rico as well as those in New York," said New York City Police Sgt. Peter Berry of the Public Affairs Office.

"Given the circumstances of the slaying, there is the possibility that an associate or former associate could have killed him or had him killed, but right now this is just speculation."

He said police have determined no motive.

Kogan, 49, was shot dead Monday morning outside the posh East 69th Street apartment house of Mary Louise Hawkins, 28, with whom he had been living since he and his wife separated about two years ago.

Thursday, Kogan's estranged wife, Barbara, 47, broke her silence and spoke with detectives investigating the case. In an interview with the New York Post, she said she is now ready "to cooperate fully" with police in helping to catch her husband's killer. They had been married 25 years and had two sons, Billy, 23, and Scott, 24.

Police said the couple were in the midst of a "messy divorce" proceeding. They also confirmed that Kogan had a $5 million life insurance policy but would not identify the beneficiary.

In the newspaper account, Barbara Kogan, when asked about her feelings toward Hawkins, said, "I have no animosity for Mary Louise. I've already spoken with her. George and I remained friends and we maintained a friendly relationship."

The report said both Barbara Kogan and Hawkins attended Kogan's funeral Friday at Riverside Chapel on West 76th Street.

Thursday, attorney Richard Golub,

George Kogan and his wife Barbara.

1982 photo

> **'. . . There is the possibility that an associate or former associate could have killed him or had him killed . . .'**
>
> — Sgt. Peter Berry
> N.Y.C. Police Public Affairs Office

Barbara Kogan's attorney, said the divorce was still being contested by both sides when George Kogan was killed.

The newspaper reports described Hawkins as a curvy, intelligent blonde, the daughter of a wealthy Long Island oil investor. She studied at New York City's most exclusive private schools and graduated from Brown University in 1986.

She went to work for a public relations agency and met the Kogans when she started handling public relations for their

classy East Side antique store.

Kogan was born in Puerto Rico and went to New York in the late 1950s. He met his wife at New York University. They were married and moved to Puerto Rico, where their two sons were born. They returned to New York a few years ago.

Among his holdings here was the Ramada Inn and Casino in San Juan, which Kogan sold about a year ago to a group of Brooklyn investors.

San Juan newspaper story about murder investigation
(Courtesy: *San Juan Star*)

Mary-Louise Hawkins
A.B. History

Mary-Louise Hawkins'
yearbook photo, c. 1985
(Courtesy: Brown
University archives)

Barbara Kogan with her attorney Barry Levin at sentencing
(Courtesy: *New York Daily News*)

Snub-nose bulldog similar to revolver used to kill George
Kogan   (Courtesy: Wikipedia Commons)

Judge Michael Obus presides over hearing
                                    (Courtesy: *New York Daily News*)

Scott Kogan addresses court at his mother's sentencing
(Courtesy: *New York Daily News*)

Barbara Kogan at sentencing, glances at the media
(Courtesy: *New York Daily News*)

Manuel Martinez during happier times
(Courtesy: Nilda Martinez)

Graduation photo of Manuel Martinez
(Courtesy: Nilda Martinez)

NEW YORK CITY POLICE DEPARTMENT

Mugshot Pedigree

NAME:	MARTINEZ MANUEL
NYSID#:	2556964R
Arrest #:	M07000668
Arrest Date#:	03-22-2007
Top Charge:	PL 1252501: MURDER 2ND: INTENTIONAL
Date of Birth:	08-18-1949
Age at Offense:	57
Social Security #:	583098608
PCT of Arrest:	005 PRECINCT
Source:	LIVE

PHYSICAL DESCRIPTION

Race:	WHITE HISPANIC
SEX:	MALE
Height:	511
Weight:	190
Hair Length:	NORMAL
HAIR COLOR:	SALT AND PEPPER
Hair Type:	CURLY / WAVY
Complexion:	CLEAR
Eye Color:	GREEN
Scars, Marks Tattoos:	
Desc:	
Location:	
Bodyside:	
Alias 1:	
Alias 2:	
Alias 3:	
Alias 4:	

Manuel Martinez Police Rap Sheet
(Courtesy: NYPD)

Farmland in Cayey, Puerto Rico (Courtesy: Wikipedia Commons)

Barbara Kogan's San Juan high-rise apartment
(Courtesy: *New York Daily News*)

Bedford Hills Correctional Center, where Barbara Kogan is
serving out her term
(Courtesy: Teresa A. Miller)

to stay on the door. I could not get involved with any other thing."

On March 25, 2008, Mary-Louise Hawkins, who had flown in from her London home, took the stand and retold the events of that day, as well as details about her relationship with George, during testimony on direct examination by prosecutor Joel Seidemann and cross-examination by attorney Strauss. Calmly and matter-of-factly, she answered their questions. She testified that she'd worked for publicist Matthew Evins, who recommended her to do public relations work for the Kogans, to counteract the bad publicity they had received because of a store robbery. Mary-Louise, she told the court, first met Barbara when Barbara interviewed her, and then George. Mary-Louise told the jury how, in short order, George began courting her. She repeated in court the words she had cried out as she stood in horror at the sight of her boyfriend sprawled out on the sidewalk nearly nineteen years earlier. "It was his wife! It's his wife!" she repeated in court.

Much had changed. By the time Mary-Louise testified at the Martinez's 2008 trial, she was forty-six, married, and living in Europe.

When asked to describe her relationship with George after he moved in with her, Mary-Louise told the court, "He was a sweet, gentle, loving person. I felt real, real sorry for him in the beginning, because he was completely damaged, incredibly shy, and I fell in love with him and was really happy to be with him."

They lived in a desirable area of Manhattan. Mary-Louise's co-op was dog friendly, so they adopted a small poodle and took long walks with him in Central Park. They went to a gym three or four times a week together, she told the court, and spent time dining out, often choosing "a different nationality of food," or staying in and cooking together. George always had his cell phone with him, and conducted business on the phone as they walked.

"We went to museums," she said. "He was really interested in art, and so was I, so we went to a lot of museums."

End to end, Manhattan is roughly thirteen miles in length and two miles across. George and Mary-Louise each Sunday chose a different part of New York, mapped it, and then walked to it, for exercise and to see as much of the city as they could. "We went to the Lower East Side," Mary-Louise said. "We went to Brooklyn. There was a lot of walking, because he needed exercise, and we went to the gym three or four times a week, but it was pretty mundane for other people, I would suppose."

They also went on business trips to Puerto Rico or to Miami, when George needed to be there. After losing her job at Evins Communications, Mary-Louise did not go back to work, and she was able to travel with him.

"How were you supporting yourself?" Seidemann asked her.

"I had an income from a commercial property I owned with my sister," she said.

"And what was George Kogan doing to support himself at that time?"

"He had small debts that he collected from people. He had some cash. In the beginning, he manipulated things a little bit to just eke out some cash, but he was more and more strapped for cash as the contested [divorce] time grew on."

She said the bank accounts were "all frozen."

"And did there come a time when he had little cash, when he was strapped for cash?" Seidemann asked. If so, he asked, did she do anything to help him?

"Pretty much, yes. I put him on as an auxiliary cardholder on all of my credit cards, so that he would be able to charge stuff and wouldn't have problems getting around. He did a lot of talking on the phone to try to move money around and try to keep assets from being foreclosed, because, since everything was frozen, properties were in danger of going into bankruptcy, really. So, he had trouble, and he would stay on the phone a lot. He would conduct business either sitting on the couch in the drawing room or on a bench in Central Park, on his cell phone."

"Did there come a time," Seidemann asked her, "when George was sued for divorce?"

"Yes, in February of 1989."

Barbara occasionally called the apartment to speak with George, Mary-Louise testified. "Usually, [it was] arguments about paying bills," she told the court. "The constant quarrels about money—it was never solved." During that time, George had fought to hang on to his properties.

The prosecutor inquired about the apartment the she and George shared, asking Mary-Louise, "Who was paying the mortgage?"

"My dad," Mary-Louise answered.

She also testified that George's relationship with his sons, especially Billy, his youngest, had been strained, because of the divorce. "He tried in every way he could to keep communications open, but Billy was pretty steadfast that he was siding with his mother and couldn't believe that his father was doing such a thing. [Billy] was understandably upset. He didn't take it very well that his father had left his mother and sided with the mother and refused to speak to George."

By the summer of 1990, things had improved some between father and son. "Billy had gotten into Cardozo Law School, and I helped him furnish an apartment that he was going to move into," Mary-Louise told the court. Billy became the mediator between Barbara and George in the hopes of settling his parents' divorce through an amicable agreement.

Scott agreed with Mary-Louise. During his testimony, he said the same: "About six months before my dad passed away, they started to become closer. My father always kept the channels of communication open, and my brother somehow just came around. And, I must say, thank God for that period of time when my brother had that closeness with him."

In an ironic twist, Mary-Louise revealed in court what Barbara Kogan had not known. "The day before [George] was supposed to meet with Barbara and Billy, we sat down and drew up the skeleton of a way to work up an agreement," she told the court. "There weren't figures mentioned in this document, but it was a way to generate figures that he was hoping Barbara would agree to."

"And what was George proposing?" the prosecutor asked.

"Basically, proposing to give her half of everything," Mary-Louise said.

That revelation, made in open court, would be how Barbara would learn, through news reports, when it was much too late, that George had been preparing to give her half of his assets to settle their divorce and be done with it.

"And can you characterize how George felt about the possibility of reaching a settlement?" Mary-Louise was asked.

"Optimistic," she answered. "He was optimistic."

Seidemann also told the court that the evidence showed, in the form of a handwritten settlement proposal, that "George Kogan the very day that he was murdered was to meet with Barbara Kogan and William Kogan, his son, in an effort to bang out a settlement agreement, and George was hopeful that that's what would happen."

Mary-Louise also testified that, once George's divorce was final, the two of them planned to marry and then move to Europe.

Throughout her time on the stand, Mary-Louise remained stoic, not allowing emotion to take over even as she talked about the October day her boyfriend was fatally shot and how she learned about it.

She told the court that after doorman Moses Crespo had knocked on her door, telling her that George was outside and wanted to talk to her, she walked outside to find her boyfriend "lying face down on the pavement. There were three holes in his back."

She also testified that George did not keep a 9-to-5 workday schedule, so it would not have been easy for a would-be assassin to monitor his daily routine. About her life afterward, she told the court that, despite George's death, she married and relocated to Europe a few years after the murder.

During his cross-examination of Mary-Louise, Strauss pointed out that Hawkins had moved in with a married man, asking her if she had "shacked up" with George. He also asked her about Barbara after she became involved with her husband. "During this time frame, had you seen Barbara?" he asked.

"Yes."

"Okay. You weren't telling her, 'Oh, by the way, I'm sleeping with your husband,' were you?"

"No, I did not," she answered.

The prosecutor, in redirect, asked about her boyfriend's funeral.

"Can you explain to the members of the jury why it was you didn't attend George Kogan's funeral?" he asked.

"On the advice of my family's attorney, I was advised to stay at home, because we had been hounded by the press and he really thought that my going to the funeral would just create a huge circus. And, in fact, a girlfriend of mine who looks a lot like me went hoping to support me, and she got followed by the press all the way down the street, because they thought she was I, me, so I did not go."

"And how did you feel about it?" Seidemann asked.

"Devastated. I wanted to go, but I saw the logic," Mary-Louise said.

On Tuesday, April 8, Ernest Bugge, by then a retired and heavily decorated detective with the New York Police Department, also testified for the prosecution. Bugge took the stand, and, upon cross-examination by Jonathan Strauss, the detective said that in October 1995, five years after the murder, he had showed Beverly Kantor a photo lineup that included Paul Prosano. Bugge admitted on the stand that Kantor was not able to identify Prosano from the lineup as the man she saw standing, holding a gun, over George Kogan.

Detective Bugge, eventually assigned to the Kogan case, assisted fellow Detective Daniel Massanova with the January 1996 arrest of Paul Prosano and his partner, Joseph McKee, for a kidnapping in which Prosano and McKee broke into the 25 Fifth Avenue ninth-floor apartment of forty-eight-year-old Frances Barnes and held her hostage for two and a half hours. Frances Barnes testified at the men's trial in 1997.

Detective Bugge had shown the same photo array that included Prosano's image to Wilmer Rodriguez, an employee in Martinez's law office who'd known Paul Prosano from his visits to Martinez's office.

"Did Wilmer Rodriguez positively identify Paul Prosano as the hit man?" Strauss asked.

"No," Detective Bugge responded.

The prosecution needed to illustrate a connection between Martinez and the alleged hit man, Paul Prosano. So Seidemann called Paul Cardone, nephew of Peter Cardone, to the stand. The senior Cardone owned, with his wife Catherine, a gun shop in Stormville, New York, and Martinez was the shop's accountant and tax attorney. When the nephew took the stand, he testified about his knowledge of the relationship between Frank Bongarzone, who formerly shared a cell in a Staten Island prison with Paul Prosano. Prosano was the one who'd introduced Bongarzone to Peter Cardone, who later hired him to do maintenance work at his gun shop. Martinez met both Bongarzone and Prosano when he stopped by the gun shop in the course of his financial work for the store.

Growing up, Paul Cardone told the court, he often spent summers at his uncle's home and regularly accompanied Peter to gun shows to learn the used- and antique-gun business. He regularly saw Bongarzone, whom he referred to as "Frankie." Cardone told the court that "Frankie was aspiring to be a gangster."

That's when Strauss objected.

"Relevance, your honor," he said.

"I'll allow it," Judge Obus ruled, and the connection between Martinez, Cardone, Prosano, and the wannabe gangster Bongarzone was made.

When it came time on March 26 for Dr. Michael Marano, the emergency-room surgeon who operated on George Kogan, to take the stand, Seidemann did the direct examination. His testimony was vital to the case, because Marano, who was also the doctor on duty who evaluated George upon his arrival at the hospital, described how hard the team of surgeons had worked to save his life. The court swore in Marano as a qualified expert witness in "operability and microscopics of firearms," according to court documents.

When it came time for jurors to hear details of the medical care, treatment, and surgery performed on George at New York Hospital, Assistant District Attorney Soumya Dayananda was the one who questioned Doctor Marano.

"I was first called to the emergency room on the date of his arrival just after the cardiac surgery team had been called, because he had been brought into the emergency room with a very low blood pressure and then suffered what we would call a traumatic cardiac arrest," Marano said. "As part of the general surgery team, it was my responsibility to evaluate patients in that situation."

"Now," Dayananda asked, "when you first saw [George], at some point was he able to be stabilized?"

"He was able to be stabilized, but it took quite a bit of effort. It took approximately an hour or perhaps a bit more to restore his blood pressure so he was stable, but in a very precarious situation."

"And once he was stabilized, what did you do?"

"Once he was stabilized in the emergency room," Dr. Marano said, "and that required quite a bit of work mostly by the cardiac surgery team, including opening his chest and trying to stop the flow of blood into the chest temporarily, trying to suture a hole in the patient's heart and restoring his blood pressure with many transfusions of blood. After that occurred, we did have at least a relatively low blood pressure enough that we brought him in the operating room to try to repair his other injuries."

"And what surgeries were performed?" Dayananda asked.

"The intent of the surgery that I was involved with was to explore into the patient's abdomen and try to repair injuries that had occurred in that location. The cardiac surgery team continued to repair the hole in the coronary arteries of the patient's heart in the operating room and then to close his chest."

The procedure, the doctor told the court, lasted about four hours. "It was quite a difficult operation for the patient," Marano continued. "He was quite unstable for the majority of it and we were able to successfully get him through the surgery, but it was clear that he was deteriorating rapidly. We got him to the surgery intensive care unit, but shortly thereafter, within fifteen or twenty minutes, the patient expired [at] approximately 4 p.m. Very aggressive efforts were employed to try to save his life."

Next, Dr. Aglae Charlot took the stand to talk about the autopsy, performed the day after George died. She testified that state's evidence, bullet number one, entered through the middle of George's back, close to the spine, and into the right side of the chest, "through the liver, and the exit wound was in the skin of the front of the chest." The bullet, she said, somewhere at the scene of the crime, was not recovered.

Bullet number two, she said, went through the right side of the back, "entered the chest, went throught the liver also, and the bullet was recovered in this area," she told the jury as she pointed to a diagram on a large screen. She said she recovered the mishapen bullet and saved it as evidence.

"Gunshot number three," Doctor Charlot said, "was on the left side of the back of the chest, and the bullet also entered the left chest cavity, went through the lung, through the covering of the heart, and it was reported to us that the bullet was recovered by the surgeon at the time of surgery." She described the bullet as "deformed."

Next, the actual damaged bullet, People's Exhibit Number 17, was shown to the jury as one of the few pieces of evidence in the case.

All told, George Kogan suffered injuries to his liver, lungs, and heart, Charlot explained: "For each one of those organs separately injured, one separately will cause blood loss, and with three of them, it just adds up. The brain was pale. There was no blood reaching the brain. It is my understanding that they tried blood transfusions, and blood was given to him in the hospital, and also fluid. It did not succeed."

Joel Seidemann asked Charlot, "Do you have an opinion, to a reasonable degree of medical certainty, as to what caused George Kogan's death?"

"Yes," she answered.

"And can you tell that to the members of the jury?"

"Yes. It was the injuries caused by the gunshot wounds and the bullets entering his body and his vital organs."

Also testifying was Detective John Kraljic. In an unusual move, Kraljic was shown a sample gun—not the one used to kill George Kogan, but one the prosecution described to the jury as "similar"—a .44-caliber, semi-automatic revolver, People's Exhibit No. 25. Investigators never found the gun used to kill George Kogan. Presentation of the sample gun to the witness made for stunning testimony. He showed the jury a large-caliber pistol that, when loaded, is powerful enough, as the LAPD SWAT officer had observed, to kill a grizzly.

Martinez's lawyer objected to admitting the gun as evidence, so the judge called counsel to the bench to discuss it, in a sidebar, out of earshot of the jury. Strauss told Judge Obus, "I'm going to object to them introducing a gun and waving it around in front of the jury. I think it's only done for the purposes to inflame the jury, and I don't think it's appropriate." Despite the defense's argument, Judge Obus allowed the gun in as an exhibit (a move that would not be lost on Martinez's appellate attorney). It was admitted as being similar to a gun used in a kidnapping and robbery perpetrated by a man named Paul Prosano, although the weapon in that case was not located either. The prosecution then asked witness Frances Barnes, one of two women kidnapped by Prosano and McKee, to help prove the point by having Frances describe to the jury a weapon she'd seen Prosano handle while he held her hostage. By calling Barnes, the prosecutor tried to illustrate for the jury Prosano's criminal background, which included the frightening episode involving Barnes and her roommate being held at gunpoint.

At 11 p.m. on March 29, 1991, Good Friday, Frances awakened in her bedroom to a stranger standing over her, pointing a gun. He told her he was a police officer, showed her his badge, and asked her if she had any weapons in the apartment. Then, a second man, also armed, brought Frances's roommate into the bedroom. They talked about a man in the building they wanted to teach a lesson to. After a couple of hours, they took the women to the roof, looking for an exit. After not finding an escape route, they returned to the apartment. Once inside again, the men explained that they had gone to the building to teach a man who lived there a lesson, because he'd gotten one of their relatives turned onto drugs. But their ploy was interrupted and, to hide, they broke into Frances' apartment, where they planned an escape route out of the building.

"They decided the best way out was for the four of us to go in the elevator together downstairs, past the doorman, and out into the street and into a taxicab," Barnes testified, "The taxicab went over to Sixth Avenue, turned up Sixth, and they let us out." The women walked back to their apartment building, where the doorman called the police. It would take nearly five years for the kidnappers to be arrested.

Then, after McKee and Prosano's January 1996 arrests on the kidnapping charges, Peter Sadadinski, Prosano's father, contacted Manuel Martinez for help in posting a $50,000 bond for his son's release from jail. The case, the prosecution pointed out, linked Prosano to Martinez through their mutual friend Paul Cardone. Also, Paul Prosano had signed a letter authorizing Prosano's brother, Peter Sadadinski Jr., to pick up Prosano's personal belongings from a police property clerk at the 120th Precinct on Staten Island. Martinez had notarized that letter, and his signature made it a documented link tying Prosano to Martinez.

In 1997, Paul Prosano and his partner Joe McKee were convicted for the crime. The prosecutor asked Barnes, a social worker and the mother of two, about the weapon she'd seen with Prosano during the kidnapping.

"Is this the gun Paul Prosano had?" Seidemann asked as he showed her the sample snub-nosed revolver.

"It looks like the kind of gun that Tony Prosano was

holding," Barnes answered, referring to Paul Prosano by his nickname.

"How was it similar?"

"It's a revolver. It's got a brown handle and the same shape, same size," she answered.

The testimony was dramatic, with the prosecutor parading a gun before the jury, even though it was not the same revolver used in the killing of George Kogan. But that didn't matter. Absent the actual murder weapon, it was as close as the prosecution could get.

Next, Beverly Kantor, thirty-five at the time of the shooting, recounted how she'd parked her car near the entrance of 205 East Sixty-ninth Street and saw a heavyset man head toward the building's awning. Another man was about ten to twenty feet behind him.

"I wanted to park in front of the awning, but the doorman wouldn't let me," Kantor testified. "So I parked here," indicating to the jury she had parked her car just past the awning.

After she was out of her car, "I see a man walking with a couple of grocery bags and then I see another man following him," she said. "It looks like he is following him, and he takes a gun out from the inside of his pants and he shoots the man three times in the back."

"And can you describe to the jury—you said you saw him take the weapon out; is that correct?" the prosecutor asked.

"From the front of his pants, yes."

"How would you describe the shooter's demeanor at the time?"

"He was very calm. He just, you know, like you were reaching for a piece of gum, he just took—he just took the gun out and *bang, bang, bang*"—she lifted her arm, as if she were shooting a gun—"and then put it back in his sweatshirt, turned around, and walked up to Third Avenue and took a right."

During the trial, in a sidebar discussion between Assistant District Attorney Soumya Dayananda and Jonathan Strauss, Dayananda asked the court's permission to question

Kantor on the stand about the statement she'd heard Mary-Louise Hawkins cry out that October morning, "It was his wife! It's his wife!" Obus ruled against allowing the statement. Judge Obus told Dayananda, "The witness is just speculating in and of itself. Make sure your witness does not volunteer it."

Kantor's response to the street shooting playing out in front of her was to recoil. "I shut my car door," she said. "I looked at the shooter first to see where he was going. He looked at me. I looked at him."

"I didn't know what he had in mind. And he ran back up toward Third Avenue, north. When I saw the coast was clear, I went to the victim. He was lying flat on his stomach."

"I tried to ask him some questions," she continued. "He had heavy breathing, and he did not respond. I could see one bullet hole. I knew three [rounds] were shot, but I just noticed one."

"Hang on," she told George. "Take it easy. The ambulance will be here soon."

She was ten feet away from Kogan when he was killed and about fifteen feet from the shooter, face to face.

"He looked right at me," she testified. "He did look at me, and I don't know if he had a thought, but he did look at me and he did look around and that was the only thing I really captured from him, was that he looked around. He did not look nervous. He didn't look scared, and then he put the gun back in the front of his pants, [pulled] the sweatshirt down, turned around, and walked up towards Third Avenue. He didn't say anything."

"Did you see him approach the victim after the victim went down?"

"He did not."

She also said the shooter was about ten feet away from George when he was shot, which didn't match the autopsy findings of Dr. Aglae Charlot that George was shot at point-blank range.

While Beverly Kantor saw most of the crime as it happened, she'd ducked when she saw the suspect pull the gun out of his waistband. Three other witnesses saw the shooter immediately after the murder, turning their heads toward the sound of the gunfire. But only one—the housekeeper on her way to work—saw the entire shooting as it unfolded. The other witnesses stood in stunned surprise as the aftermath of the crime played itself out before their eyes like a scene in a murder mystery. The housekeeper saw George—as he was shot, as he staggered, and as he fell face down on the rain-soaked sidewalk.

Questioning Kantor about the possibility of a robbery gone bad, prosecutor Joel Seidemann asked her, "Did you ever see him take any property from the victim?"

"He did not."

Next, she was asked what the shooter looked like. "It's a long time ago," she said. "All I could really remember is that he didn't really have a look. He had, you know, a flat affect, if that's—that's the best way I can describe it. Just a flat affect, and he turned around and he walked away."

Next, Seidemann, by questioning Scott Kogan and George's sister, Myrna Borus, tried to drive home the point that Barbara was uncaring after her husband was killed. As George Kogan lay in the hospital for six hours, his wife had called a friend to stay with her at her apartment. "So, you have George dying in the hospital and Barbara having her hair done," Seidemann said. But Barbara's attorney, whom she'd hired because she knew she was under investigation, had countered that accusation, saying that a friend had visited the distraught Barbara in her apartment to help her get ready to go to the hospital, in case she decided to, by combing out Barbara's hair. Seidemann told the jury that Barbara had paid $500 for that personal, in-home salon session. He did not, however, produce proof of that sum exchanging hands or even the name of the person who styled Barbara's hair—at least it was not in any of the documents filed with the court.

But that didn't matter. To the prosecution, the woman, even though she was a friend of Barbara's, was a hairdresser. During the trial, prosecutors emphasized that Kogan's wife did not visit him at the hospital. To back up the statement, on Tuesday, March 25, 2008, George Kogan's sister, Myrna Borus, testified for the prosecution. "She never came to the hospital," Borus told jurors. When Borus took the stand that afternoon, Assistant District Attorney Soumya Dayananda questioned her.

Next to testify was insurance-company lawyer Richard Lutz, who told the court that private investigators for SMA Insurance of Worcester, Massachusetts, were unable to figure out if Barbara had ordered the murder of her husband. The company filed a federal lawsuit against Barbara in 1991 challenging her right to collect the cash, but it lost the suit after its lengthy private probe turned up nothing definitive. As a result, company officials had no choice but to pay out the more than $4 million proceeds to Barbara Kogan, despite the cloud of suspicion hanging over her and despite the fact that she'd called the insurance company a week before her husband's murder. Barbara also prepaid, through an escrow account, the $2,000 premium. In the end, Lutz testified, "We were not able to determine who was responsible for the death."

Also taking the stand on behalf of SMA insurance company was Elaine Kay-Gannon, who testified that Barbara had contacted the insurance company before George's murder to see if she was the sole beneficiary. Seidemann questioned Kay-Gannon.

"Was this the first time you had someone call eight days before a murder to request replacement policies?" Seidemann asked her.

But before Kay-Gannon could answer, defense attorney Jonathan Strauss objected, and Judge Obus sustained the objection, not allowing the witness to answer.

Also taking the stand that day was Omar Quinones. Omar was Scott Kogan's roommate in Puerto Rico, in the apartment the Kogan family had lived in, while the boys were growing up. Omar, the second witness of the day, was questioned about a voice message left for Scott by his mother before George Kogan was killed. The message, intended for her son, not for his roommate, instructed Scott to give a message to his father from her.

"Tell your father to get things in order or he is going to get what is coming to him," Quinones testified. That call, he said, made him "feel uncomfortable."

Also, Quinones said that in early October 1990, he'd had dinner with George during a visit to Puerto Rico. "George was happy, in love, and looking forward to rebuilding his life," Quinones told the jury.

Barbara's sister, Elaine Siegel Sokalner, testified on Wednesday, March 26, 2008, after traveling from San Juan to New York City. She was not there because she wanted to be. She had been summoned to testify for the prosecution. She told the court her sister had nothing to do with George's murder. The bond between Barbara and Elaine was tight, and, at the time of the Martinez trial, Barbara had not yet been charged with a crime.

To the *Daily News*, as she was leaving the courthouse, Elaine said, "It was not [Barbara]. It is ridiculous."

Ridiculous or not, the issue was far from over. Assistant District Attorney Joel Seidemann was more determined than ever to dig up evidence to implicate Barbara.

And, as if hearing Seidemann's prayers that first week of the trial, the *Daily News* ran a front-page story with the headline, "Crooked lawyer on trial in '90 hit." The article began with, "An Upper East Side woman's crooked divorce lawyer went on trial Monday on charges of hiring a hit man to kill her estranged tycoon husband nearly twenty years ago." It could not have been better press for the prosecution.

On April 1, the Kogans' eldest son, Scott, took the stand. He testified, often through tears, against Manuel Martinez, but his mother was also implicated, though Barbara Kogan was not the one on trial.

Also, Scott testified about an earlier statement he'd given to the grand jury in which he recalled what he described as an "odd meeting" he'd had with Manuel Martinez while Manuel and Barbara were in Puerto Rico. His mother and

Manuel, Scott said, had stopped by Scott's apartment, and sized up Scott's stocky, muscular, square-jawed roommate, Omar Quinones, after Omar arrived home from a judo class. "He just returned from a martial arts practice session and he's a large guy," Scott testified. When Omar, six foot two and 250 pounds, walked into the apartment, Martinez told him, "You look like you could take a couple of slugs and keep walking." It was an odd thing to say, Scott said. "I've heard lots of ways of greeting people and trying to break the ice, but this doesn't seem regular."

The Kogans' oldest son also relayed that his mother at one point claimed she did not know Manuel Martinez, even though Scott had met Martinez that day in the midst of his parents' divorce. He told his mother, "The police were down here [in Puerto Rico]. They're asking about Manny Martinez." Barbara's response, Scott told the court, was, "Who's that? I don't know him."

"Mom, you know I met him through you," he told his mother. "What do you mean you don't know him?"

But she insisted, Scott told the court, that she didn't know Martinez.

Scott continued crying on the stand when he told the jury that his mother felt he had taken his father's side, and she went so far as to tell her son, who suffered from asthma, that the next time he had an asthma attack, "You should die from asphixia."

Scott testified that he'd told both of his parents that he wanted to remain neutral. "If you want someone to talk to, spend time with, I'm there," he told his parents. "But don't expect me to be involved in a slugfest or anything like that," he told them. After the breakup, he often talked to his mother on the phone. But a minute or two into the conversation, when the topic of his father would come up, she would become hysterical and hang up on him, accusing him of siding with his father. His brother William, on the other hand, wanted to be there for their mother: "I used to kiddingly call him 'the protector,'" Scott told the court. "He didn't mind that because he felt she needed protecting at that point. He was upset with my dad and didn't really want to talk with him or know [anything] about him."

In the meantime, to help control the calls from his mother, Scott said, "I bought an answering machine because she would call at all hours—morning, noon, night, you know. I bought an answering machine that would take care of a lot of these calls that came in." Also, should there be an emergency with his mother, he wanted her to be able to leave a message for him. Her emotional state, he said, wasn't good. "She would go on talking about how she felt that my father was trying to hurt her economically," he told the jury. His father talked about the divorce, too, including his financial state, once the judge froze the couple's assets. "I was aware through [my father] and through others that [my father] was being supported financially through assistance from his sister, my aunt Myrna, and his brother, Lawrence Kogan."

After Barbara filed for divorce in February 1989, Scott described how his mother flew to San Juan with her attorney Norman Pearlman and a safe-company employee who cracked a safe, installed in Scott's bedroom in his parent's former apartment, so she could remove her husband's stamp and coin collections. She also moved furniture out of the home, including Scott's bed, leaving him without a place to sleep.

"Why did your mother change so many attorneys during the divorce?" Assistant District Attorney Seidemann asked Scott.

"It coincided with the fact that during the proceedings of their divorce, my father and his attorney would try to come up with settlements to put this thing to an end, economic settlements, a deal sort of," Scott replied. "And whenever they would come to something that was doable, my mother would have to change attorneys, and another fellow would come on board, and it would take another month or so for him to become acquainted with the facts, and then sometime shortly thereafter as soon as another apparent deal was about to take place, then there was another [lawyer] change mid-course."

Defense attorney Jonathan Strauss then questioned Scott about his father's operating style as a businessman. Years earlier, when interviewed by police, Scott had told detectives he had not been surprised that his father was targeted, because of George's "aggressive business practices." During questioning at Martinez's trial, Scott explained away the remark by saying he'd meant to relay that his father had been a strong, no-nonsense businessman. Also, Scott told the jury, his parents' separation had left his mother devastated after twenty-four years of marriage.

After the direct examination by prosecutor Seidemann, during a court recess, Scott declined to talk to reporters who approached him outside the courtroom. When Scott returned to the stand, Strauss cross-examined him by presenting him with an investigative report and Scott's statement to police from 1990, asking him to read it.

"Are you familiar with those statements?"

"Yes," Scott answered, reading what he'd told police, that he was not surprised his father died violently, considering his "aggressive business practices." The defense didn't ask Scott to explain further. And neither did police. No one but Scott knew what he'd meant by that comment.

Prosecutor Joel Seidemann, as soon as Scott answered, objected to the line of questioning, saying Scott's 1990 statement to police was "speculation."

"Sustained," Judge Obus ruled.

A day after Scott Kogan testified, Manuel Martinez responded to Scott's testimony by typing out a letter, dated April 2, 2008, to his defense attorney, Jonathan Strauss. It read, in part:

> George Kogan was not the kind, loving human being presented to the jury by Frank Bonem, his divorce attorney, and Matthew Evins, his store's publicist. Scott Kogan finally admitted yesterday, between tears, that his father used "aggressive" business practices.
>
> If George Kogan owed someone $10,000, he would make them wait and wait and wait until the person fi-

*nally accepted $3,000 as debt settlement. That is the
George Kogan [the legal community] in Puerto Rico
knew well. A scoundrel. That is the George Kogan
people truly despised. That is the George Kogan Barbara Kogan experienced through the divorce. That is
the George Kogan the police never investigated because the number of suspects in his murder would
have been endless, not only in Puerto Rico. That is the
true George Kogan who purchased Scott's affection
and loyalty. People like George Kogan behave like
that as a pattern, and the jury failed to know this.*

*If I am convicted with "smoke-and-mirror" evi-
dence, what do you think will happen to Barbara Kogan who collected the $4M U.S.D. insurance policies
and was the plaintiff in the acrimonious divorce? A
long list of George Kogan's victims must be presented
as witnesses to the jury. We need help from Puerto
Rico. . . . The truth must emerge: Many people smiled
after George Kogan was executed and police misera-
bly failed to investigate all suspects.*

Throughout the four-week trial, written correspondence
like the one above was typically the way Martinez kept in
communication with his attorney, rather than conversations
before and after court each day.

Roger Wideman, the Federal Express deliveryman, was
another witness at the scene on the fateful day George Kogan was murdered. He was about to go through the service
entrance at 205 East Sixty-ninth when he heard shots fired.
Wideman sat down with a New York Police Department
sketch artist. The composite drawing of the suspect did not
resemble Paul Prosano, the man said to be the hit man. Prosano had become the elephant in the courtroom, the unofficial suspect.

But Wideman's wasn't the only artist's rendition done after the shooting. Two other witnesses, Randy Scott and Mike
Rosario, who were at Central Park just after the shooting
occurred, saw what they called a suspicious-looking man.

Authorities, however, did not want either sketch publicly released. Strauss tried to submit the police composite sketches in court to show jurors, so they could compare the images with a photo of Paul Prosano.

The mug shot of Prosano became People's Exhibit Number 29, and it was shown on a large-screen monitor to the jury. Prosano had never officially been named a suspect in the Kogan case, never charged, never arrested, yet the man in the photo was called "the hit man" by the prosecution.

However, prosecutor Seidemann argued that there were three witnesses, two sketches, and two sketch artists. "It's our position," he argued, "that you can't use the sketches in relation to those witnesses, let alone other witnesses." Then Seidemann cited the case of the People versus Robert Maldonado, where the judge in that case said, "This Court has long considered composite sketches to be hearsay." Judge Obus, in Martinez's case, ruled the same. Thus, the jury never saw the drawings of the alleged hit man, one composed by an NYPD artist with the help of witness Roger Wideman, who was delivering packages that morning and was just feet away from the killer.

Had jurors been allowed to see artists' renderings, they would have learned that none of the sketches of the gunman, according to defense attorney Jonathan Strauss, resembled Paul Prosano. On the day the trial started, without the jury present, Strauss told the judge, "The original detectives on the case . . . they received descriptions from these individuals which basically matched the composite sketches, and I'm going to cross-examine them as well about the descriptions they received as part of their jobs as the investigative assigned detectives to the case." But when it came to asking whether the witness descriptions of the gunman matched a photo of Paul Prosano, the question itself, let alone the sketches, was not allowed in court.

Despite a lack of physical evidence and eyewitnesses pointing to Paul Prosano, two days into the trial, the prosecution used its trump card to tie Manuel Martinez to the man they claimed to be the shooter. The link to Martinez was the audiotaped conversation between Martinez and Carlos Piovanetti on September 15, 1992. On that day, Carlos, while at the Westchester police station, was beeped on his pager by Martinez. Police suggested Carlos call him back so they could tape the conversation. It was 2:50 in the afternoon. After answering, Manuel asked Carlos to call back in ten minutes. Carlos was nervous, but he went along with the plan, and called Manuel back at 3 p.m. while police recorded the conversation.

Carlos told Manuel he was calling from a US post office in Manhattan at Fifty-third Street and Third Avenue. Manuel believed him. The conversation, in Spanish and translated by Virginia Blanco, who worked for the New York Manhattan DA's office, was played to the jury. The partial transcript follows:

Martinez: Hello?

Piovanetti: What's up?

Martinez: How are things?

Piovanetti: Well, so look, papa, um, um, guess who beeped me today.

Martinez: Who beeped you today?

Piovanetti: Uh, Westchester County Police.

Martinez: Yeah? How nice. And what did they tell you?

Piovanetti: Nothing, because I hung up when they called.

Martinez: Uh huh. What do they want to know?

Piovanetti: What do you think they want to know?

Martinez: Well, I was hoping that you, you, you said to me that you were going to be indicted in four, five days.

Piovanetti: Manny, I am getting indicted in four or five days.

Martinez: Great.

Piovanetti: I haven't been indicted yet.

Martinez: Uh uh. Well, that, you expected that.

Piovanetti: Well.

Martinez: That—that call, right, papa? Let's—let's dig in. I'll help you. I told you that I was not going to leave you stuck. What can I do for you?

Piovanetti: You tell me. What can you do for me?

Martinez: Well—

Piovanetti: I'm in the shit. What do you suggest I do?

Martinez: Well, let's fix it. I was supposedly meeting with Lenny Cherry on Saturday. I called him. He didn't show up. Okay. Uh, he's willing to help. Okay?

Piovanetti: How is he going to help?

Martinez: Let's get money from him. With information and money.

Piovanetti: What information do you think we can get from him?

Martinez: Everything you need. How he got to that, how that got started, etcetera, etcetera.

Piovanetti: You get me that information.

Martinez: And will deal with it. I—

Piovanetti: Yes.

Martinez: Carlos, the moment you told me, okay, "This is happening," what was my answer?

Piovanetti: Yeah.

Martinez: "I'll help you solve it."

Piovanetti: Yes, but damn, the way you solve things sometimes. Heh, heh.

Martinez: Well, Carlos, do they or don't they get solved? Don't come now telling me that, that, that you feel—

Piovanetti: No, no, but . . . what I don't want is an episode like, like—

Martinez: Like what?

Piovanetti: Like what happened to, uh, to, to this woman's husband.

Martinez: Carlos. Carlos, Carlos, Carlos, Carlos. Come on. C'mon—

Piovanetti: Don't solve it like that.

Martinez: Carlos, Carlos, Carlos, nothing will happen to you, because you have my word. Okay?

Piovanetti: I don't want to turn into a George Kogan.

Martinez: You're talking bullshit. Look, look, look. Nothing is going to happen to you, and don't think like that nor start talking shit, because that's shit, Carlos. Okay?

Piovanetti: But, remember, remember that we—

Martinez: Number one—

Piovanetti: —were told where these things came from, bro.

Martinez: Never mind, Carlos. Look, Carlos, you want solutions. I want solutions, okay? How? It isn't going to be praying, Carlos. So then—and the way all this was structured, in a very professional way, you are covered.

Piovanetti: Uh huh.

Martinez: Okay?

Piovanetti: That, I know.

Martinez: So, then, don't freak out, don't panic, because you're talking to Manny with a clear mind, a person who has his balls in the right place, who isn't, um, flying low. Okay? We'll deal, we'll— we'll solve it. He is going to bring out all the information. All that information we will use, and what has to be done will be done. If later you have to go to church and whatever, well, then, you go to church to cry and receive the Holy Communion and to hell with it.

Piovanetti: [Laughs]

Martinez: Okay? I have told you, and you have never known how to appreciate my friendship, because you don't know the extent that I'm willing to go for a friend. Okay. That—

Piovanetti: I know.

Martinez: I am, and I will, and I'll do what I have to do. Okay? Well, bro, I have my balls set in the right place. Paulie called me this morning. This morning, Paulie [Prosano] called me and he said to me: "Done." That thing, that's it, that's it. It's solved.

Thirty to forty, fifty each, that's it. Delivered, uh, it was delivered Saturday—Sunday, Monday, today is Tuesday. Sunday, Monday, Tuesday. Three days. End of story. You understand? What has to be done has to be done. Now, don't start with this or that or the other. . . . Bro, what has to be done has to be done, period. And nothing else. They beeped you, they beeped you. How they got your beeper? I have no idea. But, there's a—

Piovanetti: No, I know.

Martinez: Ah? How did they get the beeper, your beeper number? That's very strange, but—

Piovanetti: It was given by—no. Eneida [Piovanetti's wife] gave it to them.

Martinez: Oh, Eneida gave it to them. So, then, they called Eneida. Now, if Lenny starts to, you know—look, the only one there, seriously, the only link there is Lenny. You understand?

Piovanetti: I know that the only link there is Lenny.

Martinez: Well, then, what is it that has to be done?

Piovanetti: Whatever has to be done.

Martinez: That's it. So, then, um, you in the front seat, me in the back seat and we go for a ride, and he's driving, and that's it, it's over and, period. And let's cut the crap, Carlos, um.

Piovanetti: Look, the, that paper—that—that—

Martinez: What paper?

Piovanetti: —that this guy notarized, um, the one you prepared for me. That would, that would hold up in court, right?

Martinez: Of course, Carlos. Of course. Carlos, Carlos. Look, Carlitos. I have, I have given you my friendship. I have told you. I have given you my friendship. You have my word. Fuck, Carlos.

Piovanetti: I'm counting.

Martinez: No, counting, counting. Look. I'm not the type who says I'm going to do something and then I don't do it, eh? This is business. This is business, and I dig in. You can count on it. Now, I'm going to beep Lenny and I'm going to set up a meeting for tomorrow and, to get as much as I can out of him. And, then, well, that's what toilets are for, to flush things, right?

Piovanetti: Uh huh.

Martinez: You'll be fine. Stay calm.

Piovanetti: I'm counting on you, papa.

Martinez: You have my word. . . . Now, don't you chicken out on me, because we're going to have to do some things that maybe are not to your taste, but we're going to have to do them. Okay, papa?

Piovanetti: As long as I get out of this shit.

Martinez: Everyone knows it. Keep cool.

Piovanetti: Okay.

Martinez: Okay. Where are you?

Piovanetti: At the pay phone, by the post office still.

Martinez: Okay, papa.

Piovanetti: Bye.

Martinez: Bye.

The most damning language in that conversation was Carlos' mention of the murder of a "woman's husband," which Assistant District Attorney Seidemann told the jury was in reference to George Kogan's murder. In other words, Seidemann contended, Carlos was telling Martinez, "I don't want to turn into a George Kogan."

Also damaging were Martinez's words about Lenny Cherry, which Seidemann described as "the solicitation to murder Cherry."

During cross examination of Carlos Piovanetti, Strauss asked if the taped conversation Carlos had with Manuel was scripted by police or the district attorney. "You were trying actively to get your friend Mr. Martinez to inculpate him in various wrongdoings?"

"I was given a script that would inculpate him. That is correct," Piovanetti answered.

Because of the protective order, Piovanetti's name as a

witness was not disclosed to Martinez and his defense counsel until the day before Piovanetti was to testify. So, it came as a huge surprise to the defense. Martinez and Strauss sat stunned behind the defense table as Piovanetti told the jury that after George was killed, Martinez mocked him with what Piovanetti said were George's last words. Putting his hands together over his chest, Piovanetti quoted Martinez as saying, "God save me," as Martinez mocked Kogan falling to the ground. In reality, George Kogan's last words were, "I'm dying," and they were said to doorman Moses Crespo, the last one to speak to George before he fell into unconsciousness.

Martinez did not deny nor apologize for mocking George's last moments. Martinez explained his reasoning for making fun of a man who'd just been shot with this: "The irony of those words reverberated in my brain. Here was a man who . . . burned all his bridges in Puerto Rico due to his aggressive business practices, living an adulterous life contrary to his Jewish beliefs, and seeking God's salvation? Would a God-fearing man [have] done the things George did? I do not approve of his murder nor did I participate in it in any way, but I can understand it."

Also testifying for the prosecution was Chad Powell, records-access officer for the New York State Department of Correctional Services. Powell was questioned by Assistant District Attorney Joel Seidemann about the inmate records of Paul Prosano. After the record-keeper's testimony, Judge Obus instructed the jury that Prosano's incarceration record had "nothing to do with the incidents at issue in this case." It was presented during the trial and allowed in, seemingly as evidence, yet explained away afterward by the judge, who admonished the jury to not consider it. It did not make sense, other than to try to form a connection between Prosano and Martinez to connect the dots, which, basically, would have been guilt by association and not by the evidence. Because a plausible connection was not presented during the trial, Chad Powell's testimony did not add up.

When Manuel's former wife, Beatriz Oller, took the stand, she told the court that her husband had planned the murder-for-hire plot during a flight to Puerto Rico with Barbara Kogan. The problem with the statement was that Barbara and Manuel, according to court documents, did not take the same flight to or from Puerto Rico. They traveled separately, and on separate days, and met in the lobby of El San Juan Hotel and Casino, where Barbara's sister, Elaine, was the casino manager.

Beatriz also testified that she and her husband had had dinner one evening with Barbara and her companion John Lyons, and that Manuel, in the course of the conversation, had suggested that Barbara "get rid of George." On cross-examination by Strauss, Beatriz answered that she could not remember the name of the restaurant, just that it was somewhere "in New York City." She could remember the name John Lyons, whom she said she'd met just once. She could not recall, however, when the four had had dinner, what Barbara and Lyons wore, or even what Lyons looked like. But she testified she could remember the comment her husband had made that night.

It came out in court that Beatriz Oller offered that statement to police, during her two lengthy sessions with investigators, after she'd received a letter from the New York County District Attorney's office accusing her of helping her husband launder money.

In exchange for her cooperation against her husband in the Kogan case, Strauss asked if the allegations had been dropped.

"No," she responded.

The DA pursued the money-laundering charges against her. A letter to her by the District Attorney's office said she was a "partner in crime" with her husband. She was not charged in connection with the allegations, nor was her ex-husband.

Before Martinez's trial, the District Attorney's office had announced in a news release that Manuel Martinez had admitted to a friend that he'd arranged the murder of George Kogan at the behest of Barbara Kogan. In exchange, Martinez would receive $100,000.

Barbara Kogan's attorney, Barry Levin, said the allegations were "absolutely not true." No bank records were ever produced showing large sums of money were transferred from either Barbara's accounts or her parents', nor transferred to Martinez's or his ex-wife's accounts. Seidemann would cite, throughout Martinez's trial, the $100,000 and $50,000 sums, saying they were used to hire a killer. To counter the lack of documentation, Seidemann contended that Manuel Martinez had flown out of Puerto Rico with $100,000 in a suitcase. For his part, Martinez insisted that had he attempted to carry out cash in a suitcase from Puerto Rico, it would have been readily discovered at the Luis Munoz Marin International Airport by inspectors with the United States Department of Agriculture, who thoroughly inspect all personal suitcases and baggage for fruits and vegetables. To back up his claim, Martinez requested and received confirmation from the USDA that this practice was, in fact, in effect back in 1990 as well. Here is the letter, dated June 9, 2010, written on USDA letterhead:

Dear Mr. Martinez:

Thank you for your letter of May 19, 2010, inquiring about the status of our Agency's pre-departure passenger inspection program in Puerto Rico in 1990.

We can confirm that the U.S. Department of Agriculture's (USDA) pre-departure passenger inspection program in Puerto Rico was functional and operating in September and October 1990. The purpose of the pre-departure passenger inspection program is to prevent harmful exotic agricultural pests and diseases from being transported to the U.S. mainland via inbound luggage from passengers travelling from Puerto Rico. Our Agency of USDA, the Animal and Plant Health Inspection service, carries out this in-

*spection function in compliance with section 318.58
of the Code of Federal Regulations.*

Sincerely,

*Alan S. Green
Executive Director
Plant Health Programs
Plant Protection and Quarantine*

Once the trial started, Assistant District Attorney Seide-mann told the jury, "The money for the hit came from Barbara Kogan's mother, a woman by the name of Rose Siegel." The prosecution, however, did not produce bank records to show that monies of that amount were transferred to Manuel Martinez. Instead, entered into evidence were three small checks totaling $5,008 made out to Martinez and signed by Barbara Kogan.

One of the witnesses who did materialize was Nelson Ramirez, who Martinez was hoping would help his case. Instead, Ramirez testified that he'd seen Martinez's wife, Beatriz Oller, with "a bump on her forehead." Ramirez also testified that it was caused by being hit by Martinez with a skillet. But, when questioned by the defense, Ramirez, now forty-eight, a licensed nurse, and living in Hillsboro, Florida, admitted he'd never actually seen Martinez hit his wife, either with a hand or a skillet.

Still, Seidemann went so far during the trial as to compare Martinez's abuse of his wife with that of Joel Steinberg, a disbarred attorney convicted of killing his adopted daughter as well as locking up his live-in girlfriend, Hedda Nussbaum, inside their New York City apartment and beating her to the point of disfigurement. While Martinez clearly was not an angel—in post-trial affidavits, he'd admitted to shoving his wife and getting into scuffles with her—if Martinez was a wife beater, no medical reports or police accounts materialized to be admitted as evidence to back up the prosecutor's claims.

The most damaging testimony to Martinez came from

Wilmer Rodriguez, a lawyer straight out of college who'd worked as a law clerk for Martinez. Taking the stand on Friday, April 11, 2008, he testified about a telephone call he answered at Martinez's office the day George Kogan was killed. The 4 p.m. call was from Ivan Ramos, a Puerto Rican attorney Martinez had introduced Barbara to when she was looking for a divorce lawyer. The phone rang, and when Martinez's secretary didn't pick it up on the third ring, Wilmer answered.

"Is Manny there?" Ivan Ramos asked in Spanish.

"No, he is not here," Rodriguez told him.

"Where is he?"

"I don't know." Manuel had left the office about one o'clock that afternoon after he received a call, started hollering, grabbed his jacket, and, without explanation, left the office.

Ivan Ramos then asked Rodriguez, "Is he home?"

"I don't know. Call him at home," Rodriguez suggested.

"Wilmer, they killed George," Ramos said.

"Who?" he asked.

"You didn't know?" Ramos asked.

"No," he said, and then Ramos hung up.

The next morning, Rodriguez picked up three New York newspapers on his way in, because all ran articles about George's murder. He arrived at the office just after 9 a.m.

"When I got there, Mr. Martinez was in his office with his back turned toward me, looking out the window, and I walked in and I threw the newspapers on top of his desk and I pointed to them and I asked, "Did you have anything to do with this?"

Martinez turned around, Rodriguez said.

"His face was pale, ashy, and he told me, 'Wilmer, this is the first time I heard of this. I almost shitted on myself. Look, I swear on the head of my son.'"

By his demeanor "and sincere look," Rodriguez told the court, "I believed him. So I told him, 'You know, Manny, the police will come here.'"

Manny responded, "So what? Fine."

Then, a couple of days after the murder, a man called between eight and twelve times, asking, "Is Manny there?"

The final time he called, Rodriguez testified, the man said, "Tell him Paulie called."

In addition, Wilmer Rodriguez told the court that Barbara's voluminous divorce file was delivered by the office of Richard Golub, Barbara's previous attorney, sometime before George's murder. Rodriguez, curious, went through the file, which sat on top of Martinez's credenza, and read a confidential report prepared by a private investigator that detailed George Kogan's daily routine, including leaving his apartment at the same time each morning, between 9:15 and 9:35, sometimes with the couple's poodle, sometimes without, and returning around 10:15 or 10:20. The report, Rodriguez said, included "Mr. Kogan's movements from the mornings until the evening." The couple typically didn't emerge again until about 1:30 p.m., when they'd often catch a taxi. On one occasion, a waiting limousine and driver took them to a restaurant for lunch. In the evenings, they'd go out to dinner and be gone as late at 11:30 at night.

After George's death, Rodriguez told the jury he was curious and went to the file again, looking for the private investigator's report, but it was no longer there.

Wilmer Rodriguez testified that the last time he saw Barbara Kogan was shortly after George Kogan's murder, at a wine-and-cheese party for Martinez's new law office. Barbara's divorce attorney Richard Golub was there, too.

In open court, Seidemann described Martinez as living a "fantasy life as a mobster," sometimes wearing what the prosecutor described as a "fedora hat." Martinez apparently was known to wear a cowboy hat, not a fedora—a low, soft-felt hat with a curled brim sometimes associated with Prohibition-era gangsters and the FBI agents who brought them to justice.

In his testimony, Steven Cerenzio, a long-time police informant and known associate of Paul Prosano, added to the image during the trial when he described Manuel as "looking official" by wearing a trench coat, making him resemble "Inspector Gadget," a detective from the children's TV show of the same name.

One day during a recess in the case, the judge took care of some housekeeping items, including Martinez's missing legal documents. "With regard to Mr. Martinez's property that didn't make it over here to the Manhattan House when he was moved from Rikers, we have been in touch many times with Ms. Lyndz, who is the counsel to the Department of Corrections," Judge Obus said. "The last message that our clerk received is that she is advised that Corrections cannot find any additional property of Mr. Martinez. I don't doubt Mr. Martinez's statement there is such property that exists. We did advise Ms. Lyndz about the allegations or the statements in Mr. Martinez' letter about which officers had something to do with the property and his movement and I am hopeful that there is still something that we can do with this.

"If there was no property, then that's one thing. If there was property [and] it's still there, we will do what we can to get it," he continued. "I hope that there was no property that was actually dumped somewhere."

At the end of four weeks, both sides rested, with roughly fifty witnesses testifying for the prosecution. The defense, on the other hand, chose not to have any witnesses testify in Martinez's defense. It's a risky strategy, often done to send a signal that the defense believes the government has fallen short in its burden of proof. Strauss was about to learn whether or not the tactic worked.

CHAPTER 14

"Tricky, Circumstantial Case"

In his summation, delivered Monday morning, April 14, 2008, Assistant District Attorney Joel Seidemann raised his voice and told the jury, as he had in his opening statement, "This man right over here, seated right here," pointing toward Martinez, "is a murderer. If it weren't for Manuel Martinez seated here today, if it weren't for the things he did back in 1990, George Kogan would be alive today." Then, pointing out that Martinez confessed to his tenant, Carlos Piovanetti, Seidemann said, "If you believe he made that confession and that the confession was true, he's guilty."

He described Manuel's behavior before and after Kogan's murder as mob-like, saying, "His obsession was to act like a mafia don. He had one foot in the legal world and the other foot in the underworld."

Seidemann also described George Kogan for the jury. "George had grown up in Puerto Rico and was from a very rich and well-to-do family," he told jurors. "His parents owned a string of department stores and he was a very wealthy person." On the other hand, he told the jury, "Barbara was from New Jersey." She went on to live a financially comfortable life with George, Seidemann said, but that upscale lifestyle soon collapsed when "Barbara woke up one morning and discovered that the person she'd been married to for close to a quarter of a century was having an affair with somebody half her age. It was devastating. She was clearly a victim. But she lost that victim status by doing three things: She lied, she stole, and then she got together with [Martinez] in a plot to kill her husband."

Seidemann also addressed the defense's assertion throughout the trial that this was a strictly circumstantial case. "Now, much has been said there isn't any physical evidence," he told jurors. "Well, you saw sixty-seven exhibits introduced into evidence, and I submit to you that those sixty-seven exhibits are exhibits that you can touch, you can feel, and those sixty-seven exhibits provide pieces of the puzzle that show that that lawyer over there is a murderer."

To close, Seidemann said, "And in sum, ladies and gentlemen, what we have presented to you is overwhelming evidence that that man seated over there was involved in the series of events culminating in putting George Kogan in an early grave by having Paul Prosano pump three bullets into the back and killing him at the age of forty-nine."

In the defense's closing argument, attorney Jonathan Strauss attacked each of the points Seidemann presented during the trial. "It is the government's responsibility to prove that the defendant committed each and every element of the crime he is charged with, beyond a reasonable doubt," Strauss said as he stood at the jury box. "Two things matter in this case: facts and evidence. This case is not a mudslinging contest.

"There is no physical evidence to support the government's theory that the defendant was hired for money by Barbara Kogan to kill her husband or that Paul Prosano was even the shooter," Strauss continued. "Barbara Kogan was cash-poor, strapped for money, and no bank records were presented showing a substantial exchange of money from Barbara Kogan to Manuel Martinez, and no evidence of money transfer from Rose or Emanuel Siegel [Barbara's parents]. The four-million-dollar insurance policies on George's life were purchased before George met Mary-Louise. The policies were secured with George's knowledge and consent, and the insurance companies paid every dime of the policies and were unable to demonstrate Barbara's involvement in the murder under the civil standard, which is a lower standard than a criminal standard [of beyond a reasonable doubt]."

Strauss pointed out to the jury that to collect on an insurance claim, the benefactor does not need a copy of the insurance policy. Barbara Kogan needed copies of the policies, he said, for her divorce proceeding as further proof of George's assets, some of which Barbara believed George was concealing from her.

Instead of a hit-for-hire, Strauss said the evidence indicated a robbery gone bad, as evidenced by the money scattered around George as he lay on the sidewalk. Why cash was out of George's pocket was never completely explained away. "The evidence reflects a robbery that was botched, a matter that should have been investigated further," Strauss said. The evidence did not point to a hit-for-hire because of greed, he said. If the motive was money for a hit-for-hire, he continued, "Show me the bank records with this money, all right?"

At the end of his closing, Strauss reminded the jury not to speculate. "Your decision must be based on facts and evidence and not on mud that was thrown at my client, not on mud about other crimes that he's not charged with."

Judge Obus then gave the jury instructions, a set of legal rules that jurors are to follow when deciding a criminal case. Obus stated, "The People's case is based on both circumstantial and direct evidence."

The case was, in fact, exclusively based on circumstantial evidence, a point that would arise in Martinez's subsequent appeal. There was no direct evidence linking Martinez to the murder of George Kogan.

Martinez claimed that he had an alibi: he had made his 9 a.m. appearance in New York City Housing Court the same day as the murder, on October 23, 1990. Martinez was there representing client Dr. Fernando Alvarez for eviction proceedings against tenants. But Martinez's attorney was told that the records from Housing Court had either long been destroyed or would be impossible to find eighteen years later. Another problem for Martinez was that his attorney was unable to find Alvarez to use as an alibi witness.

In the defense's closing argument, Strauss brought up the recorded conversation between Manuel Martinez and Carlos Piovanetti, which investigators said was incriminating. "We are not talking about killing here," Strauss told jurors. The taped conversation, he explained to the jury, was not evidence. He also reminded the jury of their legal obligation "to determine this case on the facts in evidence" and "if you start thinking about things that are not in evidence, you could be making a decision based on things that are not in front of you, not for your consideration, and you could be dead wrong."

Strauss also emphasized that, other than notarizing a document, Martinez was not involved with Carlos Piovanetti, and Martinez was never charged in connection with the check-cashing swindle that landed Carlos in trouble. Piovanetti had wanted Martinez to represent him as his attorney, *pro bono*. When Piovanetti telephoned him the day their conversation was recorded, Martinez told Piovanetti he would assist him. But, Martinez later explained, he had no intention of helping Carlos out of the mess he'd gotten himself into.

Still, Carlos Piovanetti was a star witness in the case against Manuel Martinez even though Detective Dennis Zack headed the check-fraud investigation against Piovanetti and wrote in his report that Carlos Piovanetti was not a reliable witness. Despite that, a deal was cut with Piovanetti to testify as a witness for the prosecution at Martinez's trial. The judge ruled that Dennis Zack's opinion that Piovanetti was an unreliable witness was inadmissable in the trial. The jury would never hear it. Even so, Strauss, in his closing argument, attempted to impeach Piovanetti.

Strauss also, in his summation, reminded jurors of Mary-Louise Hawkins' testimony, during which she said that George owed "a lot of people money and was owed a lot."

In the end, Strauss reminded jurors that the prosecution

had presented nothing solid with which they could convict Martinez in the murder of George Kogan. "There is no smoking gun," he told them.

On the final day of the trial, Judge Obus instructed the jury and read them the charges against Manuel Martinez. The judge asked jurors, "in a calm and quiet atmosphere of reasoned thought," to "calmly, rationally, and objectively attempt to evaluate the evidence."

"You are a fact-finding body," he told them, and the "sole judges of the facts." He instructed them to decide whether "the body of evidence meets the people's burden of proof as to this defendant."

The jury began deliberating on Monday, April 14. Shortly after, the first request from jurors was handwritten and given to a court bailiff, who then handed it to the judge's clerk. The jury had asked for an English translation of the September 15, 1992, recorded telephone conversation between Manuel Martinez and his former office tenant, Carlos Piovanetti. The request could have indicated the jury was confused, because the defendant's exhibit of a translated version was slightly different from that of the district attorney's office, which was transcribed by translator Virginia Blanco, a New York State court certified Spanish interpreter. She had signed an affidavit on March 18, 2008, certifying that it was a "true and accurate translation."

The second request came the same day. The jury asked for a "written definition of Criminal Solicitation in the second degree." Both requests, for the transcript and the definition, clearly showed that jurors were carefully considering the charge of solicitation against Martinez.

At five o'clock, the jury foreperson sent out a third request, which asked permission "to stop for the day."

They reconvened the next morning, on April 15. By 1:56 p.m., another request made its way to Judge Obus. Jurors asked for "a whiteboard or other wall-mounted writing surface, a list—index—of articles of evidence, [and] a list of all witnesses."

Instead of a list of items that had been admitted as actual evidence, the jury was given a list of exhibits. One was the sample gun—not the one used to kill George Kogan—that was admitted to court as an exhibit. But could jurors discern the difference when they asked for an index of "articles of evidence" and were given a list titled "exhibits"?

The jury then requested, in another note, to see a variety of exhibits, which included Barbara's phone records and a chart from the local phone company, plus divorce papers served by Manuel Martinez to his wife, Beatriz Oller. At the bottom of the jury's request, they also asked for "coffee and cookies."

Jurors pored through the exhibits for the next couple of hours, then, at 4:30 p.m., they submitted another note, asking the judge to "cease deliberations for today." The last thing they saw that day was the list of exhibits.

At 10:40 the following morning, on April 16, the foreperson handed off that day's first request: "Testimony by Scott Kogan regarding Barbara Kogan denying knowing Manny Martinez, and Emanuel and Rose Siegel telling Scott Kogan they need to find Manny Martinez." It was a telling request and not good news for the defense, because it indicated the jury was examining a link between Manuel Martinez and Barbara Kogan's parents, accused of but never charged with providing money for a hit man.

At 11:25, the foreperson took another note to the court clerk. "A juror is requesting ten minutes of fresh air," it read.

In the same note, they asked, "Can we hear the audio of People's 33?" They had earlier asked to re-read the transcript of the recorded telephone conversation between Manuel Martinez and his former office tenant, Carlos Piovanetti. Now they wanted to re-listen to the audiotape of that conversation, which had been played for them March 23 during the trial. The jury returned to the courtroom, and, in the presence of the judge and the attorneys, they listened to the audiotape once more. It was becoming clear by the exhibits they were asking for that the most compelling testimony to them was that of Piovanetti and Scott Kogan. When the tape was finished playing, they quietly filed out to continue deliberating.

A final jury note, with the time of 12:45 p.m. and handwritten by the foreperson, was handed to the court clerk. It read:

"We have reached a verdict on both counts."

Then, the jury foreperson completed a Verdict Sheet, which became the court's exhibit XV. After just two and a half days, deliberations had ended. The jury returned a verdict on both charges.

Both sides were asked to return to the courtroom. "In a moment, we will have the jury step in and we will take their verdict," Judge Obus said.

Then, to the foreperson after the jury and alternates returned to the courtroom, the court clerk spoke. "Will the foreperson please stand? Mr. Foreperson, has the jury agreed upon a verdict?" he asked. The courtroom was quiet as the gallery awaited the response. Martinez looked right at the juror as he waited to hear his fate.

"We have," the foreperson said.

"How say you to the first count of indictment, charging the defendant, Manuel Martinez, with the crime of murder in the second degree?"

"Guilty," the foreperson said.

He was asked the same question about the second count of criminal solicitation in the second degree.

"Guilty," the foreperson answered.

One by one, the court polled the jurors and each, with no expression on their faces, uttered the same verdict: Guilty.

Martinez, with his attorney, sat unmoved, his face expressionless.

After thanking them, the judge dismissed the jury. As jurors filed out, they kept their eyes to the floor. But the gallery was instantly noisy as people reacted to the verdicts.

"Please, please," the judge said. "There should be no reaction from people in the audience."

With that, Judge Obus adjourned the case until Friday,

May 9, 2008, when Martinez's sentence would be handed down. "My thanks to both counsel. I'll see you on May ninth," the judge said.

With the convictions of Martinez came the final break in the case against Barbara Kogan. Two key witnesses testified under oath at Martinez's trial that he'd not only confessed to them, but he'd also implicated Barbara Kogan as a co-conspirator in the hiring of a hit man in George Kogan's slaying. With the Martinez trial behind him, it was exactly the probable cause prosecutor Joel Seidemann needed to go after Barbara.

Just before his sentence was handed down four weeks later, in May 2008, Martinez gave the impression he was willing to cooperate with the state. But it turned out he was only mocking the proceedings. He told the court, "I am willing to assist the people as much as I can. I do want to help the people get to the bottom of this." Then, Martinez added, "Let the people give me a script. I'll memorize it and I'll testify to whoever." He claimed that that was what witnesses did during his trial, reciting prepared testimony, and he voiced that opinion loud and clear in numerous letters he fired off to lawyers, judges, and attorneys.

Assistant District Attorney Joel J. Seidemann was not amused. "We don't write scripts for witnesses. If the defendant believes we would provide a script, obviously he has no intent to provide cooperation," the prosecutor said.

During the sentencing, Martinez presented a pro se motion—in the form of a letter to the court and not filed by his attorney—asking that his conviction be overturned. In it, he questioned the credibility of his ex-wife, Beatriz Oller, who was allowed to testify against him, as well as the credibility of the state's other star witness, Carlos Piovanetti. Judge Obus denied Martinez's request, telling him that it was inappropriate for that venue. The proper way to file the motion, the judge told him, would be through the appellate court.

In response to Martinez's letter asking that the conviction be reversed, Assistant District Attorney Joel Seidemann did respond, and in writing. "Defendant appears to be arguing that the verdict against him was not supported by the weight of the evidence. Simply put, defendant is wrong."

In the courtroom at Martinez's sentencing hearing, defense attorney Jonathan Strauss addressed the court. "George Kogan's murder was a tragedy. No one is disputing that. No one is arguing that. The defendant in his pre-sentence report maintains his innocence. Obviously, that's going to be a decision later made by different judges in different courts with different attorneys. All the witnesses, the substance of witnesses, that were brought against this defendant, Your Honor, were granted some kind of immunity or had some other reason to give the testimony that was given.

"I know, Judge," Strauss continued, "that the jury has spoken in this case. . . . What I am going to tell the court is that the defendant was convicted of an extremely serious crime. It doesn't get more serious than that. He is a man who in this country had never been convicted of anything. And I'm going to ask the court to consider all the factors as the court knows them to be from the testimony that the court sat through and consider giving this defendant the most lenient sentence that it could give."

Strauss also asked that the judge sentence Martinez "in a concurrent manner as opposed to consecutive."

Just before the judge sentenced him, Martinez was also allowed to speak. He once again denied any involvement in George Kogan's murder, telling the judge, "In spite of the so-called evidence, I maintain my complete innocence in this case."

"Your Honor," Manuel continued, "I did not hire Paulie Prosano or Joe Blow to kill Mr. Kogan. I don't get involved in criminal activity."

"There is no gun," he told the judge. "The people had to bring a gun, a sample. . . . How come [the prosecutor] could not bring the bank records of Rose Siegel or Emanuel Siegel or my bank records showing that I was paid fifty thousand dollars, a hundred thousand dollars, a million dollars? Where is the money?"

It was true that during his trial the prosecution had not presented witnesses or introduced evidence to prove that Barbara or her parents had paid Martinez to have George Kogan killed. In the end, though, that had not mattered to the jury. It was a moot issue, because the case had already been presented, but Martinez nonetheless pressed the court about it.

Finally, Martinez told the court, "I didn't order the execution of George Kogan. And the people who have had eighteen years to get one shred of direct evidence have been unable to. [It's] all circumstantial evidence. That's all I have to say, Your Honor."

With that, Martinez got an earful. Manhattan Supreme Court Justice Michael J. Obus, in his final words in the State versus Manuel Martinez, said the evidence was solid. "What we are dealing with here [is] a conviction for basically a premeditated assassination of an innocent person walking on the street in Midtown Manhattan, arranged by an attorney," Obus said. "There simply can be no excuse for the homicide in this case."

"To say that this is an unusual case may be the understatement of my career," he said. "To have a matter in which an attorney is convicted of arranging for the murder of the husband of a client is an extremely unusual circumstance, quite fortunately, and it is difficult to understand what would possess someone to do something like that. But a jury has found that is in fact what happened here."

Then Obus slammed Martinez with the maximum sentence. Manuel Martinez was sentenced to twenty-five years to life, the maximum allowed by law. He had thirty days to appeal.

The next day, in a document dated May 9, Martinez's attorney, Jonathan Strauss, filed a Notice of Appeal with the Supreme Court, New York County Appeals Board.

According to Barbara Kogan's defense attorney, Barry Levin, the prosecution delayed the case for eighteen years in hopes they would be able to persuade Manuel Martinez to cooperate and testify against Barbara Kogan. That cooperation never came. He never once implicated Barbara in the murder of George Kogan.

In the end, despite numerous opportunities to turn state's evidence, Martinez did not name Barbara Kogan as an accomplice. Several times, he was offered the chance to hammer out a plea deal with the prosecutor. Did Martinez not offer incriminating testimony because there was none to give? Was he so stubborn that he refused to admit his guilt even after being convicted? Or was he innocent?

The lack of a statement from Martinez saying that Barbara Kogan was involved posed a huge hurdle for the prosecution. Seidemann did not have enough evidence, at least at that juncture, for a grand jury to indict Barbara Kogan. Seidemann's hope—as it had been for many years—was that Manuel Martinez would agree to testify against Barbara. Martinez, however, refused to cooperate, even with his future uncertain, took his chances at trial, and lost.

One of the final issues Judge Obus addressed during Martinez's sentencing, seemingly in anticipation of an appeal, was to address the evidence. "The evidence was not only circumstantial, but direct, in a sense that it included the statement of evidence," he said, referring to testimony from Martinez's wife, Beatriz Oller, and his friend, Carlos Piovanetti, stating that Martinez had confessed to each of them.

The next day, New York tabloids carried the story. The *New York Post* called it a "tricky, circumstantial case complicated by the passage of 18 years."

"Convicted NYC lawyer sentenced to 25-to-life for murder," said *USA Today*'s headline. And the *Daily News* headlined their article with "Ex-lawyer's wings clipped in '90 hit job."

"The shady lawyer of rich widow Barbara Kogan was convicted Wednesday of arranging the execution-style rubout of millionaire antiques dealer George Kogan outside his girlfriend's pad," wrote The *Daily News* in its lead sentence.

The website *Above the Law* was no better. It named Martinez "Ex-lawyer of the Day."

"Divorce attorney turned hit man employer, Manuel Martinez, is *ATL*'s Lawyer of the Day," the article read. Then, quoting Martha Neil's report in the *ABA Journal*, *Above the*

Law said, "New York ex-lawyer Manuel Martinez was sentenced to 25 years to life for hiring a hit man to kill his client's husband 18 years earlier during a bitter divorce trial.

"That's *really* bitter," *Above the Law* opined.

Ten days after his sentence, Manuel Martinez was transferred from Rikers Island to the state-run Auburn Correctional Facility, a maximum-security men's prison for violent offenders. Located in Cayuga County, it was the first state prison in New York and the site of the first execution using the electric chair, conducted in 1890.

Seeking comment about the conviction from Barbara Kogan, a newspaper reporter called her apartment. A woman answered. When the reporter identified himself and asked for Barbara Kogan, the woman on the other end said, "Mrs. Kogan is not here," and hung up.

After the conviction, Manuel S. Martinez, who had been admitted to the New York Bar Association in 1985 was disbarred for life from practicing law in New York.

Martinez, state inmate number 08A2723, will be eligible for parole on March 19, 2032. In prison, he works eight hours a day, five days a week as a clerk at the prison law library. Since his incarceration in the state facility, he has feverishly fired off letters to county, state, and federal officials, including the White House, the FBI, and the Central Intelligence Agency, citing corruption in his case. He has filed complaints about misrepresentation by his attorney, Jonathan Strauss. He has filed complaints about mismanagement by the judge, Michael Obus. He has made statements to the court, only to later recant them, saying he was playing the same games the system was playing with him.

The trial in the case of the people of New York versus Manuel Martinez that began on March 18, 2008 ended less than a month later, on April 16. But the George Kogan case was hardly over, and the investigation did not end with Manuel Martinez. Police and the district attorney's office were still eager to bring to justice the one person they felt most culpable—George Kogan's wife, Barbara. Joel Seidemann was determined to prosecute Barbara Kogan, too.

As the case against Barbara was about to move forward with an indictment, the issue of Manuel Martinez cooperating with the district attorney's office cropped up again. In prison, Martinez received a letter from Claudia Trupp, his appellate attorney, asking once again whether Martinez would testify against Barbara Kogan. Claudia Trupp's letter to her client was dated August 20, 2009:

> Today, I received a phone call from the Manhattan District Attorney's office. The assistant, David Drucker, asked if you would like to testify before Barbara Kogan's grand jury with a waiver of immunity as to any information you provided. I informed him that my advice to you would be not to testify unless they were offering you consideration for your testimony. The Assistant District Attorney stated that they would offer you nothing for your testimony.
>
> The decision about whether to testify under these circumstances is of course your own. I would advise you against testifying since I can perceive of no benefit to you. Please advise me immediately if you wish to testify.

Upon receipt and in response, Martinez typed out a statement, had his signature notarized, in prison, at the bottom of his attorney's letter, and then mailed it off to her. Martinez's statement read:

> I refuse to testify against Barbara Kogan before any Grand Jury. I am willing to testify in any disciplinary proceeding against "Judge" Michael J. Obus and "A.D.A." Joel J. Seidemann for the violation of their respective oaths as Attorneys and Counselors of Law.

At Auburn, on November 9, 2009, Martinez was disciplined for attempting to contact a witness who had testified during his trial. Because he had sent the person a letter, which violated prison rules against contactng witnesses even after the trial ended, he was placed in the prison's security housing unit—twenty-three-hour isolation and disciplinary lockdown, known among prisoners as "The Box."

Seidemann, in turn, wrote to Sean Duncan of the Office of the Inspector General at the New York State Department of Corrections. "I would greatly appreciate it if you could take all legal and proper steps to prevent [petitioner] from harassing any of the People's witnesses," Seidemann said in his letter to the inspector general.

In response, Manuel Martinez was warned, in a written prison document signed by a corrections counselor, not to contact people on the prosecution's witness list.

The missive to Martinez read, in part:

> The Superintendent has directed that you immediately discontinue any form of communication with this person.
>
> Should you continue to send correspondence or packages, telephone, or attempt to telephone any person on your Negative Correspondence/Telephone List, or elicit, or attempt to elicit, aid from others for the purpose of circumventing the Superintendent's instructions, disciplinary action will be taken against you. Such disciplinary action may result in your outgoing mail being monitored and your telephone privileges being limited or suspended.

In response, Martinez immediately sent off a letter to his attorney, Claudia Trupp. It said:

> Today while I was conducting legal research at this facility's Law Library, a Corrections Officer interrupted my work and informed me that my assigned ACF Counselor needed to see me. I met with him and

he presented me with a letter from this Facility's superintendant [sic] instructing me not to contact a list of 49 individuals (list attached), practically all were the People's witnesses in my "trial." I respectfully refused to consent to the instruction, stating, in writing, that there were two persons in that list I may write to since I may file a C.P.L. Article 440.10 Motion to Vacate the Judgment. In my professional opinion, the Superintendent may be acting outside the boundaries of his legal responsibilities and the instruction could be viewed as an attempt to violate my due process right by denying me the pursuit of a defense from the baseless charges I was convicted by a deceived jury last April 16, 2008. I do not have problems with the Superintendent or any of the employees in this facility. I am focused on my legal work and overturning an illegally secured conviction.

In my professional opinion, the root of the attempted prohibition is ADA Joel J. Seidemann who, after conducting a "trial" based on sleazy gossip, innuendos, massive untrue character assassination, suspicion . . . realizes that he cannot deceive all the people all the time. The unconstitutional, illegal charade (terms I used to describe my "trial" on May 9, 2008, at Part 51 at sentencing) must come to an end with repercussions to the New York City System of Justice.

Despite the warning, Manuel continued contacting some of the people on the list, the same behavior that sent him to lockdown. He was released from solitary confinement on January 2, 2010. When he returned to his cell, number C15-19, he discovered he was missing nine envelopes, which had been stuffed, partially stamped, and addressed to five medium-sized New York newspapers and four members of the State Commission on Judicial Conduct. Martinez soon sent a letter to Andrew T. Baxter, acting US Attorney for the Northern District of New York, informing him of what Martinez called "delay or destruction of mail."

Martinez requested in a letter to New York State Senator John Sampson the appointment of a special prosecutor to investigate the "illegalities committed in my trial." It isn't known if the senator responded.

He also wrote a letter to the Honorable Theodore T. Jones, Jr., with the Wrongful Convictions Task Force of the New York State Court of Appeals. He told him, "My trial . . . is an encyclopedia of illegalities and prosecutorial misconduct that should be studied at Law Schools across the Nation. My 'trial' was about the murder of George Kogan, a rapacious, unscrupulous businessman. . . ."

Manuel wrote as well to civil liberties lawyer Alan Dershowitz, most famous for representing Claus von Bülow and O.J. Simpson, as a member of what has been called the former NFL star's legal "Dream Team." In Martinez's letter to the man some call "the top lawyer of last resort," he included a cartoon he'd enlisted a fellow inmate to sketch of Martinez in court. It was titled "N.Y.C. System of Justice & The Rotten Apples." In the cartoon's dialogue box, it said Martinez was "blindfolded at the defense table and a noose lay on the prosecution's table." In his missive to Dershowitz, Martinez described the panel as "a deceived jury." The rest of the letter read:

> The enclosed cartoon is not meant to be funny . . . My trial was a farce and a mockery to our proclaimed System of Justice. The Daily News called my trial bizarre. Corruption in the New York County System of Justice is worse than in any so-called Latin American "banana republic" because it has a devastating ingredient: hypocrisy.
> My "trial" is ideal for Law School analysis and discussion because it is rich in erroneous evidentiary rulings, gross prosecutorial misconduct, perjury, terror tactics, shameful violation of the NYS Code of Judicial Conduct, noncompliance with discovery, etc. I was railroaded in a trial "by ambush" . . . You are invited to receive my . . . Analysis of my 2,500 pages

of trial transcript I prepared over a nine-month pe-
riod for Appellate Counsel . . . enumerating most of
his errors, ommissions. . . .

Needless to say, Alan Dershowitz did not respond to Martinez's invitation. Despite how questionable the emotion-packed, finger-pointing letters Martinez regularly sent to politicians, judicial bodies, federal and state law enforcement, newspapers and law firms were, however, his case for appeal appeared to have some merit, based on points of law and technicalities during his trial. Martinez alleged judicial misconduct, insufficient evidence, and errors in jury instructions.

To aid in his defense of Martinez, attorney Jonathan Strauss had hired a private investigator, James Coffey. After the trial, in which an investigator's report was mentioned, Martinez sent a barrage of letters from jail to the court clerk, state officials, judges, his attorney, and the district attorney, asking for a copy of the report. Martinez also wanted a copy of an invoice for Coffey's services. Without a record of work performed by Coffey, Martinez contended, his defense did not properly represent him by performing investigative services. Coffey's work for the defense team was approved by the court. Martinez wrote as well directly to Coffey asking for a copy of both a report generated from his investigation and a copy of the invoice for those services. No report or invoice was ever produced.

Daniel Rosen, a court attorney assigned to Obus, sent an answer to Martinez to answer one of his many letters inquiring about who paid Coffey and for what. Martinez assumed that Coffey was assigned to his case as an 18-B panelist, a panel comprising those in the legal community who are court-approved and can be assigned to represent indigent defendants. Rosen's letter to Martinez said, in part:

I have checked further with Mr. Strauss and the
18-B panels payment office. Mr. Strauss still believes
that Mr. Coffey was assigned 18-B. The panel states
that while it has no records of payments in Mr. Coffey's

name, he has submitted vouchers in other cases—as some investigators do—in a company name, "AATJ Inc." However, they do not have records of any payment to AATJ in your case, or in any other case since 2000.

It therefore appears that Mr. Coffey did not submit a timely voucher in your case, or that he used another company name.

Manuel had expected that his lawyer and the private eye would search for records that would prove Martinez's whereabouts on the morning of October 23, 1990, when George Kogan was murdered. Martinez insisted he had an alibi and that he was in House Court representing a client in an eviction case. Martinez's case was first on the docket, at 9 a.m. He said he was there and that the House Court records could confirm it. But he'd had no luck nailing down that record. His appellate attorney, Claudia Trupp, addressed the issue in a letter to Martinez dated March 27, 2010, which basically said that while his attorney had tried to get a tape of the Housing Court proceedings, she was told it had been destroyed. She was trying instead, she told Martinez, to track down files from the court appearance that would show the time he was there. But because it was nearly 20 years earlier, "this task is proving challenging," Trupp wrote.

Finally, on July 15, 2010, Claudia Trupp sent him another letter, updating the Center for Appellate Litigation's success in learning more about the Housing Court records. She also addressed his request that they seek out witnesses at a restaurant where Carlos Piovanetti claimed Martinez had confessed his involvement in the George Kogan murder.

Trupp's letter was bad news for Martinez. In it, she let him know that she'd been unsuccessful in getting the manager of the Spaghetti Western restaurant where Martinez had met with Povanetti, to sign an affidavit. The manager, she said, did not want to get involved in a criminal case. She also said she would be seeking additional time with the court to appeal his case.

* * *

The Kogan case was a difficult one. Parts of the scene didn't add up. For example, an explanation was never given about the loose bills the doorman reported were "scattered everywhere." And a key witness, a cleaning woman, who saw the shooting as it happened, could not be located later by authorities. No one knows if the trigger man had been following George for a distance from up the street, or if he had been lying in wait for him near his apartment building.

Several hurdles remained for the prosecution in building the case against Barbara Kogan, especially because there was no direct evidence linking her to the crime. Still, once Manuel Martinez's case ended in mid-April 2008, prosecutors gathered the testimony and circumstantial evidence needed to build their case against Barbara Kogan, and, about a month later, a grand jury convened to consider the case against her.

Martinez's lawyer ridiculed the murder case as a house of cards based on no physical evidence and little more than testimony from an ex-con and the defendant's ex-wife.

In the meantime, police had proof that Barbara had contacted the life insurance company that held policies on George's life, seeking copies of those policies not long before her husband was killed.

The first contact was made on October 15, 1990—eight days before her husband was shot and killed—when Barbara called SMA Insurance. At the receiving end was Elaine Kay-Gannon, supervisor at the time for policy-owner communications. Citing three different policy numbers, Kay-Gannon, in turn, sent a letter dated October 16 addressed to Barbara but sent in care of her youngest son, William, at his Midtown address. Barbara called Kay-Gannon the following day, asking her to FedEx the policy copies instead of mailing them. She provided Kay-Gannon with her son's FedEx account number. By allowing the use of his account number, William showed he was aware of the life-insurance policies and his mother's need to show proof of assets to the court.

Kay-Gannon, in her letter, asked Barbara fill out a "lost policy" form, provided for customers who need copies of misplaced policies, which Kay-Gannon included with her letter. Kay-Gannon also asked that Barbara include a check for a $10 administration fee for each duplicate policy. She also provided Barbara with a definition of "irrevocable beneficiary," which Kay-Gannon mentioned in the letter as Barbara asking her about it when they spoke.

The next day, Barbara sent the completed form to Gannon, along with the fee, and asked that Kay-Gannon Federal Express the policies care of her son William's Fifth Avenue address.

Barbara filled out the forms, wrote out a check to cover the fee, and promptly mailed them back to the insurance company. That transaction took place before George's murder. But the copies of the policies she wanted would not arrive until after his death.

Meanwhile, on October 24, 1990, a man telephoned the insurance company and identified himself as "John Lyons." Elaine Kay-Gannon took the call. Lyons told her he was Barbara Kogan's accountant and wanted to know if the copies of the policies had been mailed out to Barbara. Kay-Gannon told him she would look into it and get back to him. In that conversation, Lyons did not inform Kay-Gannon that George Kogan had been murdered the day before.

Lyons called back the following day, on October 25, to see what Kay-Gannon was able to learn about the status of the policy copies. She told him she was still "looking into it." Again, Lyons, according to Kay-Gannon, did not tell her that George Kogan was dead.

Kay-Gannon looked into it and called Lyons back, but he didn't answer. She left a message telling him the replacement copies had been mailed.

On October 29, John Lyons telephoned the insurance company once again and spoke with Elaine Kay-Gannon. He asked again where the copies of the policies were. She told him she'd mailed them out, via regular mail—not overnight Federal Express, as Barbara had asked. He'd called because the copies Barbara had first requested on October 17 to be overnighted had not yet arrived. So, Lyons again requested that the policy duplicates be expedited.

On October 31 John Lyons called the insurance company to inquire again where the copies of the policies were. Kay-Gannon called the mailroom at the insurance company, got the tracking number, and gave it to John Lyons.

In early November, the highly anticipated copies arrived at Barbara's son's apartment.

Kay-Gannon was unaware when she sent the package that Barbara's husband had been murdered a week earlier. Still, because of the number of queries made to the insurance company and per company protocol, Kay-Gannon made note of each call asking about George Kogan's life-insurance policy.

Finally, on November 2, Barbara's attorney contacted the insurance company to notify them of George's death. During the same call, he requested payment to Barbara of the policies' proceeds—one for $2 million and two others for $1 million each.

The SMA insurance company, an affiliate of State Mutual Life Insurance Company of America, was immediately suspicious of Barbara when they learned she had not visited her husband in the hospital and because of the phone calls and requests she made a week before George's murder. So, the company contacted attorney Richard Lutz to handle the case.

"There were questions about whether Mrs. Kogan was in any way involved with that homicide," Lutz later said.

He filed a request in court asking that insurance proceeds be retained by the company to give them time to investigate "as to what had transpired." Lutz hired retired Nassau County Detective Roy McMillian to investigate the case on the company's behalf. According to New York law, if a person kills the insured, he or she cannot benefit from an insurance policy, although the policies had been purchased in the early 1980s with George Kogan's knowledge and approval.

But while Barbara may have been off the hook with the insurance company—finding no fault, they paid out the insurance money to her—the criminal investigation into who killed George Kogan was far from over for the police and, especially, Assistant District Attorney Joel Seidemann. He would not rest until he could officially hold Barbara accountable.

CHAPTER 15

A Likely Suspect

From the start, Barbara Kogan was considered a person of interest in her husband's murder.

On that fateful October morning, Billy Kogan, at the time a college student, called his mother from the hospital and, when she didn't answer, left a message telling her that his father had been gravely wounded.

Afterward, at 11:52 a.m., Barbara, who would later describe herself as distraught, telephoned her parents, Emanuel and Rose Siegel, at their home in Puerto Rico, purportedly to tell them the bad news about George. Her parents had lived in San Juan for twenty years and, at the time, were in an apartment next door to their oldest daughter, Elaine. Emanuel had built up a decent public-relations business and also published a popular tourist newspaper. If Emanuel and Rose were wealthy, it didn't show. As they had when their daughters were growing up in New Jersey, the Siegels lived conservatively.

"George has been shot," Barbara told her parents.

She spoke to them for a total of seven minutes. The shortness of that call, and a series of others that same day, led police to suspect that the calls weren't merely to comfort a grieving daughter, but, rather, were regular and sporadic updates on George's condition, which Barbara was getting when hospital personnel called several times asking her to visit her husband, because his odds of surviving his injuries were low.

At 12:10, eighteen minutes after Barbara's initial contact, Barbara's father returned her call. They spoke just three minutes.

Then, at 3:02 p.m., Barbara rang them again to give them an update. During that conversation, Barbara spoke for eleven minutes with her parents. She called them again an hour later, at 4:01 p.m., and, when they didn't answer, left a brief message. She tried again at 4:40 and spoke with them for eight minutes.

At 5:38 p.m., Barbara once again telephoned her parents, apparently to tell them that George had died, after the hospital had notified her. She called back again at 7:01 p.m. and talked for another eleven minutes. Then, her parents called her at 8:43 p.m. That call lasted seven minutes. Finally, Barbara spoke with her parents one last time that night, at 9:07 p.m., for about ten minutes.

But more noteworthy to investigators were the long-distance phone calls that morning originating from the Siegels' Puerto Rican home to Manuel Martinez's law office in New York City. Manuel was the attorney Barbara had hired a couple months earlier to find her a divorce lawyer in Puerto Rico. The Siegels' calls to Manuel were short, indicating that they were messages left on an answering machine. They took place before Barbara had called her parents. The first one, at 10:18 a.m. on October 23, was a minute long and placed from the Siegels' home phone to Martinez's office. At that point, George had been shot just a few minutes earlier and the family hadn't yet been notified. At 11:02, a fifty-second call was placed to Martinez's office from the Siegels' home, which Manuel later said was made by Barbara's father, Emanuel.

Then, at 11:17 p.m., a call that lasted four minutes was made from the same number at the Siegels' home to Martinez's residence. It was the last call of the day that interested the police. Martinez later said the calls to his office, which his answering machine had picked up, proved that he was in

House Court that day and not in his office. Martinez explained away the calls as Barbara's father wanting to have documents notarized and said it was coincidental that the calls began just minutes after George's death.

That same afternoon, John Lyons, the man Barbara had been seeing and who had accompanied Manuel Martinez to George's funeral, also telephoned Martinez. "[John] called me at my law office in the afternoon of October 23, 1990, [and] told me George Kogan had been shot and was still alive at the hospital," Manuel explained.

What Barbara wouldn't learn until later was that John Lyons was a CIA agent. As the murder investigation closed in on Barbara, Lyons was suddenly transferred to Afghanistan as a "State Department official."

"I originally thought he was Barbara's accountant," Martinez said. After he got to know Martinez better, Lyons told him he was "an international salesman of military equipment."

"He told me he had completed a sale of military hardware to North Korea. I never knew he worked for the CIA until [years later]," Martinez would later say.

When it came to John Lyons, it was difficult to tell fact from fiction. Martinez said he didn't know where Barbara had met Lyons. But Barbara utlimately told a judge that it was Martinez who'd introduced her to Lyons.

Martinez changed his stance and later said it was Barbara who'd introduced him to Lyons. "I met John Lyons through Barbara," Martinez explained, saying he "spoke with [Lyons] over the phone several times." He also said, "I met him with Barbara once for Sunday brunch. He played second fiddle to Barbara, who carried the conversation."

However Martinez and Barbara had met quiet John Lyons, he became a curious background character in the case, one who'd been a companion, and possibly a confidant, and who spent time with Barbara in the weeks leading up to her husband's murder.

To the outside world, Barbara's relationship with John Lyons seemed cordial, almost professional, not romantic.

They didn't display affection toward each other, yet they were constant companions. Because of his connection to Barbara and Manuel Martinez, Lyons would later play a significant, albeit absent, role as a figure in the George Kogan murder case.

Barbara and George Kogan's acrimonious divorce was no secret. The divorce was not Barbara's idea, but since her husband had fallen in love with another woman, there was no stopping it. Setting the pace for the murder investigation were Mary-Louise Hawkins' words at the murder scene, "It was his wife!" From that moment on, Barbara became the key suspect in her husband's murder.

In fact, she appeared to be the *only* person of interest, at least for the first few years. It's common practice for police to look at family members—especially spouses—as suspects, mostly to rule them out, so they can move on to other clues. In the Kogan case, Barbara's involvement appeared to be the main scenario investigators probed.

Nevertheless, it would hardly be an overnight case. It would take nearly two decades and two criminal cases to move the investigation from the district attorney's office and through the criminal court system.

It wasn't just May Louise's statement that caught detectives' attention. It was Barbara's actions, as well.

Just one day after the murder, a Wednesday, a police detective told the *New York Times* that Barbara's silence, and her seeming avoidance of being interviewed, were hampering their efforts. The detectives thought Barbara's behavior suspect, especially her absence at the hospital after the shooting. 19th Precinct officers and homicide investigators from the Manhattan North Homicide Squad began piecing together the mystery.

Publicly, detectives said they "had little to go on" from witnesses. Detectives were frustrated from the start, stunned by the lack of information they were able to gather from witnesses on that busy Manhattan morning. Several people at the scene only saw the immediate aftermath of the crime. The housekeeper had witnessed the shooting and the police had taken her statement, along with the others. The housekeeper's statement, however, would later prove to be inadmissible and hearsay when police discovered that she had left the country and they were unable to locate her.

Police had, however, determined early on that the killer was a hired gun. "All indications are that [Kogan] was an intended target, and it was an assassination," said police spokesperson Captain Stephen Davis, citing the use of a large-caliber revolver and the gunman's cool demeanor. "Whoever wanted to kill George Kogan remains a mystery."

A day after the shooting, Detective Mike Sheehan, a veteran homicide cop, drove to Barbara's apartment and asked the door attendant to call her apartment. Barbara answered the phone and said she would meet him downstairs. "She never came down," Sheehan reported. From their vantage point, Barbara appeared to be avoiding the police.

In his will, George had left the minimum legal amount of money to his wife, which was the interest on one third of his estate, the balance to his sons, which was split, and nothing to Mary-Louise Hawkins. But Barbara did not learn about George's will until after his death. Before the murder, Barbara hired Norman H. Donald III, a prominent estate attorney, to help with the asset portion of her divorce. After George's death, Donald arranged for Barbara to meet with detectives.

So, a day and a half after the murder, on that Wednesday night of October 24, three detectives from the 19th Precinct drove to the Times Square offices of Norman Donald, a partner with the law firm Skadden, Arps, Slate, Meagher & Flom—later considered a giant in the legal field—to speak to his client, Barbara Kogan, about her husband.

The detectives arrived that evening at Skadden's skyscraper offices on Third Avenue between Fifty-fifth and Fifty-sixth Streets and interviewed Barbara with her attorney present.

"When was the last time you spoke with your husband?" a detective asked her.

"The night before he died," she answered.

She also told detectives, "I was shocked when I was told [George] had been shot. It was terrible."

Barbara explained that she'd spoken with George on the phone the night before his death to discuss divorce details. The former couple's conversation had been pleasant, police later recounted to reporters. She and their son Bill had an appointment the next day, on the twenty-third, to hammer out a settlement. It had been long in the making, and Bill, especially, was anxious to get his parents past the divorce. He was worried about his mother, because she was still so upset about the split.

Mary-Louise Hawkins also told police that the conversation between Barbara and George the night before his death was uneventful. Mary-Louise was in the room when George spoke with Barbara, and nothing seemed amiss, she told them.

To a reporter, Barbara described her conversation with police as "amicable."

On October 25, two days after the murder, *The New York Times* reported on the status of the case in an article headlined, "No Suspects in Killing of East Side Businessman." The story quoted police as saying that as of late Wednesday, the same evening Barbara had spoken with detectives, while they had no suspects, their efforts "were being hampered in their investigation by the silence of the slain man's estranged wife."

That came as a surprise to attorney Norman Donald. A couple days later, in interviews with reporters, Donald repeated what investigators had told his client, that she was not a suspect in her husband's death. Detectives told Donald that they had contacted law enforcement officials in San Juan, Puerto Rico, where George had lived most of his life and still had real estate and business holdings. They were looking into his financial interests.

At that early stage of the inquiry, information was being leaked to the media about the possibility of some of George Kogan's negative business dealings turning deadly. "We are still looking at a number of possibilities," a detective familiar with the case told *Newsday* reporter Mitch Gelman. "But the focus of the investigation is on his business partners. He owed a lot of people a lot of money."

In an interesting aside, very early in the inquiry, police also publicly said that George Kogan had mob connections. This was reported in a *Newsday* article by Gelman and dated a couple days after the murder.

Another possibility was that the murder could have been a robbery gone bad. Cash—bills and change—was all over the sidewalk that morning. Could all that cash have popped out of George's pockets from the force of being shot?

What police did know was that George had been shot at close range. But the case was baffling. It didn't at that point add up to a robbery-turned-murder scenario and it didn't fit the M.O. of a mob hit, nor did the wife seem likely to have done it. With no murder weapon, no real description of the shooter, and no hard evidence, it was a particularly difficult case to solve.

Still, as George Kogan lay on his deathbed in the hospital, police said his estranged wife was busy summoning a hairdresser to her Fifth Avenue apartment. They soon focused their attention on Barbara.

CHAPTER 16

"I'm an Innocent Woman"

By 1995, with few leads, the police moved in a new direction with the case and linked Manuel Martinez to Barbara Kogan as a co-conspirator to hire a hit man. They also attempted to link Martinez with Paul Prosano, believed by authorities to be the hired gun in George Kogan's murder. Information saying just that was leaked to the press through an unnamed source, who claimed that Prosano told Martinez George's last words were "God save me," and that when the hit was made, Prosano called Martinez to say, "It's done."

In an interview with the *New York Post* for the same story, Prosano, thirty-seven years old and in jail for an unrelated conviction, denied any involvement in George's murder or even knowing Barbara Kogan. But Prosano said he knew Manny Martinez and that he had once fumigated his law office. "I was his exterminator. That's the only relationship I had with him," Prosano told the *Post* from Rikers Island.

Prosano was being literal when he said he was an "exterminator." While investigators took the statement to mean that Prosano had killed—or exterminated—for Martinez, Prosano in actuality owned a pest control business called Technical Extermination Method, and he operated it from his parents' home on Avenue U in Brooklyn, New York. After Prosano refused to cut a deal with prosecutors to make monitored telephone calls to Martinez and others as part of the district attorney's probe, Prosano was convicted of kidnapping Frances Barnes in a spree of robberies.

In 2008, investigators finally closed in on Barbara Kogan. By now, she had started her own company and called it Clementine Holding Corporation. She needed to continue earning a living. Barbara could no longer afford the lavish lifestyle to which she'd been accustomed. She was spending thousands a week on her attorney, and she'd cut back drastically on daily expenditures. Gone were the expensive salon visits, massages, and meals at top-rated Manhattan restaurants.

Twenty days before Barbara's arrest, the court record showed that the prosecution had filed a voluntary discovery document dated October 30, 2008, in the case of The People of the State of New York against Barbara Kogan, defendant. On the disclosure form, Joel Seidemann wrote that the prosecution had scientific and medical reports, including ballistics, serology, fingerprints, and the medical examiner's reports. The prosecution also included photographs and drawings, as well as tapes and electronic recordings. Barbara knew from her attorney that he was expecting her to be indicted. She was at her wit's end.

Just before Barbara's arrest, her good friend Dawna Cole was in the city. Dawna was staying at her Manhattan apartment, which was a second home for her. Barbara, who was still living in her East Fifty-fifth Street apartment, wanted to talk, so, on a Sunday afternoon, she went to Dawna's apartment. Barbara threatened suicide and was so out of sorts that Dawna was frightened for her friend. Dawna worked at a Binghamton hospital and talked Barbara into going home with her to Binghamton, New York, where Barbara could enjoy the picturesque setting, surrounded by high hills, and relax. Barbara was more than uneasy about her future, what with the investigation and the looming indictment against her, and she needed a change of scenery. Plus, she hoped that spending time with a good friend would help relieve the pressure.

Binghamton, Barbara agreed, might be the answer, at least for the time being. Located about 180 miles north of Manhattan, it was a world away from her problems. Once they arrived, Cole took Barbara the next day to the psychiatric ward of Binghamton General Hospital, where Barbara checked in as an outpatient.

While Barbara may have been anxious, her activities while at Dawna's didn't reflect it. On November 11, Barbara had her nails manicured for $16 at Asian Nails in Vestal, New York, near the Pennsylvania state border—again, a world away from the extravagant beauty spas Barbara was accustomed to. She shopped the same day at a Target store in Vestal, according to her bank statement, obtained by police. Also the same day, she returned to Binghamton and, at 10:30 a.m., ate at South Side Yanni's, a neighborhood restaurant and bar, and spent just under $20 for the meal.

That same day, the *New York Daily News* reported that a grand jury had been deciding whether to indict Barbara for the murder of her husband. The paper reported that a panel, after convening for several weeks, had been voting for a week and a half, but it "was unclear if it handed up an indictment against Barbara Kogan."

On November 13, Dawna and Barbara had dinner at the Moghul Fine Indian Cuisine restaurant in Vestal.

Barbara also made three trips to fill prescriptions at the CVS Pharmacy in Binghamton, as well as two stops to mail packages from the United States Post Office, also in Binghamton.

Then, on November 15, 2008, from Dawna's home and using her own laptop, Barbara got online and ordered two sweaters from Woman Within. The cardigans, one heather gray and the other royal purple, cost $19.99 each. She had them shipped to Dawna's home. On November 16, according to posted charges on her account, Barbara also paid two bills online.

At the same time, while Barbara remained in Binghamton, the New York City tabloids reported that a warrant was about to be issued for her arrest.

The pressure became too much for Barbara; she was an emotional wreck. Dawna took Barbara to the hospital once again, this time not as an outpatient. Barbara was admitted involuntarily as a psychological patient at the upstate mental hospital. As her arrest grew closer, she became mentally unhinged.

Meanwhile, her attorney informed reporters that Barbara would turn herself in for booking, and be arraigned the following day, even though Barbara was still in the hospital.

On the evening of November 20, 2008, New York City police detective Raymond Brennan, on the NYPD force since 1972, interviewed Dawna Cole. He caught up with Dawna in the parking lot at Binghamton Hospital, where she had been visiting Barbara. As Dawna left the hospital and walked to her car, she was approached by Brennan, who had been assigned to the Kogan case since March 2007.

"I asked her about [her] friendship with defendant Barbara Kogan," Brennan wrote in a sworn affidavit dated December 9, 2008. "Ms. Cole made a one-page written statement while seated in my vehicle." Brennan wrote that Cole stated: "Several weeks ago, I let [Barbara] know I'd be in Manhattan. We met on Sunday and it was auspicious for her to come at that time since she had no plans. That evening in my home, she became hysterical, crying, stating she wanted to die and would I go with her to Oregon where she could be euthanized with an injection. I knew she needed help, and I brought her the next morning to our hospital where she was admitted and has been since."

The next day, on November 21, Alan Wilmarth, the director of New Horizons, a wing of the hospital, handed over Barbara's passport—to prevent her from fleeing—to Detective Brennan. Barbara's passport listed her last name as Bodine, the surname of her second—and former—husband. Also, Barbara's date of birth was listed as February 10, 1945. While at the hospital, Detective Brennan talked on the phone with Assistant District Attorney Joel Seidemann, who told Brennan that he'd been in contact with Barbara's attorney,

Barry Levin, and was aware that the defendant had been admitted for treatment.

The next day, Detective Brennan paid Dawna Cole a second visit, this time at the Greater Binghamton Innovation Center where Dawna worked, to ask her follow-up questions about her relationship with Barbara and issues surrounding George's death. At the end of their conversation, Dawna, while sitting at her desk at work, hand-wrote a second statement, this one two pages long.

"In a portion of this statement," Brennan wrote in his affidavit, "Ms. Cole stated, 'On the day Barbara's husband was killed, she called me frantically in Norwich, where I was living at the time, to tell me what had happened. She was hysterical. A mutual friend in our organization had killed her husband in self-defense and Barbara asked me who her lawyer was, if she needed one. I believe it was Michael Dowd.'"

Dawna Cole's statement matched Barbara's phone records obtained by investigators. The records show that at 5:32 p.m. on October 23, the evening of the day George Kogan was shot, an outgoing phone call was placed to Cole's Norwich, New York, home. Brennan also verified that Michael Dowd, the attorney mentioned by Cole, did, in fact, represent a woman by the name of LuAnn Fratt, an Upper East Side socialite who had been charged with stabbing her wealthy husband in December 1989. Fratt, who claimed self-defense, was acquitted.

In fact, LuAnn Fratt, a mother of three and a wealthy Upper East Side Manhattanite, had walked the three blocks to her estranged husband Charles's Park Avenue apartment and fatally stabbed him. Then she reported it to police.

Fratt hired Michael Dowd, who has been described as a "scruffy-looking" downtown attorney known for representing battered women. Fratt pleaded self-defense, because she claimed her husband had attempted to rape her, so she stabbed him. A jury believed her, and LuAnn Fratt was found not guilty.

But Barbara Kogan ended up not retaining Michael Dowd,

who at that time was still practicing criminal law in New York. Instead, she hired Barry Levin.

The day came, on November 25, 2008, when Barbara and attorney Levin arrived at the New York County District Attorney's Office, so Barbara could turn herself in. Detective Raymond Brennan was there to assist in the arrest. Brennan worked at the time in the technical branch of the District Attorney's Office Squad, or DAOS, known as the Wire Room, which houses an inventory of electronic equipment, including surveillance. While it operates within the DA's office, it is officially a unit of the NYPD and falls under the purview of the chief of detectives. The unit—and Brennan—had assisted in the investigation of Barbara Kogan, just as it had in the investigation of Manuel Martinez's role in the murder. Brennan had joined the Kogan case, along with Donald Kennedy, after taking over the case from the investigative team of detectives Ernie Bugge and Joseph Buffalino. Despite their time on the case, Bugge and Buffalino would not be the ones to arrest Barbara. Instead, Detective Brennan assisted, and Barbara Kogan was officially arrested and charged with a single felony count of murder, a violation of New York penal code 125.25. The one-page indictment listed Barbara as five foot five-inches tall, 140 pounds, sixty-five years old, with black hair and brown eyes.

After booking Barbara, Detective Brennan, who discovered the wrong birth date on Barbara's passport, filed the following affidavit:

"On November 25, 2008, during the arrest process at the New York County District Attorney's office, while asking defendant pedigree information, defendant stated her date of birth was February 10, 1943," he wrote in the affidavit. "I then asked her if her date of birth was February 10, 1943, or February 10, 1945, as it stated on her passport. Defendant stated that she listed her date of birth on the passport as 1945 for job purposes, but her real birth year is 1943." Later, when Levin requested bail for Barbara, the discrepancy in her birthdate would be used as one of the reasons—this one dishonesty on her passport—to deny bail and keep her in custody.

It was a big day for the district attorney's office and a long time in the making. The DA issued this news release:

Manhattan District Attorney Robert M. Morgenthau announced today the arrest of BARBARA KOGAN for murder in the 1990 contract killing of her husband, George Kogan.

The defendant was returned to New York State Supreme Court on a bench warrant to face a charge of one count of Murder in the Second Degree, a class A-I felony.

The investigation leading to today's arrest revealed that KOGAN, 65, plotted with her lawyer, Manuel Martinez, to hire a hitman to kill her husband with whom she was in the midst of a divorce. George Kogan was killed on October 23, 1990 in front of his girlfriend's apartment building on East 69th Street. Upon his death, BARBARA KOGAN collected approximately $4.3 million from four life insurance policies on her husband's life.

Martinez admitted [during a police-taped conversation in September 1992 with a friend and associate] to arranging the murder at KOGAN's behest in exchange for money. Martinez was subsequently convicted for the murder in April 2008, and is serving a sentence of 25 years to life.

KOGAN, who faces 25 years to life in prison, was remanded. She is scheduled to be arraigned tomorrow afternoon before Judge Michael J. Obus in Part 51.
Defendant Information: BARBARA KOGAN
    2/10/1943
    1503 Ashford Avenue
    San Juan, Puerto Rico

On November 26, Barbara was removed from the holding area at the courthouse and housed at the Rose M. Singer

Center. In the inmate van as it crossed the bridge to Rikers Island, she was greeted by the sign "Rikers Island, Home of the Boldest." Barbara stayed in one of Rikers Island's ten prisons until December 2, when she was placed on suicide watch and relocated to the Elmhurst Hospital Prison Ward on Broadway in Queens, New York. According to the prison Web site, Elmhurst houses "female inmates requiring acute psychiatric care."

Eventually, Barbara was transferred again, back to the Rose M. Singer Center jail at Rikers, where 1,100 detained and sentenced female adults and adolescents are housed. But Barbara was placed in a protective custody—locked away and segregated twenty-three hours a day—so corrections officers could keep an eye on her and prevent her from a suicide attempt. She was tucked safely away from the general population. At the same time, she was in nearly complete isolation from the outside world.

At Barbara's bail hearing, lead prosecutor Joel Seidemann told Manhattan Supreme Court Justice Michael Obus that Barbara Kogan, after being shut out from her bank accounts, "became so overwhelmed that she and Mr. Martinez chose to sort of litigate the divorce through the bullets of a gun rather than through the good offices of the court."

Barbara's attorney, Barry Levin, was at first unaware of the indictment. When asked by reporters if his client had been indicted by a grand jury, said, "I would hope not." He also said that a criminal case against Barbara was weak. If it were true that she'd been indicted, he said, "I would surrender her, present a bail package to the county, and look forward to a quick and speedy trial. I intend to represent her zealously. I think she will be acquitted. I think the entire case is based on innuendo and gossip."

Soon after Levin received a phone call from the Manhattan district attorney's office, telling him that his client had just been indicted on one count of murder. Levin's response to further requests for comments by reporters was similar to what he'd told them earlier, that prosecutors had no "substantive evidence" to tie his client to the killing. He insisted his client was innocent. "I look forward to the trial and having my client vindicated so she can put eighteen years of stress behind her," he said.

His protests appeared to be true. No murder weapon. No eyewitnesses who could ID the shooter. It was anything but a slam-dunk case for the DA, which is why they waited nearly two decades to indict first Martinez, then Barbara.

Levin countered the allegations by suggesting that George Kogan's disgruntled and former business associates, whom Levin never named, had killed George.

Levin explained away Barbara's inquiry to the insurance company, which was about to be used by the state as circumstantial evidence against her. He said that Barbara had initially contacted the company in need of a copy of the policies for her divorce battle, in which the equity in at least one of the policies was considered an asset. "George had taken all the paperwork from their home in Puerto Rico," Levin said. "Barbara needed the policies, because she wanted them to be a part of the matrimonial settlement."

At the time that Barry Levin took on Barbara Kogan as his client, he had been practicing criminal law for twenty-three years, much of it specializing in drunken-driving cases. He was determined to prove Barbara's innocence. Ultimately, though, the case appeared headed for a trial and a jury of her peers. Would a jury buy the prosecution's side of the story that Barbara Kogan was a greedy, cold-blooded killer who had had her husband murdered for his insurance money, or was she instead the victim of an overzealous prosecutor who looked at no other suspects except the wife?

She hardly seemed the type to orchestrate a coldblooded murder. Soon, however, tabloids began referring to Barbara as the "Black Widow."

Stanley Goodman, Barbara's divorce attorney, also insisted the case was shaky, old, and circumstantial. "She's not well. She's not a flight risk. She's been living in New York City," Goodman said after news broke with details about Barbara's impending arrest. His statement that Barbara was not well was the first hint at Barbara's declining mental condition. In a phone interview, Levin said Barbara had been on medication, but he did not go into detail.

Barry Levin arranged with the DA's office that his client would surrender to authorities on Tuesday, November 25, 2008, to face a charge in the shooting death of her husband. Levin said, "There is no substantive evidence of my client's involvement in the death of her husband. If the DA wants to create a soap opera, I can't stop them. George was an individual who did business with everyone and paid no one." He insisted there was nothing to link his client to her husband's death.

Barbara arrived at New York State Supreme Court, on the warrant to face a single charge of murder in the second degree, in a black luxury SUV, her attorney by her side. George Kogan's widow stepped out of the SUV, prepared to turn herself in.

Awaiting her arrival outside the seventeen-story Art Deco courthouse was a throng of reporters and photographers as sheriff's deputies, along with Barbara's attorney, escorted her into the courthouse at 100 Centre Street, the nexus of all criminal prosecutions in Manhattan. It's also where hordes of New York's paparazzi and mainstream photographers show up for high-profile arraignments, where the accused are taken, from either a police precinct or Central Booking, for arraignment before a Manhattan criminal court judge. Defense attorneys for good reason have unofficially and universally referred to the booking area as "The Tombs."

Newspaper reporters shouted "Did you do it?" and "Are you innocent?" while photographers took pictures of Barbara stepping out of the SUV.

"I'm an innocent woman, oh, absolutely," Barbara answered as she and Levin passed the reporters on their way from the sidewalk to the courthouse.

Eighteen years after her husband's murder, Barbara was fingerprinted, and, within a span of minutes, she got her booking number. She was officially inmate number 09289727J.

Then her mug shot was taken. She was handcuffed and escorted through the entrance of the courthouse for her 9:30 appearance. She went inside to a thirteenth-floor courtroom for the five-minute arraignment before Judge Michael J. Obus. She looked around at the courtroom, simple except for its wood wainscoting.

The court clerk asked Barbara to stand.

"How do you plead?" the judge asked.

"Not guilty," she said quietly.

Thus, the charge of one count of murder in the second degree, a class A-I felony in New York, was official. Because of the lengthy passage of time, the statute of limitations for filing conspiracy and larceny along with the murder count had long since expired.

Barry Levin was hoping Barbara would be released the same day on bail so she could help prepare her defense. But that would not be the case. The judge held Barbara over, sending her to jail with no bail, pending a hearing the next day.

Barbara, stunned because both she and her attorney had expected she'd be given bail, did not stay long in the courtroom. The hearing was over almost as soon as it had started. By late morning, Barbara Kogan was officially added to New York State's court system as a "violent felony offender."

At that juncture in the investigation, defense lawyer Levin was not aware of any hard evidence against Barbara. In a voluntary disclosure form, the state soon released particulars leading the prosecutor to seek an indictment, which revealed to Levin what evidence the state had—and didn't have—against his client. The evidence, at least what the state had presented at that time, consisted of "scientific and medical reports"—the medical examiner's report, ballistics results, a blood serum report, and a fingerprint report. The prosecution also presented photographs, drawings, tapes, and electronic recordings. Prominently missing, again, was the murder weapon. And the person who fired it.

The two sides battled in court in a lengthy hearing over bail. During the explosive proceedings, the defense requested that instead of jail, Barbara be placed on house arrest and wear a GPS monitoring bracelet attached to her ankle. Levin also pointed out that Barbara had no prior criminal record.

Instead of helping her, however, Barbara's lack of prior arrests hindered the defense's case for bail. The prosecution argued that because the defendant had never before been arrested, the court had no history of Barbara showing up for hearings and proceedings. Therefore, she could be a flight risk, especially considering she lived part of the time in Puerto Rico. Also, the incorrect birth date on Barbara's passport, discovered by police during her arrest, was used as reason to deny her bail.

Barbara's release was not to be. In a decision dated December 12, 2008, Justice Michael Obus sided with the prosecution. For the second time since her arrest, he ordered Barbara Kogan be held indefinitely without bail. The judge's three-page decision spelled out his reasons:

> *Defendant's motion for bail is denied.*
>
> *Defendant has been indicted for murder in the second degree on the theory that she arranged for the 1990 murder of her husband in the course of a contentious divorce. In reviewing her bail application, the court has considered the lengthy oral arguments and written submissions of both parties. Having presided at the trial of Manuel Martinez, who was convicted of second-degree murder based upon his role as the alleged intermediary between this defendant and the actual shooter, the court is further familiar with the background of the case and the proof expected at defendant's trial.*
>
> *Obviously, the denial of bail is not lightly done in general and it is not lightly done in this case. The court is well aware of the age of the alleged crime, defendant's opportunity to flee before indictment, her lack of criminal record and her offers to post significant bond secured by others' property and to undergo GPS monitoring. However, a review of the nature and*

strength of the case, defendant's background and character, and the remaining factors compel the court to conclude that the defendant presents a significant risk of flight if released.

The People have presented evidence that in the course of collecting the life insurance proceeds on her husband's death, her own subsequent bankruptcy proceedings and alleged relevant conversations with others, defendant has apparently been untruthful. By defense counsel's admission, she also suffers from psychiatric conditions which have resulted in her recent involuntary commitment to a hospital and which require a number of medications, and the People have alleged that she threatened suicide. While defendant has worked, her jobs have been short-term and have involved much travel and many contacts outside of this country. Her residences likewise have changed frequently. Having collected over $4 million in life insurance benefits and having been denied a discharge in bankruptcy, her financial resources are disputed, and apparently involve foreign bank accounts. When arrested, defendant was also in possession of a passport containing a false date of birth.

As stated, defendant has no prior criminal record. Because she has no record and was remanded in this case, she also has no history of nonappearance or flight in a criminal proceeding, either positive or negative. The court does note, however, defendant's alleged failure to appear for an examination before the bankruptcy court. Her offer to surrender in this case does not establish that bail is appropriate.

As also stated, the court presided at the trial of defendant's purported accomplice and has reviewed the People's account of the similar evidence they expect to introduce at defendant's trial. While the court has yet to review the minutes of the grand jury presentation against defendant, the People appear to have assembled a substantial circumstantial case on

which a jury could convict. If defendant is in fact con-
victed after trial, she faces a significant sentence of
incarceration, a minimum of 15 years to life impris-
onment.

Finally, the proposed bail package, while substan-
tial, is based upon collateral pledged by those other
than defendant, and the court is not satisfied that GPS
monitoring would guarantee knowledge of her where-
abouts or presence in court.

In summary, the character of the defendant, nature
of the offense, probability of conviction and possible
severity of sentence establish that defendant poses an
appreciable risk of flight. Bail is denied and remand
is continued.

It was a hard hit to the defense.

Wording in the decision mentioned an "actual" shooter, when in reality no one had yet been identified. It was an odd insertion. Of course, the fact that a shooter was not brought to justice didn't change the outcome in Manuel Martinez's trial. It did not bode well for Barbara's case, either.

Barbara first met Manuel at his New York law office seeking an attorney to represent her in her divorce case. "She went to Manuel's office in New York," said Nilda Martinez, Manuel's sister. "After speaking with her and telling her that he did not take divorce matters, he said she could go to Puerto Rico to several law offices that he knew. She asked him to accompany her, and he presented her to several law firms, including one of Manuel's ex-professors, Lino Saldaña."

"We spent three days in Puerto Rico," Manuel later said. Manuel stayed at El San Juan Hotel and Casino, compliments of Elaine Siegel, who at that time was still the hotel's casino manager. After the Kogans sold their controlling shares in the Ramada San Juan Hotel for $11 million in 1986, Elaine went to work as general manager of Hotel El Convento, a smaller luxury hotel. Barbara and Manuel went to the Chase Manhattan Plaza to meet with Julio Aguirre at the law office of Fiddler, Gonzalez and Rodriguez. They also met with law professor Saldaña at Banco Popula Center, and attorney Ivan Ramos. In addition, Manuel met privately with attorney Francisco Troncoso.

But it was Kermit Ortiz Morales, whose law office was located in the Golden Mile in Hato Rey where the major banks in Puerto Rico's capital city are located, that Martinez said Barbara retained. Barbara needed to see what her husband's financial holdings were in Puerto Rico, because it appeared that George Kogan had tried to hide his assets after the couple's separation. Barbara was convinced that an attorney in Puerto Rico could better help her locate those assets. She wanted her share of the couple's assets; if it took hiring an attorney in San Juan to help her, then that's what she'd do. She willingly traveled to Puerto Rico to get closer to her goal.

Even so, this trip is where prosecutor Joel Seidemann contended the deal to kill George was consummated. Barbara, if the prosecutor's theory was to be believed, had gotten $100,000 in cash from her parents to give to Manuel Martinez, so he could pay a gunman to kill George.

"The Siegels did not give me $100,000 or 100,000 pennies," Manuel insisted in a letter he wrote from prison. No record of $100,000 changing hands was listed in Barbara's bank accounts. Only a $3,000 payment, for notary and other services, paid out to Martinez by Barbara, and two $1,000 payments, were ever found.

Yet, at Martinez's trial, the prosecutor continually mentioned large sums of money paid out by Barbara to Martinez. In turn, the prosecution contended, Martinez paid $50,000 to hire a hit man. It was a serious accusation, and Barbara knew she needed a lawyer with a big name and a successful track record to represent her, which is why she had hired criminal defense attorney Barry Levin.

CHAPTER 17

The Defense

Three years before Barbara Kogan's indictment, in the spring of 2005, defense lawyer Barry Levin was making headlines in another case. Media coverage of that case was how Barbara learned about Levin and eventually contacted him to ask that he represent her.

In Levin's previous and equally high-profile criminal probe, he represented Albert Pirro, husband of Westchester District Attorney Jeanine Pirro, who was described by the *New York Daily News* as a "GOP powerbroker."

In the Pirro case, Albert claimed his innocence, including specifically denying saying anything to DePalma about the officer. But according to FBI surveillance tape released to the public, DePalma and his associates said otherwise. At an October 2004 meeting at a restaurant, DePalma conferred with mob associates, including reputed soldier Robert Vaccaro. The men discussed Frank DellaCamera, a Mamaroneck police officer who'd been charged by the Westchester district attorney's office three days earlier on drug and stolen-goods charges. FBI documents accused the officer of helping the mob in auto-insurance scams and paying tribute to the Gambino family. On tape, DePalma said, "The DA's husband told Bobby Persico that Westchester district attorney's office investigators have been following [DellaCamera] for one year," according to the FBI documents, made public by the *New York Daily News*. Mobster DePalma appeared furious that Albert Pirro had not told the gangsters earlier that DellaCamera was being followed, saying on tape, "He tells you now. He could have—" Vaccaro interrupted him with, "Watch the pinch," referring to a potential arrest.

In an e-mail to the *Daily News*, according to the newspaper, Albert Pirro denied having such knowledge and passing it on to others. In 2002, as a lobbyist, he had represented Persico, a Westchester contractor. Pirro also denied any knowledge of Persico and his mob ties, even though in 1998 prosecutors publicly labeled Persico an associate of a crime family.

In 1994, Levin defended Alphonse Persico, son of Carmine Persico, who at the time headed the Colombo crime family—one of New York's five Mafia groups. In federal court, prosecutors accused the younger Persico, known on the street as "Allie Boy," of plotting from prison a Colombo family war that sparked bloodshed on the streets of New York. The six-week trial ended in an acquittal of Persico—and a major win for Barry Levin.

The cost to defend high-profile clients like Pirro, who was ultimately convicted of tax fraud and served time in a federal penitentiary, and Persico, later convicted of a variety of offenses and sent to prison, is expensive. Murder trials like Barbara Kogan's are even pricier to defend, and her legal expenses added up quickly.

Levin, who began his legal career as a prosecutor, said shortly after Barbara retained him that he looked forward to representing her through the trial. But a few weeks before Barbara was indicted and after she'd retained Levin, she was still paying an earlier defense team she'd had on retainer.

On April 7, 2008, Barbara paid civil and criminal defense attorney Jay Goldberg a $3,267 fee. At the time, Goldberg, a graduate of Harvard Law School, was with the firm Levitt & Kaiser specializing in criminal law. Two days later, on April 9, she paid a retainer fee of $75,000 to Goldberg, according to her business checking account records with Chevy Chase Bank, which were provided to the court. Also on April 9, she wrote a check for $600 to Nick Kaizer, a partner at the firm. The check was endorsed by Jay Goldberg. She wrote another check to Levitt & Kaizer on April 12 for $2,120, another on April 25 for $29,000, one on May 1 for $2,500, and yet another, written for $760, on May 27. Also on May 27, Barbara wrote a final check for $30,000 to Nick Kaizer with the memo noting "Fee."

In early May Barbara wrote Levin a check for $5,000. Ten days later on May 12, 2008, she wrote out another check to him for $100,000. On the memo line of the check she hand-wrote "Retainer Payment in Full."

The next month, on June 30, Barbara cut a check to Levin for $30,000 with the memo notation "Toward Fee." On July 30, she wrote a check to him for an additional $10,000 and, on August 19, another check for $10,000. On September 8, she issued a check to him for $25,000 with the handwritten notation "Retainer." In October, she paid Levin $13,310 with the notation "Client Contract."

Prior to trial, Barbara paid attorney Jay Goldberg, who'd represented her for two months, and the firm of Levitt & Kaizera, a total of $143,247. And to Barry Levin, she paid a total of $183,310. The grand total of $326,558 paid out to attorneys had, at that point, just gotten her past her bail hearing. Barbara, who'd earlier filed for bankruptcy, but was denied because the court said she'd hidden her money, was running out of funds.

Still, Barry Levin fought for Barbara and was confident he'd win. "This is a kooky case," he said in a telephone interview. "This is not a cut-and-dry case. There is no evidence against Barbara. I was a prosecutor when I started out, and there are a lot of prosecutors who wouldn't have taken this case."

He went to court and argued on behalf of Barbara for the dismissal of the murder charge, citing the years'-long delay in indicting his client. "The defense has lost its ability to call several material witnesses that would have been able to rebut the prosecution's theory, because they are either deceased, unable to be located, or have had their recollection compromised as a result of the long delay," he argued.

In his eleven-page motion for dismissal, dated March 25, 2009, Levin pointed out that Barbara's parents, Rose and Emanuel Siegel, "who would have been able to testify as to their relationship with Mr. Martinez and why they had made calls to his home office on October 23 and 24, 1990, are now deceased."

Also dead was Lorenzo Munez, a trustee appointed to oversee the proceeds of George's sale of the Ramada Hotel and Casino in Puerto Rico. The brief stated that Munez was accused of "mismanagement in his oversight of the proceeds of the sale."

Norman Perlman, a divorce lawyer for Barbara Kogan, had also since died. Perlman, Levin pointed out, "would have been able to rebut the testimony of Scott Kogan regarding the events surrounding the parties' divorce proceedings."

Three times in his motion for dismissal, Levin cited the "eighteen-year delay" as a violation of his client's rights. "The prosecution is wrong on both points," Levin argued. "Such mischaracterization of longstanding precedent is an absurd attempt to fool this Court in order to salvage an 18-year delay and is in violation of defendant Kogan's constitutional rights to a speedy and just prosecution." New York has recognized similar cases, he wrote, since 1948.

"The District Attorney's Office has had the same quantum of evidence against defendant Kogan since the grand jury presentation against Manuel Martinez in 1996," Levin wrote.

In fact, Levin emphasized that "the only substantive difference between the evidence in the people's possession in 1996 and the grand jury presentation in October 2008 is the claim that a witness will testify that defendant Kogan was getting her hair done after being informed her husband had been shot. The evidence against Kogan is, at best, a weak circumstantial evidence case consisting of two admissions made by Mr. Martinez to his then-wife, Beatriz Oller, and his former business partner and friend, Carlos Piovanetti, that he had committed the murder for Ms. Kogan. As this court is aware, Mr. Piovanetti is a convicted felon, a drug dealer, and a con artist whose testimony is highly suspect. Secondly, Ms. Oller is a woman who has a history of mental illness and was both mentally and physically abused by Mr. Martinez. Their testimony has substantial credibility issues."

For those reasons, Levin asked that the court dismiss the murder charge against Barbara. He ended the motion by asking Judge Obus to "grant the defendant's motions in their entirety."

Levin's argument worked. The court dismissed the single charge of murder in the second degree on a technicality, because of failure to charge Barbara in a timely manner. In July 2009, State Supreme Court Justice Michael Obus ruled that the DA had empaneled a grand jury in 2008 but had not gotten the court's permission to do so.

Levin said, in a telephone interview, that because the court had tossed out the charge and there were no new charges pending against his client and it was a new case, he again requested bail for Barbara Kogan while awaiting her trial. He was confident that, this time, bail would be granted and she'd be released from Rikers Island.

But the judge also included in his ruling an opportunity for the prosecutor to re-file the charge. First, Seidemann would have to get permission, after the fact, to empanel the 2008 grand jury. Levin explained Obus's move, saying, "Like all judges in New York, he compromised. The judge gave the prosecution the opportunity to resubmit the charge."

However, Levin pointed out, "They have to do this whole thing all over again. It will take them months. Barbara will probably be out on bail or on her own recognizance by early August."

Levin was so optimistic about his client's chances that he and Barbara even planned where she would live after she got out of Rikers. "If she is released, she'll be staying with friends who have a place on Park Avenue," Levin said.

But it was not to be. About a week later, the court's answer came: "Denied."

"Her bail was denied," Levin explained, "because the judge ruled she was a flight risk because she'd been staying in San Juan, Puerto Rico, at the time the indictment was issued. Records, however, show that Barbara Kogan also had an apartment in New York."

Thus, Barbara Kogan became one of the forty-six out of forty-seven defendants charged with murder in 2008 in New York County who were not awarded bail.

In addition to denying bail, the judge ruled that Barbara should remain in isolation and under suicide watch at Rikers Island. Barbara remained in jail, without the formality of any criminal charges against her.

Levin commented that once a new charge was filed, "I'm going to go in and argue that they violated the speedy-trial statute. They have one hundred and ninety days to charge my client." But Levin predicted in a phone interview that the prosecution would not re-file the charge until late December 2009, which, he said, would give him and Barbara more time to prepare. He was off on his prediction.

No sooner had the charge of murder been dismissed against Barbara than it was re-filed by the District Attorney's office. In September 2009, the same charge was filed and accepted by the district attorney's office, which had, after the fact, received permission to empanel a grand jury. Assistant District Attorney Seidemann then re-filed the lone charge against Barbara. The tables had turned, and now it was the defense that was back at square one. Levin said while he had anticipated the re-filing, he had not expected it so soon.

Still, he was adamant about going to trial and vigorously defending Barbara. Levin regrouped and said he was ready.

"I'm going to give them Manuel Martinez in my opening statement. Martinez's conviction has nothing to do with my client. If Martinez is guilty, so what? What does that have to do with Barbara?"

Levin would have his answer to that question soon enough.

CHAPTER 18
The Prosecutor

Over the course of Joel J. Seidemann's nearly thirty years at the Manhattan prosecutor's office, he had tried twenty-two homicide cases by late 2009. Of those, twenty had ended in convictions. Law.com once called Seidemann's style a "take-no-prisoners advocacy" that's "pugnacious, unrelenting and highly effective."

"Emotion is the key to getting convictions," Seidemann told Law.com in an October 2009 interview. "You can prove guilt beyond a reasonable doubt, but if no one was hurt, the jury will just say 'so what.' It's easier to prove a murder than a shoplifting."

In Seidemann's book *Guilty By Reason of Stupidity*, published in 2008, he wrote about dozens of cases, but didn't include the George Kogan homicide—the one he'd spent, by that time, nearly eighteen years on.

Even so, to his peers, Seidemann lists Manuel Martinez among his biggest cases. Seidemann also handled the prosecution of cabbie Ronald Popadich, who is serving a sentence of up to twenty-five years after pleading guilty to killing a neighbor. Popadich was accused of running down twenty-five New Yorkers in Midtown and shooting a cabbie during a three-day crime spree.

According to defense attorney Barry Levin, Barbara Kogan's was the one case Seidemann wanted to see end in a conviction. "The Barbara Kogan case is *the* case of Seide-mann's career," Levin said. "He wants to retire with a con-viction. He's obsessed with the case."

Obsessed or not, Seidemann, then in his late fifties, was determined in his efforts to close the book on the George Kogan murder. For him, Manuel Martinez was peripheral. Nabbing, or even identifying the gunman seemed unlikely. Most of all, Seidemann wanted Barbara.

Joel Jonathan Seidemann joined the New York Bar Associa-tion in 1980 after getting his juris doctorate from George Washington University. Before that, he'd earned a bachelor's degree from Cornell University.

For three years before joining the district attorney's of-fice in 1982, he was an associate in the trusts and estates and corporate banking departments of Shearman & Sterling. Then he moved from Midtown to 100 Centre Street in the Criminal Courts Building shared with the Manhattan Crim-inal Court and the Office of the District Attorney, among other agencies.

Seidemann's second book, *Guilty by Reason of Stupidity*, was named "Best Book of 2008" by *National Jurist*, a mag-azine for law students. The publisher, Andrews McMeel, in its description of the author, said, "Joel J. Seidemann is a district attorney who has seen his share of courtroom stu-pidity during his twenty-five years of practice." His first book, *In the Interest of Justice: Great Opening and Closing Arguments of the Last 100 Years*, published in 2005, was more serious, highlighting dramatic summations.

Vanity Fair quoted Seidemann in a sentencing statement he gave at a December 2009 hearing in the Brooke Astor case. Seidemann, describing Tony Marshall's scheme to separate the Alzheimer's-addled Mrs. Astor from her $187 million fortune, told the court, "He had the help of a crooked lawyer and the support of his wife. Grand theft Astor was a team effort."

Writer Meryl Gordon took notice of Seidemann's color-ful statement. "If he puts out a new edition, the Astor trial might well merit a new chapter," Gordon wrote in her *Vanity Fair* piece.

In his book's acknowledgments, he called the Manhattan DA's office "the most prestigious prosecutor's office in the country."

Since 1989, Seidemann has been senior trial counsel responsible for trying murder cases and other serious and complex crimes. His appointment was right in time for the George Kogan case when, on October 23, 1990, Seidemann was on homicide call at the DA's office the morning Kogan was gunned down. "Back then," he would later say, "I was a lot thinner." But not much else had changed in the two decades of Seidemann's time on the case. He was still as zealous about solving the Kogan murder and bringing the perpetrators to justice as he was on that fall morning so long ago when he arrived on the scene at East Sixty-ninth.

CHAPTER 19
The Unofficial Hit Man

The contract killer in the George Kogan murder has never been arrested. Despite that, prosecutors contended that Barbara hired Manuel Martinez for $100,000 and that Martinez, in turn, hired Paul Prosano to carry out the murder for $50,000. Publicly fingering a man for a crime but not charging and prosecuting him was a bold move by the district attorney's office. But it didn't stop them from charging Martinez with hiring the supposed hit man or from leaking to the press Paul Prosano's name.

Prosano's wife, Christine, was none too pleased that her husband had been called a killer in the press, even though he hadn't been named a suspect or even a person of interest and, more significantly, had not been charged with the crime. In an interview, Christine said her husband was not involved in George Kogan's murder.

Being unofficially named a killer, however, was the least of Paul Prosano's troubles. He and Joseph McKee were arrested in January 1996 and charged with kidnapping, burglary, and armed robbery.

The thing McKee had going for him was being unarmed when he committed the 1991 crime, so he was given less prison time. Prosano, on the other hand, was identified as carrying a gun. This gun had been suspected to be the same weapon used to kill George Kogan, although no solid evidence was ever presented because Prosano's gun was not located.

McKee's appeal, filed in May of 2002, was denied by that Supreme Court of New York's appellate division, because, the court said, three eyewitnesses, including the two hostages, had identified McKee as the robber. The court ruled that McKee's appeal lacked merit.

Paul Prosano and Joe McKee each filed appeals. McKee first filed a writ of habeas corpus, claiming that his kidnapping, burglary, and robbery convictions were not proven beyond a reasonable doubt. In March of 2002, the US District Court for the Southern District of New York denied his claim.

A jury convicted Prosano, who was charged with kidnapping in the second degree, burglary in the first degree, robbery in the first degree, and unlawful imprisonment in the first degree. In January 2001, the same court that had denied McKee's appeal denied Prosano's request for a new trial. Prosano's appeal asked that the case be thrown out, due to the testimony of his wife in which she mentioned his prior record and prejudiced the jury. He also appealed because of a five-year delay in his arrest, from 1991 when the crime was committed, to 1996, when he was arrested. But the Supreme Court Appellate Division ruled that the delay was not unconstitutional.

In an eerily similar case to George Kogan's, this one out of Brooklyn, a housewife who had paid her brother $20,000 to kill her husband was convicted of second-degree murder after waiting a decade to confess. On July 11, 1990, Anthony Suarrcy died in a hail of bullets while sitting in a car parked in front of his Bay Ridge house, a home he'd once shared with his wife, Joan Bongarzone-Suarrcy.

Joan's brother was none other than Frank Bongarzone, who once shared a cell at a Staten Island prison with Paul Prosano. Prosano was the one who introduced Bongarzone to Peter Cardone, who later hired him to do maintenance work at his Trap & Skeet gun shop in Stormville, which had a shooting range in the basement. Manuel Martinez was the store's accountant.

Frank Bongarzone, or Francis, his given name, was described by police as "a wiseguy wannabe." Beginning in 1984, according to prison records, Bongarzone was serving five years at Arthur Kill Correctional Facility, a medium-security prison in Staten Island, for conspiracy, criminal solicitation, and leaving the scene of an accident. The charges included conspiracy because he tried to hire an undercover cop to kill a witness who was scheduled to testify against him. After Bongarzone's conviction, he was sent to the Staten Island prison, which was when he shared a cell with Paul Prosano. While he was there, Joan Bongarzone visited her brother in prison. It was where she was introduced to Anthony Suarrcy, her future husband, who was serving out his time for drug- and cigarette-related convictions.

Similar to the Kogan murder, Bongarzone's was a contract hit by a disgruntled ex-wife, with greed as a motive, executed in broad daylight outside a home, and a life-insurance policy paid out upon the victim's death. Most interestingly, the shooters in both cases have not been charged.

Was George Kogan's murder a copycat hit-for-hire? The contract hit of Anthony Suarrcy went down three months before George Kogan's murder. In the Suarrcy case, the ex-wife was accused of hiring the hit man. In this case, it was her brother, Frank Bongarzone, who was hired on the promise of a $20,000 payment from Joan's husband's $200,000 life-insurance policy.

The case remained unsolved for a decade, until Peter Cardone, who'd been having an affair with Joan Bongarzone-Suarrcy, killed himself. He left a suicide note that said Joan had admitted to having her husband killed and that she'd threatened to do the same to Cardone if he didn't continue paying her thousands of dollars each month.

Joan Bongarzone-Suarrcy, in her own statement to police, named her brother Frank as the shooter. In addition to later being a cellmate of Prosano's, Frank Bongarzone lived on the same street as Paul. Frank also was an associate of

Manuel Martinez. In the taped conversation between Carlos Piovanetti and Martinez, they each referred to a person named "Frankie." Martinez later confirmed the "Frankie" he referred to was Bongarzone.

Joan Bongarzone-Suarrcy, fifty-two years old at the time and referred to in the media as a "Bay Ridge housewife," faced up to twenty-five years to life in prison for asking her brother do her a "big favor" and kill her husband.

The husband, a forty-year-old concrete salesman—who had served time for illegally transporting cigarettes, selling fireworks, and drug possession—was gunned down outside the couple's Bay Ridge home on Wednesday, July 11, 1990, in what police believed initially was a mob hit. At the time of Suarrcy's murder, two factions in the Colombo crime family were warring, and police thought Suarrcy might have been a victim in the battle, NYPD Lieutenant Alfred King told *The Times Herald-Record*. "They were killing each other. We'd get five, six bodies a day."

Bongarzone-Suarrcy played the grieving widow until June 5, 2001, when she walked into a state police barracks in upstate New York and confessed.

Paul Prosano lived in Bay Ridge in Brooklyn, New York, before he was incarcerated.

On August 15, 2005, Paul Prosano's wife, Christine, a corporate travel agent, told *The New York Times* that her relationship with her imprisoned husband, incarcerated since March 1992 on the robbery and kidnap convictions and not eligible for parole until August 2016 at the earliest, was "on hold." She continued, however, to stand by her man, including when he was injured in prison.

On March 19, 2006, Paul Prosano hurt his neck when a pole supporting a four hundred-pound punching bag in the recreation yard at the Sullivan Correctional Facility in Fallsburg, New York, fell and landed on him. Prison officials took photos of the apparatus and the bag. Prosano didn't immediately file a claim. But he and his wife, who were given the nod by the state to file a late claim, did so in 2009, asking for damages. In the meantime, the punching bag and the apparatus that held it were disposed of, and the photo taken of the apparatus was misplaced. A metals scientist, Richard F. Lynch, inspected the bag and the apparatus that held it up and told the court that "the pole was in a degraded condition caused by red rust corrosion, which further weakened the pole and the four spot welds in particular. The pole was rusted from being kept outside in the rain and not properly maintained."

Even so, a New York State Court of Claims judge ultimately denied the request. In her July 8, 2009, decision, Judge Catherine C. Schaewe wrote, in part: "It is undisputed that on March 19, 2006, claimant was injured when the Support Apparatus broke and hit the back of his head as it fell to the ground. There is also no question that defendant took pictures of the Support Apparatus immediately after the accident, and then removed both the Support Apparatus and punching bag from the yard. Further, approximately four months after the incident, the Support Apparatus was removed from Sullivan and taken to a landfill. The original photographs of the Support Apparatus have also apparently been lost or destroyed.

"Further, (Prosano) has admitted that he was aware of the corrosion on the Support Apparatus, and that by using the punching bag with said knowledge, he exercised poor judgment."

"Claimant's Motion No. M-76340 is denied in its entirety," the judge ruled.

Soon after he filed a claim, Prosano was moved from the Sullivan prison, where the Son of Sam killer, David Berkowitz, was serving out his sentence at the same time.

As the criminal case against Barbara became reality, she, too, was about to see her day in court. Coincidence or not, the judge in her case was Michael Obus, known as the no-nonsense jurist who had presided over the Manuel Martinez case. In New York, as in many other jurisdictions, judges receive cases randomly. Such was the case, the courts insisted, with the

Martinez and Kogan trials. Obus had been appointed in December 2007 to the post of Administrative Judge of Manhattan Supreme Court and took the bench on February 1, 2008. A month after the appointment went into effect, Obus was officially presiding over Martinez's criminal proceedings.

But in early 2010, Barbara Kogan's case was switched from Judge Michael Obus's courtroom at 100 Centre Street to Judge Roger Hayes's sixth-floor courtroom across the street, at 111 Centre. The move was a smart one. It could help prevent appeals by both Martinez and Barbara for having the same judge preside over their separate trials.

Roger Hayes, now presiding over Barbara's case, had an important matter to take care of before Barbara's trial, which was set to begin at the end of April. The judge wanted to ask Manuel Martinez a question. Judge Hayes summoned Martinez to his courtroom. On March 26, 2010, a Friday, Martinez was bused 250 miles from the Auburn Correctional Facility to Judge Hayes's courtroom. By Manuel's side was appellate attorney Claudia Trupp.

"Hayes was very polite," Martinez said later about the short session.

Martinez and his attorney, Claudia Trupp, sat at the defense table as Hayes addressed Martinez. He had just one question to ask. The issue had come up before. But Hayes wanted to hear it directly from Martinez, and in person.

"If you are asked to testify in Mrs. Kogan's trial, will you plead the Fifth Amendment, right?" the judge asked.

"Yes," Manuel answered.

Then Judge Hayes asked a second question, prompted by a March 24, 2010 letter from Barry Levin to Judge Hayes in the defense's attempt to prevent Beatriz Oller from testifying at Barbara Kogan's upcoming trial. It marked the second time that Levin had brought up the pesky issue of Oller potentially testifying against Barbara at her trial. It could prove to be a repeat of the testimony Oller gave during Manuel Martinez's trial. The testimony could prove damning, as it had been to Martinez. Levin wanted it ruled out before that could happen.

Oller's statement to police was that in July 1992, shortly before she and her husband Manny separated, Martinez told her he had convinced Barbara Kogan to have her husband killed. She also testified that Martinez told her the hit man was Paul Prosano. The statement helped convict Martinez. Levin's letter to Hayes read:

> As a follow up to my correspondence of March 23, 2010, I write to address the court concerning an additional basis to prevent Beatrice [sic] Oller from testifying to confidential communications between herself and her then-husband, Manny Martinez. Beatrice [sic] Oller testified in the prior trial that in July of 1992, Mr. Martinez took a Xeroxed copy of a photograph of George Kogan from a file cabinet and stated, ". . . if the police ever came looking for him that I had proof that . . . the photograph had been given to him by Barbara Kogan when he suggested in the trip to Puerto Rico that he knew somebody, Paulie Prosano, who could . . . who would do the hit, who can kill George Kogan. . . ." New York State has long recognized confidential communications are privileged between spouses.

Levin then cited the law, which states that "a husband or wife shall not be required, or without the consent of the other, if living, allowed to disclose a confidential communication made from one to the other during the marriage."

Levin ended his letter with this:

> To the extent the prosecution will argue that Barbara Kogan does not have standing to raise the issue of privilege, I submit that Mr. Martinez has previously raised the issue himself both at his sentencing before Judge Obus in 2008 and in the CPL 330 motion to set aside his conviction. The issue for this Court is whether Martinez intends to rely on his statutory privilege to prevent Beatrice [sic] Oller, his wife at the time of

disclosure, from testifying to his confidential admissions where he provided her with a Xeroxed photograph of George Kogan and stated that the photograph was given to him by Barbara Kogan after he had suggested during a trip to Puerto Rico that he could have somebody kill George Kogan.

I respectfully request this Court to allow the parties to inquire tomorrow of Mr. Martinez whether he has ever waived the marital privilege for confidential communications.

Manuel Martinez has adamantly denied saying to his then-wife Beatriz Oller that he had anything to do with getting a photo of George Kogan to the hit man. "Ms. Oller's testimony at my trial claiming I had a photo of George Kogan is completely false," he wrote in a letter from prison.

CHAPTER 20

The Trial That Was Not

A couple weeks before Barbara Kogan's trial, scheduled for April 1, was to begin, the start date was changed to April 29. Yet, the court calendar didn't show anything going on for either of those days. A telephone call to the clerk's office did not clear up the confusion. The case had already been moved from Michael Obus's court to Judge Roger Hayes's, so the judge wasn't the issue. The trial appeared to be in limbo as April 29 drew closer.

"I know the case is adjourned, but I don't know why," said associate court clerk Mary Cassidy.

A more definitive answer would soon be made public as the State of New York versus Barbara Kogan quietly recommenced in Judge Hayes's courtroom on the afternoon of Thursday, April 29, 2010. Nothing was officially scheduled on the court calendar; nevertheless, members of the Kogan family were instructed to attend the proceeding—an important one—with the media left unaware.

Barbara Kogan was tired. And worried. On that late April day, when her trial was to begin, she sat stoic, almost docile, and so calm that she appeared to be medicated. Diagnosed with bipolar disorder and depression, she had been on meds even before she had gone to jail. Wearing a simple dark-colored suit, eyeglasses, and her now salt-and-pepper medium-length hair tied back in a small bun, Barbara had a studious appearance about her. Barbara looked almost beaten down and her outfit matched her mood—an off-white round-necked rayon blouse under a dark-brown suit jacket. Gone was the heavy makeup she had worn two years earlier at her arraignment. At the defense table, she did not speak with her attorneys. This time, she was flanked by two lawyers—Lori Cohen on the right and Barry Levin on the left. Two attorneys in the courtroom was a surprise. But, it later came out, Barbara had had a dispute with Levin and it was too late at that juncture to fire him and get another attorney. So, the court appointed Cohen to represent Barbara, in addition to Levin.

During the homicide probe, the words from Barbara that stood out were her continual denials. "I deny any knowledge of my husband's murder," she'd told the *Post*. "I want everything fully investigated, and I hope they find the people responsible for this," she said in 1995, in the midst of the lengthy investigation. And, again, in 2008 after her indictment, "I'm an innocent woman," she'd told a throng of reporters. Barbara had also once said to a newspaper reporter that the investigation into her possible role in her husband's death was "shameful."

So, it was unexpected for Barbara, on the eve of her May 1, 2010, trial, to plead guilty at a hearing at which the media were not present, a session that was not officially scheduled nor listed on either the DA's or court's daily calendars for April 29.

On the afternoon of April 29, in what one newspaper called "a secretive hearing," a plea allocution—not a trial—commenced. Barbara Kogan's case was about to become one of the roughly ninety-five percent of all felony convictions in the United States that result in a plea bargain—an agreement between the prosecutor and the accused where the defendant pleads guilty in exchange for a reduced charge. It was a surprise hearing that no one, including the media, saw coming.

Like a scene from a Hollywood movie, in a small courtroom inside the State Supreme Court in Manhattan, Barbara, who appeared calm, walked to the witness box, raised her right hand, and promised to tell the truth, the whole truth, and nothing but the truth. Then, in a strategic and pivotal moment in the hearing, Barbara Kogan admitted to what she had denied for nearly two decades, that she had indeed played a role in her husband's murder.

Days earlier, the discovery had prompted the hastily scheduled court proceeding. Barbara Kogan and her lawyer, Barry Levin, had learned that prosecutors had recordings of Barbara having several conversations with a friend on a jailhouse telephone. Those taped conversations, authorities insisted, implicated Barbara. The recordings spanned her eighteen-month isolated incarceration at the Rose M. Singer Center women's jail on Rikers Island. Details of the recordings were not made public, but both sides—the defense and the prosecution—listened to the tapes, and what they heard was passed on to Barbara.

Thus, for the first time since her indictment in 2008, Barbara Kogan took the stand, but not in her own defense. She was there to plead guilty for her role in her husband's murder nineteen years earlier.

It was a stunning admission. And it was a big day for the prosecution. At the table with Assistant District Attorney Joel Seidemann was his former colleague, former Assistant District Attorney Soumya Dayananda, who'd sat beside Seidemann during Manuel Martinez's trial and helped the People of New York win the case against Martinez. Dayananda had since retired, but for Barbara's allocution and sentencing hearings, she returned, one last time, to her place next to Seidemann.

Also seated in the courtroom, expecting Barbara's trial to begin the following Monday, was Jessica Chen, an attorney for the Center for Appellate Litigation. Representing Martinez, for information purposes, she, too, was surprised at the switch from a trial to a plea allocution. Even more stunning to Chen was an accusation Barbara was about to make concerning Martinez.

Prosecutor Joel Seidemann approached the witness stand. The judge explained waivers to Barbara, then reminded her that she was under oath. When she took the stand, she was calm and strikingly unemotional.

"We're going to ask you a lot of questions," Judge Hayes told her. "If you have any questions, please stop me. Everybody has worked a long time on this. Take your time. We're not in a hurry."

Barbara, stoic, looked almost like a schoolteacher. She was mild-mannered, as she had been during her bail hearing months earlier, listening to the proceedings. "You would have trouble believing she was conspiring to kill," said author and crime writer E.W. Count, who attended the hearing.

"How did you meet Mr. Martinez?" Assistant District Attorney Joel Seidemann asked Barbara.

"Through John Lyons," she answered.

"Did there come a time when Mr. Martinez and you discussed having your husband killed by hiring a hit man to do that?"

"Yes."

"Did Mr. Martinez tell you he was going to hire a hit man?" Seidemann asked Barbara.

"Yes," she answered.

"Did you agree with him to participate in the killing of your husband?" Seidemann asked.

"Yes."

"John Lyons called the insurance company for a replacement policy. Is that correct?"

"Yes."

"Did you give a photo of your husband to Mr. Martinez?"

"No. I gave a photograph to John Lyons. He gave it to Manuel," Barbara answered, which could possibly implicate Lyons as a person of interest in the case. But the fact that Barbara had given a photo to Lyons, who, in turn, gave it to Martinez, wasn't anything cocounsel Lori Cohen had expected her new client to be asked.

So, with Seidemann's line of questioning, Cohen jumped out of her chair, walked up to the judge with the prosecution right behind her, then looked at Seidemann and said, "I went over all of this with you." The rest was out of earshot of the gallery, but, after that, no other questions were asked of Barbara about the photo. The prosecution, however, was not yet done with the matter of John Lyons and continued questioning Barbara about him.

"Did you and Mr. Martinez travel to Puerto Rico to pick up a hundred thousand dollars from your father to pay for the hit?" Seidemann asked Barbara.

"Yes," she answered.

"Did you ever meet the hit man?"

"No."

"Do you know who the hit man was?"

"No," she said.

"Does John Lyons know who the hit man was?" Seidemann continued probing.

"Yes," Barbara replied.

It was a monumental moment in the case. With Barbara's statement, the police and district attorney's office had probable cause to pursue John Lyons as a person of interest in the murder because of his alleged knowledge of the hit man's identity.

After that line of questioning, Judge Hayes began asking Barbara questions.

About her deposition, which Barbara gave on July 31, 1991, to SMA Insurance Company as part of its investigation into whether they should pay out the money to Barbara, the judge asked, "[The insurance company] asked you if you knew anyone who might have wanted to kill George, and you said, 'I don't know.' Is that correct?"

"Yes," Barbara replied.

"You told police you had no knowledge of the murder?" he asked.

"Yes."

The judge then began winding down the hearing.

"Did you do this [plea agreement] under pressure?" Judge Hayes asked.

"No," Barbara answered.

"Are you satisfied Mr. Levin did his best to represent you?"

"Yes."

He then talked about Barbara's time at Rikers Island, where she'd been incarcerated in solitary confinement the last two years.

"Do you want to stay in protective custody?" he asked.

"Yes."

With that, the judge turned his head and said to his clerk, "Protective custody. That continues."

Barbara Kogan's cocounsel, Barry Levin, interrupted the proceedings at one point and said, "This is the longest allocution in history."

While it may have been the longest in Levin's experience—one hour—it was setting forth Barbara Kogan's future in prison. It was as if, one spectator pointed out, Levin was in a hurry for the hearing to end. Barbara's future hung in the balance even as her attorney pointed out the time it was taking.

Next, the judge explained to Barbara her rights and what she was giving up in exchange for her guilty plea.

"By pleading guilty, you give up many rights you could have had should you have gone to trial. Instead of pleading guilty, you would be entitled to a bench trial or a jury trial. If you wanted to have a trial, you would be represented by an attorney and you'd have the right to cross-examine witnesses. You gave up that right to a trial. You'd have the right to remain silent. You would be presumed innocent. By pleading guilty, you give up every one of those rights and give up your right to present any defense. You give up your right to appeal on this case. You have been required to waive your right to appeal."

The judge also explained to Barbara what an appeal was. Then he said, "Your right to appeal is negotiated away by you."

Also during the allocution hearing, the judge dropped the first-degree murder charge against Barbara, and she, in exchange, pleaded guilty to Class B felony charges of first-degree manslaughter, second-degree conspiracy to commit murder, and first-degree grand larceny. Another coup for the prosecution was that the statute of limitations on conspiracy had expired after five years, in 1995. That was why Barbara had been indicted with just one charge, murder. Now, with the plea deal, Barbara agreed to waive the statute of limitations and accept the charge of conspiracy—a charge the district attorney's office was denied in the Martinez case, because of the lengthy passage of time.

"The court's intention is to sentence you to an indeterminate sentence of eight to twenty-four [years] for manslaughter," Judge Hayes told Barbara at the plea hearing. "Conspiracy two is an indeterminate sentence of four to twelve consecutive [years], to manslaughter one. However, you do get credit for time served from November 24, 2008."

The judge scheduled Barbara's sentencing for May 19, 2010.

Behind the scenes, according to court sources, Barbara was promised that she would serve no more than a total of ten years in prison before she would be eligible for parole, because of the two years' credit she was receiving for the time spent in custody since her arrest. It meant she would be out of prison no later than 2020, at the age of seventy-seven. By contrast, a jury convicted Manuel Martinez of second-degree murder, with the judge handing him a twenty-five-to-life sentence.

After the hearing, Lori Cohen said she was privy to the recorded jailhouse conversations between Barbara and a friend. "I listened to the taped conversations," said Cohen. "I cannot comment on the content of those conversations." But when asked if the conversations were so incriminating that they prompted Barbara to plead guilty, Cohen said, "[Barbara] did it because of her children. I don't think the evidence against her was strong. It wasn't because of that. Not everyone who pleads guilty is necessarily legally guilty. I think [prosecutor Seidemann] overstated the strength of his case, and he thinks she pled guilty for a number of reasons."

Following her brief representation of Barbara, Cohen said she was not the only one who negotiated the plea deal, even though the judge had told the gallery, almost offhandedly, during the allocation hearing that he had appointed Cohen to the case to hammer out a deal with the defendant.

"[Barbara] was talked to about it with both of us. I advised her. There were specific legal reasons," Cohen said afterward, without volunteering those details.

When asked if Barbara was okay with the decision she'd made, Cohen said, "She has no choice. The decision was made. I think she's doing fine."

As for John Lyons and the potentially incriminating testimony Barbara gave against him, Cohen was more definite about that. "I'm not the police, and you'd have to ask them, but I think that's the real story. Why hasn't John Lyons been charged? If they can't find him, that doesn't mean they can't charge him," she said.

Why, indeed? The prosecution had indicted Manuel Martinez eight years before they were able to take him into custody, because they couldn't find him, yet Lyons had not been charged.

When asked in a telephone interview whether the district attorney's office planned to pursue an indictment against John Lyons for his alleged role in the Kogan murder, Joel Seidemann replied, "The investigation got this far because we kept it quiet. Do you think it would be smart to discuss something that law enforcement might be working on? I don't feel comfortable talking about John Lyons. And I'd rather not get into the investigation."

Police declined to say whether an investigation of Lyons was prompted by Barbara's incriminating statements in court. But by mid-2011, no investigation into Lyons's possible role had been opened by the NYPD or by the DA's office.

When asked about the nonpublic way in which the plea hearing was done, Lori Cohen said, "I'm not in the habit of alerting the media." However, she said, Seidemann seemed to "play to the media in court."

With the announcement of her guilty plea, many wondered why, on the eve of trial, Barbara Kogan would cop a plea in a circumstantial case in which, for nearly two decades, she'd maintained her innocence.

Among those surprised was former felony prosecutor Robin Sax, who, during her tenure as a deputy DA at the Los Angeles County district attorney's office, has seen her share of plea bargains in murder cases. "In a case with this type of sentence, with two years already in custody, and her increasing age, why wouldn't she just go to trial?" Sax asked. "It seems to me that she should have just taken it to a jury. I am not saying she is not guilty—I don't know, and certainly there are compelling reasons to think she may be [guilty]—but this is not a case that should have gone down without a fight. She seems to have a pattern of poor legal advisors. If I were the defense lawyer, I would never have pleaded it, and if I had, it would be for a definite term and not an indeterminate time period prior to sentencing."

Legal scholar Stephen Bright, a defense attorney and a visiting professor at Yale Law School, talked about the plea-agreement process in an interview with PBS's Frontline show in June 2004. "Everyone [in the courtroom] knows the answers to the questions and everyone knows that if you answer the questions incorrectly, the whole thing will blow up and the judge will yell at you and you might not get the bargain that you're going to get. So everyone answers, 'Yes, yes, yes,' to all the questions, and the judge says, 'Well, I find that this is a knowing, intelligent, voluntary plea.' The fact is, the client probably didn't even understand the process. . . . The prosecution completely controls what happens: what crime the person pleads guilty to, and what the sentence is."

When a PBS reporter asked Bright why an innocent person would plead guilty, Bright said, "I think that for somebody who is innocent to plead guilty is going to torment them for the rest of their life. They're always going to think, 'I shouldn't have done that. I've been branded now as a murderer, [and] I had nothing to do with the murder.' But it's really a Hobson's choice, because spending the rest of your life in prison is not very good either."

Getting Barbara Kogan to admit to a role in her husband's slaying was a coup de grâce for prosecutor Joel Seidemann, who called the plea agreement "a good disposition to the case."

However, when Seidemann was asked if the case was pleaded out because it was circumstantial and, because of that, difficult to try, he said, "I'm not afraid to try cases."

For his part, Barry Levin, who for two years had represented Barbara and who had successfully gotten the original murder charge dismissed—a huge accomplishment—appeared to have given up. Barbara's telephone conversations taped at Rikers were sealed and never made public. Still, the worst-case scenario was that the conversations reportedly implicating her would have complicated the trial—but they may not have derailed her case. Apparently, though, the recorded conversations were the final straw that drove Barbara, who once adamantly and confidently told reporters, "I didn't do it," to fold.

Levin spoke briefly, in a defeated tone, after the plea hearing. When questioned by reporters, he said, "It was a circumstantial case in which [Barbara] was her own worst enemy."

He added that she took the deal because the case "had been weighing heavy on her mind. She decided she wanted to put this behind her. Barbara was always concerned that she'd have to face her children on the stand. She didn't want to have to see her two sons testify, so that was always a concern. Secondly, they didn't really make an offer to lessen the indictment until the eve of the trial, at which time we discussed it and she made a decision that she would plead guilty and hopefully get out of jail within the next ten to twelve years."

Then, to CBS 2 TV in New York City, Levin said, "She herself is not healthy, and I don't think she could have handled the stress of the trial." Despite the lack of strong evidence against her, aside from the taped phone calls, Barbara chose to accept a plea that all but guaranteed parole in ten years.

In the end, she still faced one of her sons in court. To

allow Scott Kogan, her adopted son, to travel from his home in Puerto Rico for his mother's sentencing hearing, the prosecution requested a delay in Barbara's sentencing. One day before her May 19 sentencing, the hearing was postponed until June 4, a Friday. Everyone knew, if Judge Hayes stuck to the original bargain, that Barbara would be sentenced to twelve to thirty-six years in prison.

For the Kogan family, it seemed hardly enough. The court expected Scott to describe how his mother's actions had harmed his family. But what also weighed on the minds of Scott and the rest of the Kogans was the recommended sentence. They wanted a longer sentence.

For the family—George's two sons, brother Lawrence, sister Myrna, niece Taryn, nephew David, and a dozen cousins—Barbara Kogan's conviction had been a long time coming. "It's sad it took this long," commented one family member to a reporter. Taryn Kogan, who'd described her uncle as "my best friend," commented, "It's been a very challenging twenty years. I was very close to him."

On the afternoon of Barbara's plea, Manhattan District Attorney Cyrus R. Vance issued a statement in a news release about the case:

DISTRICT ATTORNEY VANCE ANNOUNCES GUILTY PLEA IN MURDER FOR HIRE

Barbara Kogan Pleads Guilty to Planning Murder of Her Husband

   The defendant's guilty plea brings to a close a difficult, nearly 20-year-old murder case. The group of current and former NYPD detectives and individuals within the Manhattan District Attorney's Office responsible for today's announcement showed extraordinary perseverance in their dogged investigation of this case, which led them from New York to Puerto Rico and finally to court today. Since 1990, Assistant District Attorney Joel Seidemann has tenaciously pursued justice in this case, which this plea delivers today.

KOGAN, 67, plotted with her lawyer, MANUEL MARTINEZ, 60, to hire a hit man to kill her husband with whom she was in the midst of a divorce. George Kogan was killed with three gunshots wounds on October 23, 1990, in front of his mistress's apartment building on East 69th Street. KOGAN subsequently collected approximately $4.3 million from her husband's life insurance policies.

MARTINEZ was convicted for murder and criminal solicitation in April 2008 and is serving a sentence of 25 years to life. A grand jury indicted MARTINEZ in 1996 on these charges but he was required to serve out a jail term in Mexico on unrelated charges before being extradited to the United States in 2007.

Defendant information:

BARBARA KOGAN, 2/10/1943

316 East 55th Street

New York, NY 10022

Charges:

Manslaughter in the First Degree, a class B felony, punishable by up to 25 years in prison

Conspiracy to Commit Murder in the Second Degree, a class B felony, punishable by up to 25 years in prison

Grand Larceny in the First Degree, a class B felony, punishable by up to 25 years in prison

Included in the press release was a "thank you" to all the people involved—lawyers, detectives, prosecutors, administrators. In the press statement, District Attorney Vance specifically thanked NYPD detectives Don Kennedy and James Zaccari and former NYPD investigators Ernie Bugge, Joseph Buffalino, and Raymond Brennan, who'd all worked the case in the early years of the investigation. The DA also thanked those who helped prosecute it, including Assistant District Attorneys Joel Seidemann, Mirella deRose, and David Drucker, with "assistance from former Assistant District Attorney Soumya Dayananda."

Lori Cohen, appointed two days earlier, had been responsible for the negotiations between Seidemann and Barbara Kogan. Brought in at the eleventh hour to help negotiate the plea, Cohen sat at the defense table on one side of Barbara while Levin sat on the other. Yet, the district attorney's office did not include Cohen's name in his news release.

Manuel Martinez, incarcerated at the Auburn Correctional Facility upstate, was paying close attention to Barbara's case from his prison cell. Appellate attorney Jessica Chen, who represented Martinez, sent him her assessment of the situation and the guilty plea in a letter, later released by Martinez, dated May 4, 2010. The statement by Barbara in court and under oath that John Lyons knew the identity of the shooter was a particularly interesting piece of information to Chen. In order to stay on top of the proceedings, Chen had gone to court expecting Barbara's trial to begin. Instead, the trial was changed to an allocution hearing without prior notice.

Chen's letter, on Center for Appellate Litigation letterhead stationery, to Martinez was a status report of The People versus Barbara Kogan. In it, she explained that the trial was scheduled to begin on April 29 and that she'd gone there that day to observe the trial. On that day, however, she told him Barbara instead pleaded guilty to the charges against her, and she listed the charges and the sentences they carry. She also let Martinez know that Barbara's sentencing was scheduled for May 19 and that Chen would not be attending.

She explained that Barbara had pleaded guilty after learning that phone conversations between Barbara and a friend in which they'd discussed the crimes had been recorded, prompting Barbara to enter into a plea deal to avoid going to trial.

In her letter, Chen also gave Martinez a heads-up that during the plea allocution when Assistant District Attorney Joel Seidemann asked Barbara whether she'd hired, through Martinez, a hitman to kill her husband, Barbara said yes. Also, Chen continued, when asked whether Barbara had given a photograph of her husband to Martinez, Barbara answered no, that she had given one to John Lyons, who, in turn, handed the photo of George over to Martinez. Chen also passed on to Martinez that Barbara told the court she had gone with Martinez to Puerto Rico to pick up $100,000 from her father to pay for the hit.

Manuel Martinez responded to Chen with a letter two days later, on the same day he received Chen's letter in prison:

May 6, 2010

Dear Ms. Chen:

Thank you for your May 4, 2010 letter received today.

Let me assure you on my word as a man of the following facts:

1. *Barbara Kogan never hired a hitman [sic] through me.*
2. *My trip to Puerto Rico was not to pick up $100,000. She could have wired to any bank account worldwide. We spent three days in P.R. I stayed at El San Juan Hotel & Casino, courtesy of her sister Elaine Siegel who was then the hotel's casino manager. We visited Julio Aguirre, Esq. of Fiddler, Gonzalez & Rodriguez at the Chase Manhattan Plaza, Law Professor Lino Saldana at Banco Popular Center, Ivan Ramos Esq., Kermit Ortiz Esq., and I met Francisco M. Troncoso Esq. on my own.*
3. *I met Emanuel Siegel once and his wife Mrs. Rose*

Siegel at their home at Barbara's invitation. The murder or payment for the murder was never discussed with either. I never received a dime from Mr. Siegel not even for my billed legal services to Barbara.

4. *John Lyons, Barbara's boyfriend or companion back then, informed me that he was an international salesman of military equipment. In those days, he told me he had completed a sale of military hardware to North Korea. I never knew he worked for the CIA until now and he never gave me George Kogan's photo, which I never had. I doubt Mr. Lyons, as a CIA official, would be involved in the murder of a U.S. civilian. He called me at my law office in the afternoon of October 23, 1990, told me George Kogan had been shot and was still alive at the hospital. I met John Lyons through Barbara. Never knew him before. I have no idea how to get in touch with John Lyons except by writing to the Personnel Department at CIA Headquarters in Langley, Va. and asking them.*

It seems that A.D.A. Joel J. Seidemann used his classic Gestapo tactics on Barbara (just like [Carlos] Piovanetti and [Beatriz] Oller testified he did to them via the NYPD) forcing [Barbara] into entering a "suicide deal." Who is the Psychiatrist treating her and what are her mental illnesses? I pray you are doing your investigation work to bring out the truth in this miscarriage of justice.

Respectfully,

Manuel Martinez, DIN #08A3723
Auburn Correctional Facility

After Barbara Kogan pleaded guilty, the headlines screamed it from the rooftops of New York City. There was as much coverage for Barbara pleading out as there had been for the shooting nearly two decades earlier, and even more than when Manuel Martinez was convicted in 2008.

"'Black Widow' Barbara Kogan Pleads Guilty to Hiring a Hit Man," one headline read. "Barbara Kogan Faces Sentencing In Real Estate Tycoon Husband's 1990 Hit Job," another said. "Barbara Kogan Admits Role in 1990 Double-Indemnity Murder of Husband," yet another read.

CHAPTER 21
The Sentencing

On a sunny June morning in downtown New York City, the family of George Kogan arrived at Manhattan Supreme Court Justice Judge Roger Hayes's sixth-floor courtroom, Room 621, at 111 Center Street. It marked the last time the family would gather in court for anything to do with Barbara Kogan and her husband's murder. The final chapter in the case that had lingered for nearly two decades was finally coming to a close.

Along with the rest of the Kogans, Barbara returned to the courthouse near Foley Square on Friday, June 4, 2010, to learn her fate. She had been told she would get the minimum, but there was still a slim chance the judge could change his mind and sentence her to more time.

Barbara sat at the defense table, flanked as she was at the plea hearing by attorneys Lori Cohen, in a seersucker blue pantsuit, and Barry Levin, broad-shouldered and tall in a navy suit, white shirt, and tri-colored tie. Levin clearly was the largest person at the hearing, even among the row of cops—who had all worked on the Kogan case at one time or another over the years—lining the back of the courtroom. Barbara stared straight ahead, seemingly unemotional and calm.

Before the session began, a uniformed court bailiff told those in the gallery, "I remind you, no cell phones." But every reporter continued busily typing into their smartphones throughout the proceeding.

Attorneys sat in the first row, and all the rows on both sides of the room were filled. Three women assistant district attorneys, there to observe the action, sat a couple rows back, behind the prosecution's table.

Occupying the jury box was a camera technician with CBS's New York City affiliate, a pool videographer with the only video camera allowed in. Family members sat in the third row, behind the media, who showed up *en masse* to cover the hearing. The bailiff, again politely, directing his request to reporters, asked that "all cell phones and electronic devices" be turned off. The reporters appeared to ignore him. "The reporter next to me, one across the aisle, and at least two [other] people were on BlackBerrys," said E. W. Count, a journalist and author in court for the proceedings. A fourth reporter, Count said, "was a whiz with his laptop." Waiting outside, because the courtroom was full, were more members of the press.

Because it was full, the courtroom seemed small. Mary-Louise Hawkins, George Kogan's mistress, did not attend, but she spoke through a letter. It was Hawkins's first public statement since the 1990 murder. Joel Seidemann rose from the prosecution table and read her words.

"This is a moral tale that has no positive lesson whatsoever to offer," Mary-Louise wrote, saying she had stayed in touch with the Kogan family, including George's two sons, who were still in college when their father died. "I have enjoyed watching his kids grow and develop. That they have had to live with their mother's depravity all this time has surely taken its toll on both men in ways they cannot begin to imagine. They had to accept the reality that it was their mother who was responsible. Nearly twenty years have passed, and I doubt any of the individuals would have recovered by now—no one who was close to George Kogan. Bill and Scott must grapple with this quandary their entire lives."

"I do not have to live with this curse looming in perpetuity over my family. I am fortunate to have changed worlds,"

Mary-Louise's letter continued, acknowledging that she had since moved out of the country to Europe. "But even I struggled . . . to comprehend how such an act of wanton evil could be perpetrated by a woman who once claimed to love George Kogan. It was Barbara who lost more than she realized. The real irony is that in having George [killed], Barbara Kogan lost the one person who understood that she was in need of special care and who tried all of their married life to indulge her material desires and keep her safe." That, Hawkins said, was the true tragedy for Barbara.

Myrna Borus, who testified for the prosecution in Manuel Martinez's trial, could not attend the sentencing, but her son David, who did not speak, attended in her place. Prosecutor Seidemann, before giving his own statement, quoted David Borus, saying that David would "never forgive" Barbara for the loss of his uncle, and he would "never forget. I don't wish this on anyone. I object to the sentence. I want to make sure the sentence fits the crime. [Barbara] wanted the kids to love her and hate George."

Then it was Seidemann's turn to give his sentencing statement. He talked about why the prosecution opted not to go to trial and pleaded out the case instead. "It's a twenty-year-old case that's circumstantial. We didn't want George Kogan's life to be dragged through the mud," he said, acknowledging George's reportedly bad dealings in the casino business hinted at over the years but never thoroughly investigated—at least publicly. "If there had been a trial, [his life] would have been dragged through the mud."

The plea agreement with Barbara Kogan, Seidemann said, "was making the best of an imperfect system. It is a bitter-sweet day as a prosecutor. I have been witness to an ocean of misery. I have witnessed the worst that man can do to man. [The agreement] is the best we could hope for and the best we could achieve."

As soon as Seidemann finished his presentation, the three female assistant district attorneys from Seidemann's office quietly slipped out the courtroom door while the hearing was still in session.

Then, it was Scott Kogan's turn to address the court. The hearing had been postponed so that Scott could be there. He'd traveled from his home in San Juan, Puerto Rico, where he worked as a certified public accountant. He arrived late, just as the session was about to begin, and sat in the last available seat in the packed gallery, in the last row.

When the prosecutor called his name, Scott stood up and walked to the front of the gallery, then stepped between the defense and prosecution tables and stopped at the lectern. Informally dressed in gray twill pants and a sporty plaid shirt, with his wire-rimmed eyeglasses hanging from his shirt and a yarmulke on his head, he appeared on the verge of breaking down. He stood before the court as a man who had lost both parents.

With his back to the gallery and trembling as he addressed the court, he turned and looked at his mother, who had adopted him when he was a baby.

Scott nodded, then said, "Mom." But his mother did not return the glance as he called her name. She stared straight ahead, looking sad, as if she, too, were on the verge of tears.

Now in his forties and recently divorced, Scott had lost his father while in his early twenties and in college. Now, on this June 2010 day, Scott was losing his mother, too, to prison. His voice cracked as he began to speak, recalling his father's love and their relationship that was cut short. "For nearly twenty years, I have suppressed strong thoughts of suspicion, anxiously focusing elsewhere. Today, here in the darkened room of despair, I see newfound room for forgiveness and hope. I turn to seeking peace and closure and forgiveness."

He then spoke in Hebrew about his father, saying (translated into English), "May his memory be as his blessing."

"I was in the last semester of my bachelor's degree when it happened, and my brother William was in law school," he said. At that point in Scott's life, just before his father's death, he had felt "a bright new page" was turning in his life—nearly finished with college, facing graduation, and about to embark on a career in accounting.

After their father's death, he and his brother grew closer to their mother, closer as a family. Even so, Scott said, "It seemed like nothing was ever enough for her."

Before his father's death, William even went so far as to try to help his mother and father settle their divorce. His mother embraced William, Scott told the court, rejecting Scott, her oldest son. He'd taken sides, he told the court, "because I loved my father." And, Scott emphasized, "I still love my mother."

He said she benefited from his father's death. "She didn't pay for the funeral or the burial. She claimed to be destitute."

Turning toward his mother again, he spoke about his parents: "I loved them both. I still do."

"Today," Scott continued, "I offer my love and support to my mother, as a son. May the day soon come when Barbara Susan Siegel Kogan is welcomed as a different person." He also said he hoped the court's sentence for his mother "honors my father."

Earlier during the thirty-minute proceeding, Barbara turned toward the gallery to catch her son's eye. The *Daily News* would report Scott's sentiments as, "He lost his father to a hit man nearly twenty years ago. Yesterday, he lost his mother to prison—because she ordered the murder."

Speaking next was George Kogan's niece, Taryn Kogan. Attractive and dressed conservatively with a shoulder-length haircut and a sleeveless black cotton dress, she stood trembling, holding back the tears as she spoke publicly for the first time about the death of her favorite uncle, who no doubt would have been proud of her that day.

Taryn was just twelve years old when her uncle—younger brother to her father Lawrence—was killed, but she remembered the moment as if it were yesterday. As she spoke, Barbara's attorney, Barry Levin, with a pensive, almost sad look, turned his chair toward Taryn.

Taryn, George's little niece, now a young woman of thirty-one, stood at the lectern facing the judge and said to the court, "I adored him." She recalled the excitement she'd felt when her uncle picked her up on Sundays to take her to Serendipity, a landmark ice cream parlor and gift shop, and *the* in place to go. It was ideal for an uncle and niece on a Sunday afternoon outing. Near Bloomingdale's on East 60th Street, it was just nine blocks from George's apartment. Taryn lived on Staten Island, so going to the city to see her uncle was a special treat.

George had given Taryn "a little pink antique pillow" from his antique store. "This is the only thing I have left of him that I can hold and touch," she said.

Immediately after Taryn's uncle was shot, she was called out early from school and told he'd had an accident. The next day, Taryn learned what had really happened when she read a front-page newspaper story. She'd always remembered it as the last time she saw her uncle, in that photo on the cover of the *New York Post*. Then, she said, came the funeral service.

"I will never forget the funeral, because Barbara occasionally smirked at me as I mourned and wept," she said, the emotional trauma still fresh in her voice despite the lengthy passage of time. "Who smirks at a loved one during her husband's funeral? [George Kogan] was a loving father, a best friend, a son, an uncle, a little brother. The rest of us loved him. She removed him from our lives. She changed our lives forever."

This day, there was only one thing Taryn wanted from her one-time aunt. She turned her head sharply toward Barbara Kogan. "For twenty years, I have fantasized about this day, when I could face you, Barbara, and be able to call you a murderer, a villain, to your face. But it still won't bring my uncle back."

Then, to the judge, Taryn said, "Your Honor, please, this is an admitted assassin. If not for Barbara, my uncle would not have been murdered that day. I wonder why Barbara's sentence does not reflect the crime, why her sentence was not taken as seriously as that of the attorney or the hit man. I want Barbara kept in prison so no one can run into her on the street." Taryn turned to walk back to her third-row seat in the gallery, but she first stepped to the back of the court-room where her cousin Scott was sitting. They shared, as observer E. W. Count described the moment, "a warm, strong embrace."

Throughout Taryn Kogan's statement, Barbara stared straight ahead, until, for one brief moment, Barbara turned her glance toward Taryn. After the hearing, Taryn said, "It was hard to look at her, but at one point she finally looked back." Taryn had gotten what she'd wanted.

Prosecutor Seidemann began his statement with a quote, which he first cited in Hebrew, reading Deuteronomy 16:20:

צֶדֶק צֶדֶק, תִּרְדֹּף--לְמַעַן תִּחְיֶה וְיָרַשְׁתָּ אֶת-הָאָרֶץ, אֲשֶׁר-יְהוָה אֱלֹהֶיךָ נֹתֵן לָךְ

Then, in English, he translated: "Justice, justice shalt thou follow, that thou mayest live, and inherit the land which the Lord thy God giveth thee."

The veteran prosecutor said he was honored to be in the presence of the NYPD detectives who filled the last row of the courtroom, lining the back wall. Seidemann had been on call on the day of the murder, because his office rotated the schedule of assistant DAs to go out into the field as serious cases unfolded. That day, sitting in his Centre Street office, he was on duty for what at the time was a "homicide call."

"It is, perhaps, the understatement of the century to say this day has been a long time coming," Seidemann said as he addressed the court. *New York Times* blogger John Eligon later described Seidemann's delivery as "a lengthy and metaphor-filled statement from the deputy DA who five years earlier had penned a book about courtroom statements titled *Great Opening and Closing Arguments of the Last 100 Years.*"

Joel J. Seidemann reflected on the length of time it had taken to reach finality in the case. "The point has been to pursue justice, even though it took twenty years. I thank the court for reviewing the case and understanding it," he said.

He noted that Barbara and George Kogan's publicist, Matthew Evins, had testified before the grand jury and recounted how Barbara "once told [Evins] that she wished to 'destroy George,' even if it meant depriving her kids of their father.'"

"Why was Barbara in such a rage?" Seidemann asked the court. "Her fury was intense and mean-spirited and this fury became venomous as Barbara Kogan's love for George turned to hate. She basically adopted a 'scorch the earth' policy."

As for George's affair with Mary-Louise, Seidemann said he wasn't "peering into the bedroom." But when Barbara learned about her husband's affair with Mary-Louise Hawkins, "Barbara had every right to feel hurt and angry. On the other hand, we shouldn't take her on as a virginal victim, because she was dating John Lyons."

The aside hinted that Barbara had been dating outside the marriage when, in truth, she had met Lyons after she and George had separated. And it was never confirmed that she and Lyons were romantically involved. Barbara's friends said it appeared to be more of a friendship during her divorce, when she'd needed someone to lean on.

Seidemann continued. "In the probation report, Barbara Kogan claims the murder was a sudden impulse. It wasn't. It was the result of a long, simmering rage," he said.

Seidemann said the murder motives were, number one, that Barbara was held up to ridicule, because she was concerned about her image. "The other motive was money. Instead of going through the nasty divorce litigation, she decided to kill him."

"Her American Express bill was five figures each month, so Barbara Kogan demanded five thousand a week in alimony," Seidemann said. "As her husband lay dying after the shooting, she did not go to the hospital. Instead, she brought in a fancy hair stylist and had her hair done for five hundred dollars."

By contrast, for her appearance in court for her hearing that day, Seidemann said, "Recently, Barbara had her hair done at Rikers for three dollars. How the mighty have fallen."

At that point, Levin stood up at the defense table, looked at the judge, and said, "This sounds like a summation at trial and not a speech at sentencing. I'm not sure it's relevant to the proceeding." The judge dismissed Levin's protest and allowed Seidemann to continue his statement.

Seidemann contended that Barbara began "elaborate planning" to have her husband killed after a judge denied her hefty alimony request, saying, "Barbara's anger only grew." And that planning included a trip to Puerto Rico. "One must call it what it is. It's a cold-blooded murder, the ultimate evil, a contract killing," he said. "Justice delayed is not justice denied."

He went on to say that "Martinez, Prosano, and Barbara are now living in a gated community." The prosecutor failed to point out that Paul Prosano, long called the hit man in the case but never charged, was not in prison in connection with George Kogan's murder, nor had he ever been arrested or charged in connection with it. Prosano at that time was serving a sentence for a strong-arm robbery and kidnapping case unrelated to the Kogan murder.

When Seidemann finished, the court clerk asked Barbara to stand so the judge could impose the prison sentence. Barbara stood solemn, still looking straight ahead, as Judge Hayes handed down his sentence of twelve to thirty-six years, with the possibility of parole.

Despite a plea from George Kogan's niece to the judge for a tougher sentence than had been agreed upon, Justice Roger S. Hayes stuck to the agreement made with Barbara and her attorneys, giving her the opportunity to serve out just one-third of her thirty-six-year maximum sentence in exchange for the plea of guilty. Hayes explained that he believed it was "fair to everyone involved and does protect the public interest."

Then, Barbara's lead defense attorney Barry Levin spoke, asking the judge to continue the mental treatment she had received at Rikers Island when she moved to state prison. "She's been in suicide watch at Rikers and in protective custody," Levin said. "She has been diagnosed with bipolar disorder and has been hospitalized repeatedly, including three times in the past five years. I don't say this to excuse this crime, and in no way to minimize murder, but I bring that out because I don't think that Barbara Kogan had or has the capability today to think through all of her actions."

But the judge's order was clear: "General population."

Now that the case was out of the court system, Hayes did not order continued suicide watch or the protective custody Barbara had had at Rikers. Doing her time in an upstate prison, she'd be treated like all the other women inmates.

Levin also told the court that if Barbara "didn't cause trouble behind bars" and "if her children refrain from going to the parole board [to speak] against her," she could be free in ten years.

Later, in response to Levin's veiled appeal for Barbara's sons not to speak against their mother during probation and parole hearings, Taryn Kogan spoke plainly. When asked if she would attend Barbara's parole hearing in the year 2022, Taryn answered, "Without a doubt."

At Barbara's sentencing, after everyone else had spoken, the judge directed a question at Barbara.

"Do you wish to say anything?" he asked.

"No," Barbara answered, with her eyes down, in a barely audible voice.

The judge's final statement, to a uniformed court bailiff, was, "You can take charge, officer."

With that, the hearing was over.

And so was the case that had for two decades wound its way slowly through the judicial system, haunting George Kogan's family and everyone else involved, and keeping the attention of a Manhattan prosecutor who refused to let it go. Judge Hayes's words unceremoniously marked the end of the twenty-year journey. Barbara had no recourse, no grounds for an appeal, because of the airtight plea agreement she'd signed. She was guaranteed to be in prison for the next ten years, until she was about seventy-seven.

The bailiff stood next to Barbara as she lifted her hands and held them together so he could handcuff her wrists in front of her. Then, he walked Barbara, with eyeglasses in one of her cuffed hands, through the courtroom. Hunched and in a slightly protective stance as if to ward off a potential blow, she slipped out a side door with the bailiff, and out of the courthouse. There was a sadness in her gaze as she turned for one last glance, this time at the media.

The following morning, on June 5, 2010, the *New York Post*'s photo caption of Barbara called her "heartless."

Then, on a summer day in a prison bus, Barbara, her hands and feet shackled, headed one hour outside of Manhattan to New York's only maximum-security prison for women. Once there, Barbara officially became state prisoner number 10G0497.

Thus began Barbara Kogan's lengthy stint inside the walls of the Bedford Hills Correctional Facility in Westchester County. It is the same prison housing Joan Bongarzone-Suarrcy, also convicted of hiring a hit man—her brother, Frank Bongerzone—to murder her husband. Bedford is a designated mental-health level-one facility, which means it's able to provide intensive mental-health services.

Six months after Barbara pleaded guilty, her good friend Clarissa Barth made the trip from Hollywood, Florida, to visit her in Bedford Hills. "I had never been to a prison, so I was scared half to death," Clarissa, tan with long blonde hair, said shortly after, "and this was a maximum security women's prison where every guard says to you, 'It's your first time?' How did they guess?"

The two had not seen each other in several years. "She looked great and was happy to see me," Clarissa said. "She had been in the infirmary a great bit of time and was just released by chance the day before my visit. She didn't know I was coming. I never could find the words [to write to her]. I'm glad I was able to visit her. It was like old times."

As for Manuel Martinez, his fight is not over. From his prison cell, he continues to cry foul and fight for a new trial. Before Martinez could even file an appeal, a judge denied it. "There is no question of law or fact presented which ought to be reviewed by the Appellate Division," Helen E. Freedman, justice of the appellate division, first department, wrote in her September 17, 2010, decision, ". . . and permission to appeal from the order of the Supreme Court, New York County, is hereby denied."

It was an interesting move, since Martinez's attorney had not yet filed an appeal. Martinez, nonetheless, vowed to continue his fight to higher courts. Even Barbara Kogan's guilty plea would not deter him.

"Barbara Kogan's conviction does not affect Manuel Martinez's appeal," Joel Seidemann countered. "But it affects his ability to retry his case."

Time will tell whether Martinez will be granted a new trial. His appellate attorney, Claudia Trupp, up until she withdrew from the case in spring 2011, believed there were valid reasons to file an appeal. On March 5, 2010, Trupp e-mailed a letter to Martinez's sister, Nilda, in response to a question about the viability of her brother's appeal. Trupp wrote, in part, "I have to say that as far as my confidence in being able to help your brother, after many years working in this area, I can only tell you that it is difficult to overturn a murder conviction. That said, I do believe that serious errors occurred in your brother's trial."

While Barbara Kogan and Manuel Martinez have now been convicted in connection with hiring a hit man to kill George Kogan, no one knows for sure who the actual killer was—the man who followed George on the street that cool October morning and pulled the trigger of a snub-nosed revolver, firing three high-caliber bullets into his back. The prosecutor attempted to answer the question about who had George killed, but the man he accused, Paul Prosano, was never charged.

Even George Kogan's family has questioned why Manuel Martinez—the convicted middleman—was prosecuted, while the man who supposedly pulled the trigger was never brought to justice. For some, including George Kogan's family, that part of the puzzle has never made sense.

"The thing that struck me as bizarre, and you could put your finger on it, was how they'd go after the middleman without having indicted the person who actually committed the crime," said one of George's cousins. "It was so odd to get the middleman [Martinez] instead of the actual shooter."

Paul Prosano, the unofficial gunman, is currently serving out a twenty-year sentence at the Great Meadow Correctional Facility in Comstock, New York, after being convicted of two counts of robbery in the first degree, second-degree kidnapping, and first-degree burglary. He is eligible for parole in August 2016. If not granted parole, Prosano is scheduled for release at the end of his term in December 2024, when he is sixty-four years old.

Barbara Kogan and Manuel Martinez are in prison, convicted of hiring a hit man. But until the day a shooter is officially and legally held responsible, whoever shot George Kogan remains unknown and the killer remains free, at least on those charges. The lack of a shooter in custody leaves a single, nagging question: Who pulled the trigger and killed George H. Kogan? As the case now stands, that question remains unanswered.